DAILY LIFE IN THE ABYSS

War and Genocide

General Editors:
Omer Bartov, Brown University; A. Dirk Moses, University of Sydney

In recent years there has been a growing interest in the study of war and genocide, not from a traditional military history perspective, but within the framework of social and cultural history. This series offers a forum for scholarly works that reflect these new approaches.

"*The Berghahn series* War and Genocide *has immeasurably enriched the English-language scholarship available to scholars and students of genocide and, in particular, the Holocaust.*" —**Totalitarian Movements and Political Religions**

For a full volume listing, please see back matter

DAILY LIFE IN THE ABYSS

Genocide Diaries, 1915–1918

Vahé Tachjian

berghahn
NEW YORK • OXFORD
www.berghahnbooks.com

Published in 2017 by
Berghahn Books
www.berghahnbooks.com

© 2017, 2019 Vahé Tachjian
First paperback edition published in 2019

*This publication was made possible by a generous grant
from the Dolores Zohrab Liebmann Fund*

All rights reserved. Except for the quotation of short passages for the purposes of criticism and review, no part of this book may be reproduced in any form or by any means, electronic or mechanical, including photocopying, recording, or any information storage and retrieval system now known or to be invented, without written permission of the publisher.

Library of Congress Cataloging-in-Publication Data

Name: Tachjian, Vahe, author.
Title: Daily life in the abyss : genocide diaries, 1915–1918 / Vahe Tachjian
Other Titles: War and genocide ; v. 25.
Description: New York, NY : Berghahn Books, 2017. | Series: War and genocide ; volume 25 | Includes bibliographical references and index.
Identifiers: LCCN 2016054890 (print) | LCCN 2016057538 (ebook) | ISBN 9781785334948 (hardback : alk. paper) | ISBN 9781785334955 (eBook)
Subjects: LCSH: Armenian massacres, 1915–1923—Personal narratives. | Pogharean, Grigor—Diaries. | Tavukjian, Nerses, 1870–1934–Diaries. | Armenians—Syria—Diaries. | Armenians—Turkey—Diaries. | Armenians—Relocation—Syria.
Classification: LCC DS195.5 .T223 2017 (print) | LCC DS195.5 (ebook) | DDC 956.6/20154—dc23 LC record available at https://lccn.loc.gov/2016054890

British Library Cataloguing in Publication Data

A catalogue record for this book is available from the British Library

ISBN 978-1-78533-494-8 hardback
ISBN 978-1-78920-065-2 paperback
ISBN 978-1-78533-495-5 ebook

Contents

List of Illustrations and Tables	vi
Acknowledgments	viii
Introduction	1
Chapter 1 The Diarist, his Environment, and the Reasons for Keeping a Diary	15
Chapter 2 The Deportees in the Region of Bilad al-Sham: A Race Against Time at Breakneck Speed	51
Chapter 3 The Circle of Salvation in Extreme Conditions: Money-Food-Connections	80
Chapter 4 Descriptions of the Deportees' Decline: The Deaths of Shoghagat, Hagop, Krikor, Diruhi, and Many Others	128
Chapter 5 From Forced Islamization to Emancipation: Two Historical Episodes and their Contradictions	155
Afterword	184
Glossary	199
Index	201

List of Illustrations and Tables

Illustrations

Figure 0.1. Map of the Ottoman Empire.
Map prepared by Eric Van Lauwe. ... x

Figure 1.1. Ayntab, Vartanian school. Graduating diploma given in 1912 to Krikor Bogharian
(Source: Haigazian University Library, Beirut) ... 20

Figure 1.2. A view from Hama in the 1920s
(Source: AGBU, Nubarian Library, Paris) ... 33

Figure 1.3. The Bogharian family, early 1920s.
(Source: Annie Kambourian family collection, Paris) ... 44

Figure 2.1. A view from Hama in the 1920s
(Source: AGBU, Nubarian Library, Paris) ... 57

Figure 2.2. Krikor Bogharian
(Source: Krikoris Bogharian family collection) ... 65

Figure 2.3. A view from Hama in the 1920s
(Source: AGBU, Nubarian Library, Paris) ... 74

Figure 3.1. Krikor Bogharian's Lebanese identity card, 1926
(Source: Haigazian University Library, Beirut) ... 86

Figure 3.2. A view from the region of Hama in the 1920s
(Source: AGBU, Nubarian Library, Paris) ... 99

Figure 3.3. Aleppo, 1923.
(Source: Grégoire Tafankejian collection, Valence) ... 108

Figure 4.1. A view from Hama in the 1920s
(Source: AGBU, Nubarian Library, Paris)   137

Figure 4.2. Father Nerses Tavukjian
(Source: Kevork Sarafian, ed., Պատմութիւն Անթէպի Հայոց
[History of the Armenians of Ayntab], vol. 1. Los Angeles, 1953)   143

Figure 5.1. Krikor Bogharian
(Source: AGBU, Nubarian Library, Paris)   163

Figure 5.2. Father Karekin Bogharian
(Source: Krikoris Bogharian family collection)   172

Figure 5.3. Aleppo, ca 1923, Armenian religious leaders.
(Source: Mihran Minassian collection)   176

Figure 5.4. Homs, 15 November 1933.
(Source: AGBU, Nubarian Library, Paris)   179

Figure 6.1. Ruins of Baalbek (Beqaa Valley, Lebanon),
August 24 1928. (Source: Krikoris Bogharian family collection)   195

Tables

Table 3.1. The price of wheat in the Hama district,
December 1915–October 1918.   89

Table 3.2. The price of bread in the Hama district,
December 1915–April 1917.   90

Table 3.3. The price of flour in the Hama district,
December 1915–April 1918.   91

Table 3.4. The price of yogurt in the Hama district,
January 1916–April 1918.   92

Acknowledgments

This book was essentially written during my tenure as a research fellow at the Zentrum für Literatur- und Kulturforschung in Berlin. I thank my colleagues from those years, as well as the staff of the Center's library, for their collaboration and support.

The English translation of my book would not have been possible without a financial grant graciously provided by the Dolores Zohrab Liebmann Fund, for which I thank the members of the Fund's staff and jury. I also express my gratitude to the Hrant Dink Foundation's History and Memory Research Fund for awarding my work the historical research prize established by the Foundation.

Many different individuals contributed to my project with advice and assistance of various kinds, for which I am greatly indebted in particular to Taner Akçam, the late Krikor Chahinian, Nanor Stepien, Michel Paboudjian, Vahram Shemmassian, the late Vazken Yacoubian, Nazan Maksudyan, Eric Van Lauwe, Hans-Lukas Kieser, Kevork Bardakjian, Gabi Jancke, Vartan Tashjian, Arsen Guidanian, Nadine Méouchy, Mihran Dabag, Peter Hrechdakian, Heghnar Zeitlian Watenpaugh, Toros Toranian, Mohamed Al Dbiyat, Rosemary Russell, Krikoris Bogharian, and Hovan Simonian.

I am grateful to Berghahn Books for its willingness to publish my work. I thank its senior editor, Chris Chappell, for very competently preparing the text for publication. I also thank the anonymous reviewers of the manuscript, from whose suggestions I profited greatly in revising the text. I am also grateful to Rebecca Rom-Frank and Alina Zihharev of Berghahn Books.

My gratitude also goes to the former director of the Nubarian Library, Raymond H. Kévorkian, its current director, Boris Adjémian, and a member of the Library's staff, Megerditch Basma. I am indebted to the people at Haigazian University who kindly put Krikor Bogharian's personal archives at my disposition. My thanks go especially to those responsible for the University's Derian Armenological Library, Vera Gosdanian and Sonia Sislian.

I thank Archbishop Shahan Sarkisian, the Armenian Prelate in Aleppo, who—at a time when the city was not in the deplorable state it finds itself in today—offered me an opportunity to carry out research in the Aleppo Prelacy Archives. The conversations I had with the Archbishop in the course of my work unfailingly proved to be both interesting and useful.

Mihran Minassian's contribution to the preparation of this book was fundamental. It was thanks to him that I gained access to the original version of Father Nerses Tavukjian's diary. With his many suggestions, comments and criticisms, and elucidations of various points, his help in securing primary materials, and his final review of the whole book, Mihran constantly contributed to developing and enriching my research.

I also thank G. M. Goshgarian, who proved to be an invaluable interlocutor with whom I discussed a great many of the problems raised by my work.

Finally, I am deeply indebted to my wife Elke Hartmann. My conversations with her were enriching and a source of inspiration, and my work took final form under their direct influence. In that sense, Elke made a fundamental contribution to this book.

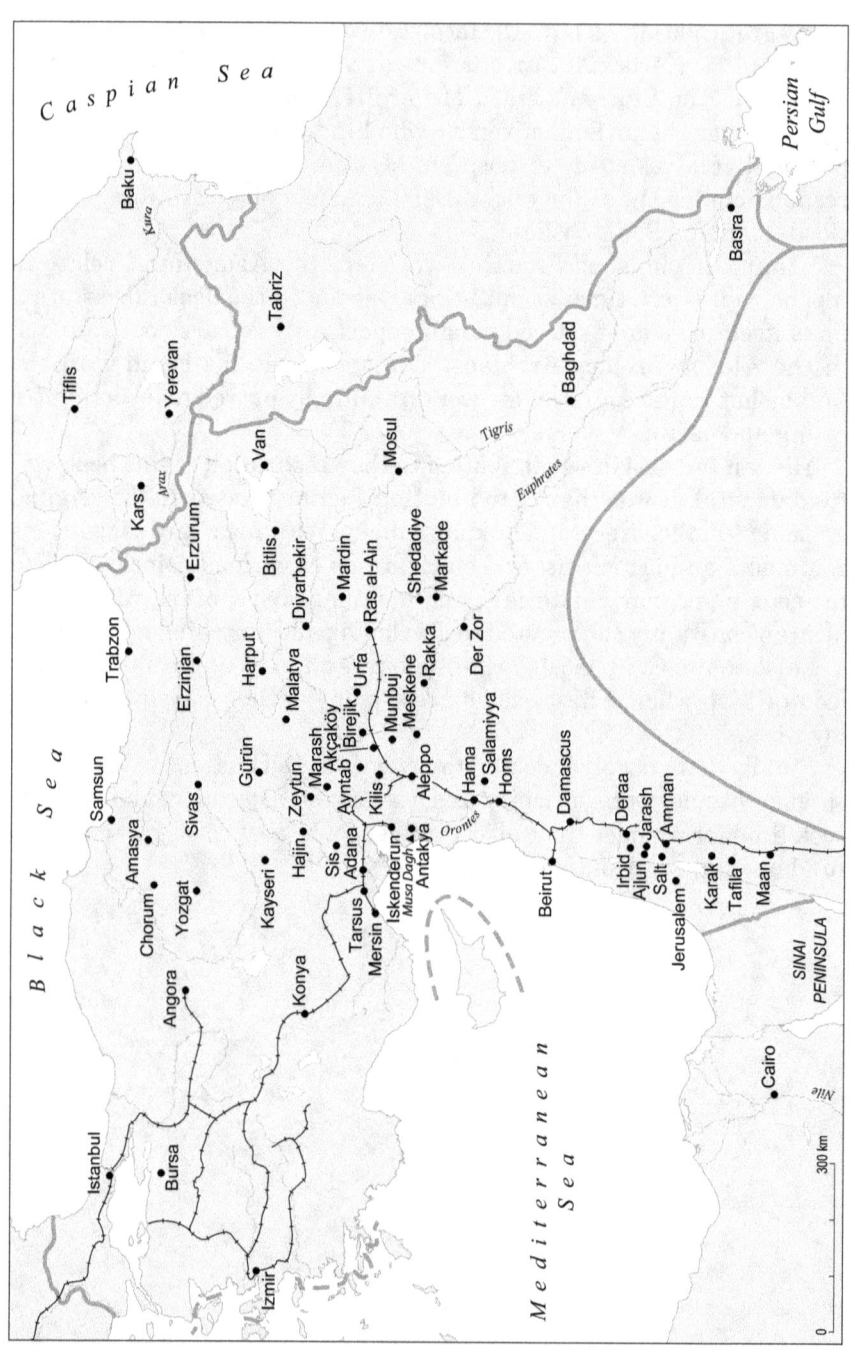

Figure 0.1. Map of the Ottoman Empire. Map prepared by Eric Van Lauwe.

Introduction

Beginning in May–June 1915, when the plan for the Armenian genocide was put into practice under the Ottoman authorities' supervision, the region of Bilad al-Sham saw an influx of tens of thousands of Armenian deportees. There is no precise information as to how many people there were in this mass of deportees, and I do not intend to enter into the debate about numbers here. What is certain is that those who arrived in this area represented a sizable proportion of the Armenian population of Cilicia and the towns and villages to the east of it. The new arrivals in the area also included human wrecks from Central and Western Anatolia as well as the Armenian High Plateau. Bilad al-Sham was an extensive region, roughly encompassing what is today western Syria, Lebanon, Israel, the Palestinian territories, and Jordan. It was in this vast region of the Ottoman Empire that, for more than three years, the Armenian deportees would wage a struggle to survive.

With the end of World War I in autumn 1918, it rapidly became apparent to an international public that Bilad al-Sham was the region harboring the largest concentration of Armenian genocide survivors. All had witnessed a human catastrophe. Death, disease, and misery had reigned uncontested over their environment. An entire social system was in shambles there. The deportees had found themselves needing to adapt to extreme conditions and comply with the pitiless laws of survival.

The present work sets out to reconstruct these historical times, in a sense. It proposes to examine a form of human existence bound up with the period in question, reconstruct the deportees' social environment, with its many-sided internal relations, and study the human reactions flowing directly from the spirit of the times and the singular conditions then created. It therefore stands to reason that the main axis of this study should be the Armenian deportees' day-to-day existence or, more precisely, the day-to-day concerns imposed by their struggle for survival. In that sense, the deportees are also the main protagonists of the present work, and the subject examined here is their peculiar world, in which prevailing conditions were harsh and survival had become a special art. For the same reasons, the focus here is not on the policies implemented by the chief architects of those extreme conditions—the Ottoman authorities and in particular the Ittihat ve terakki or Committee of Union and Progress (CUP), the party that held absolute power in the empire. Doubtless, we need to know the ruling party's political and ideological line, the Unionists' attitude toward the Ottoman Armenians, the way the genocidal project was carried out, and the various stages of its unfolding in order to arrive at an exact understanding of the overall situation of the Armenian deportees concentrated in Bilad al-Sham and the conditions of existence that flowed from it. Nevertheless, in no way do these factors, taken alone, open a window on the deportees' singular world. They do not allow us to observe and study the traumatized Armenians' daily lives and comprehend their inner state of mind under the extreme conditions, or the means they mobilized to cope with the catastrophe, or the unequal battle they waged against epidemics and dire poverty. None of these realities can appear straightforwardly or authentically in Ottoman state communications or reports, other Ottoman official documents, state laws, or even the Unionist leaders' secret correspondence.

For a minute examination at the level envisaged here, it is the deportees' personal testimony, their self-narration, that is of the greatest significance. In this perspective, diarists will not only be one of the present work's main themes but will even, as individuals giving an account of their own inner world, become our most important primary source. Under catastrophic conditions, diarists portray a collectivity whose mode of life and daily existence are, to say the very least, caught up in a process of radical change. In this sense, Andrea Löw notes that one of the most pertinent questions is the progressive disintegration of such a collectivity's frame of reference, which had been, under normal conditions, a factor promoting these people's security.[1] Such disintegration is a hellish process that leads toward death. The best witness to it and its best interpreter is, I submit, the diarist.

In the case of the Armenian genocide, eyewitness testimony can take the form of retrospective narration, in which a survivor attempts to reconstitute his or her lived experience and transform it into common knowledge, whether in the guise of memoirs, correspondence, interviews, or art. When that happens, the narrative—apart from already being personal testimony with its own inherent value— simultaneously becomes subject to the influence of its present, that is, post-catastrophic times, and displays the traces of historical reconstruction. The language it uses is that of the personal testimony of its day; by the same token, the way questions are framed and the dominant conceptual approach correspond to the spirit of the times.[2] In addition to eyewitness accounts of this type, we also have texts written in the days of the catastrophe itself—diaries, letters, minutes of the meetings of public institutions or their account books—by writers who, facing an uncertain future, were incapable of prophesying their fate. What preoccupied them was their daily round, which survivors' memoirs do not, as a rule, emphasize to the same extent. Such quotidian events are especially observable in diaries, which contain texts and narrations whose ends and logical conclusions are very often unknown to their authors. According to Philippe Lejeune, the diarists here consent to work hand in hand with an unpredictable, uncontrollable future.[3] They offer us scraps of real life, which, while undoubtedly subject to authorial self-censorship at the moment of their transformation into text, nevertheless manifestly bear the stamp of the authenticity of the moment. To be sure, what we see is not a live-action video, yet it *is* a life process in which we can very well observe a gradual transformation of the prevailing conditions, internal shifts, and manifold influences in their wake to which diarists and their associates were subject.

The present work does not reduce diaries to the role of mere ancillary documents that can provide confirmation of a historical event. On the contrary, it treats diaries as fundamental primary sources or "monuments," to use Marc Nichanian's expression; as such, these works of self-narration shed their status as purely factual, archival documents and are invested with new and enduring value.[4] Throughout the present investigation, diaries will serve as our basic travel companions and guides. It is by way of diaries that we will be able to penetrate to the level of day-to-day life and expose the most minute yet simultaneously essential details. Diary entries will show us a family's struggle to obtain its daily bread, the gradual impoverishment that deprived it of basic nourishment, the mutual assistance family members gave each other and its limitations, the deaths of loved ones, and the conversions or other moral compromises made for the sake of survival. In their daily jottings, in a word, the diarists studied here depict a process—the gradual deterioration of day-to-day existence—whose culmination is unknown to them, although they know they are living through a human catastrophe, that death is pitilessly mowing down their loved ones, and that they themselves are helpless in the face of it all.

The diary regarded as a primary source acquires its full value when it proves possible to situate it in its true social and temporal context. Then we can comprehend personal testimony, illuminate its various and sometimes obscure facets, bring out its contradictions, underscore the novelties it transmits, and transform seemingly insignificant details into keys for deciphering events and situations. Carlo Ginzburg might never have succeeded in recreating Menocchio's sixteenth-century microcosm,[5] had he not also had expert knowledge of the sects flourishing in the Friuli region in the medieval period. In other words, Ginzburg was closely acquainted with both the times of the miller who is his book's main protagonist and the social context he lived in. This allowed him to put Menocchio back in his native habitat, illuminate the hidden recesses of his personality, and penetrate to the heart of the thoughts he expressed.

From the standpoint of microhistory, I have also tried to respect this principle throughout the present work. That is, I have focused on individuals whose experiences and testimony shed light on a particular historical period. Our Menocchios are two diarists, Father Der Nerses Tavukjian and Krikor Bogharian. In the years of the deportation they lived in the same places, Hama and Salamiyya, today neighbouring towns in Syria. By focusing on just one small area in Bilad al-Sham, their self-narration throws a spotlight on the day-to-day life of those deported there and, more generally, on the environment in which their struggle for survival took place. Nevertheless, as the other sources used in the present study show, my investigation of the situation of the Armenian deportees then living in Bilad al-Sham and the two localities just mentioned is part of a wider-ranging research project. This made it possible to place the Hama-Salamiyya microcosm in a broader social, economic, and political framework and to examine it in that perspective.

There is, of course, good reason for turning to this kind of description in two voices, based on a pair of diaries. Not only did Der Nerses and Bogharian find themselves in the same geographical areas, but their diaries are complementary. While Der Nerses's penetrating observations and psychological-intellectual analyses create scenes of moral dereliction and catastrophe sui generis, we gain intimate knowledge, thanks to Bogharian, of the economically unusual state of local markets, the process of Islamization, and other fundamental matters of the kind that the priest from Ayntab rarely stops to consider. Here and there, moreover, the two diaries are interlinked, for the Tavukjian and Bogharian families had been on very close terms in Ayntab. Information about the Tavukjians appears in Bogharian's diary, and vice; I even found correspondence between the two families from the war years. All this explains why I have opted for the variant of a description in two voices: it is the most appropriate way to present a faithful picture of the deportees' everyday lives.

The two diarists at the center of the present study show us a tripolar social field that emerged under extreme conditions. These two deportees waged their own struggle for existence within the boundaries of that field. The first pole is the diarist himself, with his personal preoccupations, memories of the past, uncertainty about the future, constantly fluctuating moods, and moments of happiness and despondency. The second pole is his family, that immediate nucleus in which, on various levels, a spirit of cooperation prevails. That same nucleus is where the everyday trials and tribulations of the catastrophic environment come emphatically to the fore to be depicted in their true colors: epidemics, lack of food, consequences of dire poverty, deaths of loved ones. The third pole is the diarist's wider circle, which in the present case comprises the other deportees in Hama-Salamiyya, who in some sense constitute a prolongation of the life of his community of origin, as well as indigenous inhabitants, the local economy, prices of basic foodstuffs, and the town itself. Here the diarist is most likely to record impressions of his environment, portraying his compatriots' mode of life and efforts to adapt to local conditions and engage in remunerative economic activity; and describing the pervasive poverty, the unburied bodies, and the many different facets of the deportees' degradation and decline. In sum, the diaries allow me to chart the evolution of this tripolar microcosm, following an individual and familial experience while also observing the deterioration of environmental conditions, gradual disintegration of a social system, and especially, the dire impact that the extreme situation had on the deportees' way of life.

Without a doubt, Der Nerses's and Krikor Bogharian's diaries pertain chiefly to what these men saw and experienced in the three years and more of their deportation: the events that took place in their field of vision. The interpretations they offer surely also depend on their personal worldviews and their mood on the day a given diary entry was made. Phenomena of this sort, however, are not peculiar to diaries or the genre of self-narration in general. Rather, as I see it a subjective factor is at work in all forms of textual expression, whether a letter, memoir, or state official's political report. Consequently, what is essential is not the primary source itself, but the methodology of the scholar utilizing it, that is, the extent of his or her familiarity with the subject under investigation and skill at locating it in a broader context. When the second desideratum is lacking, the scholarly work seems to lose its authenticity and fail in its attempt to reconstitute an accurate picture of the past. In this perspective, moreover, there is no difference between the intellectual productions of a scholar who consults thousands of documents in a state archive and another who bases his entire work on an eyewitness account by a single individual.[6] In the case at hand, making diarists into main protagonists is an essential requirement flowing from the need to make the narrative as authentic as possible. On a topic of this kind, a deportee's insider's perspective is likewise indispensable, as it enables us to study and understand the influences at work in a given social structure, the individual strategies deployed in it, and many other details of the rapid transformation of a human life environment.

Throughout this study, it will be crucially important to set microhistorical observation in its wider context.[7] Properly understood, the Armenians' environment in Hama-Salamiyya was never an isolated world. Its history was intimately bound up with the situation of Armenian deportees in other towns and villages of the Bilad al-Sham region. Of course, disparities between the peculiarities and distinct social systems of the various localities made for varying conditions in the villages and towns of Bilad al-Sham and their indigenous populations, and highlighted the differences between the groups of Armenian deportees that settled in them. For example, a majority of those deported to the agricultural district of Salamiyya were urban Armenians from Ayntab (present-day Gaziantep), whereas the big commercial city of Damascus was settled by substantial numbers of deportees from rural Western Anatolia, although it, too, saw the arrival of large numbers of urban deportees from Cilicia. Under these circumstances, local characteristics combined with the Armenian deportees' origin and character to create singular situations that heightened the disparities between the various places of deportation in Bilad al-Sham.

Naturally, this diversity contributed to shaping the deportees' strategies of survival. Armenians in Damascus could sometimes practice a trade or open a small business to earn a living. In contrast, large numbers of Armenians from Ayntab were forced to leave Salamiyya, which was basically an overgrown village, for the nearby town of Hama, where they expected to find job openings in their trade, weaving. All these phenomena underscore the importance of the local history of every one of the Armenians' deportation destinations. Thus there is no gainsaying the significance of microhistorical study of the population centers in which the Armenian deportees found themselves, including Damascus, Amman, Homs, Jarash, Rayak, Salt, Aleppo, Hauran, and many others. Such study will surely shed new light on the extreme conditions generally encountered by the Armenians in this region. Yet, major disparities of this kind notwithstanding, it seems likely that the deportees faced the same basic problems no matter where they found themselves in Bilad al-Sham: epidemics, a steadily worsening economic crisis, the fear that they would be displaced again, steadily increasing food prices, the draft. These problems formed a whole. They appeared simultaneously throughout Bilad al-Sham with virtually the same intensity and evolved along the same lines. This points to a certain homogeneity in the environments in Bilad al-Sham in which Armenian deportees were struggling to survive, so that the essential difference resided in the means adopted to overcome the dangers that all faced.

Both Krikor Bogharian's and Der Nerses's diaries were published, and both were released in Beirut: Bogharian's in 1973, Der Nerses's in 1991. Bogharian's published diary comprises a chapter in a general work entitled Ցեղասպան Թուրքը, վկայութիւններ բաղուած հրաշքով փրկուածներու զրոյցներէն (The genocidal Turk: Eyewitness accounts culled from the accounts of people who were miraculously saved). This chapter is eighty-one pages long (the pages measure 5.5 by 9.4 inches, or 14 by 21.3 centimeters). Der Nerses's diary, edited by Toros Toranian, begins in 1909 and continues, with interruptions, up to 1933. In all, the diary contains 393 pages (6.3 by 9.3 inches, or 16 by 23.5 centimeters). Entries for the three years from deportation to liberation take up 95 pages. Efforts to obtain the manuscript of Bogharian's diary were unsuccessful, but I had better luck in Der Nerses's case. Thus the diarist is known to have settled in Aleppo in the early 1920s and continued to live there until he was murdered in 1934. After his death, one of the priest's sons, Kevork Nersoyan, undertook to have the diary recopied, with the obvious intention of publishing it. This task was accomplished by Father Kalusd Ekmekjian, who prepared a manuscript, that is, a typed copy of as much of the diary as was contained in the notebooks put at his disposal. Missing from Ekmekjian's typescript are the entries covering the period from October 1911 to May 1915. It might be supposed that the priest from Ayntab did not keep a diary in this period. However, the periodical Հայ Անթեպ [Armenian Anteb] contains information that tends to invalidate this assumption: the single issue published in 1965 reproduces a diary entry for 14 November 1913 under the title "Extracts from Father Der Nerses' Tavukjian's Diary." This entry merely provides supplementary biographical information about Bishop Papken Gyuleserian (the future Catholicos of Antelias Papken I).[8] But the very fact that it exists suggests that Der Nerses most probably kept his diary without interruption and that the entries for the nearly three-year period encompassing the pre-war and early war years are simply missing from the typed variant of the text. It is highly likely that the notebooks containing these entries had been entrusted to compatriots of Der Nerses's from Ayntab who later prepared various publications about the town, to which the information in the priest's diaries would have represented a very valuable contribution. It would follow that it is by no means simple happenstance that the 1913 entry turns up in Հայ Անթեպ, a journal published in Beirut: Krikor Bogharian was the editor of the journal, which contains only material about Armenians in Ayntab. The rest of the notebooks containing the diary may well have met a very typical end, going from hand to hand, never becoming available to Kalusd Ekmekjian, and eventually being lost without a trace.

What remains at a scholar's disposal, besides the published text, is thus the typescript of Der Nerses's diary, comprising a total of eight hundred pages measuring 8.3 by 11.7 inches (21 by 29.7 cm). Entries for the period running from the deportation to liberation comprise eighty-four pages. It is most fortunate that this variant was available, for there are major discrepancies between the typed and the published versions of the text. The editor of the published book evidently cut many entries about the illnesses and, especially, epidemic diseases that befell Der Nerses's family, as well as scenes in which the sick received care. Also occasionally excised are evocations of the degradation the deportees underwent under the extreme conditions they faced. This is unfortunate, because information of this kind sometimes holds the key to understanding Der Nerses's day-to-day life, the conditions of his and his family's existence, and their struggle for survival.

It should be pointed out here that while conducting research for the present study I was able to consult, besides Der Nerses's and Bogharian's diaries, other writings by the two men that shed further light on the deportees' environment in the Salamiyya-Hama area. These are personal testimonials, such as letters written during the years of the deportation or thereafter, autobiographical notes written thereafter, and essays and books that, in aggregate, lead to a better understanding of our two diarists, their personalities, and their times. In Bogharian's case, it proved possible to obtain (in addition to his many published articles and books) some of his personal papers, housed in the archives of Beirut's Haigazian University. As for Der Nerses, the portion of his legacy that may be characterized as personal testimonial consists instead in the countless letters he wrote, many of which it proved possible to find in the seat of the Catholicos of the Great House of Cilicia in Antelias (near Beirut) or in the central archive of the Armenian General Benevolent Union in Cairo. Other important material was available in the archives of the Armenian Prelacy of Aleppo, which house Armenian community institutions' minutes and account books from the period of the deportation. Although they rarely directly concern the Hama-Salamiyya area, these documents nevertheless proved to be precious primary sources for understanding the fundamental problems facing deported Armenians in Bilad al-Sham and for retracing the complicated operations required to provide assistance to the traumatized people there. In the final analysis, all these documents served the same ultimate purpose: they are a means to understand the strategies of survival developed by the deportees in the Hama-Salamiyya area, the many obstacles in their path, and their daily battle to obtain food and stay alive.

At the same time, research done for the present study showed that the genre of the diary has been badly neglected in studies of the Armenian Genocide. Deportees who kept diaries are far from rare; Der Nerses and Bogharian were but two of many. In particular, these diarists include priests (I have no special explanation for this), along with well-read young people like Bogharian and still others who had only an elementary school education. In a word, keeping a diary during the genocide appears to have been a widespread practice among Armenians from nearly every social stratum. The essential question, however, is how these diaries were ultimately utilized. Many who found it inappropriate to publish their survival experiences in diary form; instead reworked their diaries, transforming them into autobiography. As a result, to borrow Philippe Lejeune's and Catherine Bogaert's expression, their writing "lost its essential feature, namely, the authenticity of the moment."[9] Hayg Aramian's book is a text of this kind: clearly the author based this work on his diary, but thoroughly revised the day-to-day entries decades after the events took place, introduced new analyses, and published the whole in the form of a memoir.[10] Although Vahram Dadrian did not go to the same extreme, he too later revised his diary, which he began to keep at the age of fifteen. Thus, entries dated between 1919 and 1922 and consisting of succinct notes were expanded, and narratives by other eyewitnesses were grafted onto them, and thereby the "authenticity of the moment" was, in short, dealt a heavy blow.[11] As we shall see in Chapter 1, Bogharian's diary likewise holds traces of later editing. The field of Armenian Genocide studies includes many other texts of personal testimony that were later edited and prepared for publication, not by their authors, but by others. Editors have often seen fit, in Krikor Beledian's phrase, to "make these texts acceptable," that is, to "upgrade" them by rewriting them, given that their authors were not writers, historians, or college graduates.[12] The publicist Vahram Mavian, son of a priest from Zeytun (present-day Süleymanlı) named Der Hagop Mavian, opted to publish only selected entries from the notebooks containing his deported father's diaries; what is more, he included them in a work in which his own memoirs and his father's diaries are paired off and interwoven.[13]

All this, of course, testifies to a lack of awareness of the inherent value of diaries. However, I am convinced that, in some circumstances, this underestimation of diaries also stems from what might be defined as an extreme sense of shame or self-accusation. For instance, an attentive reading of Der Nerses's or Krikor Bogharian's diaries justifies the supposition that the two of them recorded episodes (personal or not) or moral compromises made for the sake of survival that would be regarded as unacceptable and blameworthy, both from the standpoint of the reconstructed Armenian historiography of the postwar period and, more generally, when measured against the social norms prevailing in their community. These are diaries whose authors, together with some members of their immediate families, were genocide survivors. The fact that they had to give accounts to postwar Armenian society very probably weighed quite heavily on these individuals and their descendants. They would consequently have felt a pressing need to revise their or their relative's work, insert explanations, bring the text into line with the spirit of the times, publish only excerpts or, going still further, simply leave them unpublished, with the result that entire diaries have been lost with the passage of time.

Meanwhile, another factor that also has to do with the domestic Armenian climate in the postwar period is the genocide's transformation into a tale of martyrs and heroes. It is evident that the countless victims led off to slaughter were the martyrs, while the heroes were those who leveled rifles at their executioners, fought with arms in hand, and fell on the field of unequal battle. However, as Yehuda Bauer rightly notes about the Jewish Holocaust, "there is no justification for turning Holocaust history into a hagiography of the victims."[14] Bauer continues: "It is wrong to demand, in retrospect, that these tortured individuals and communities should have behaved as mythical heroes."[15] In an atmosphere of this kind, the survivors' self-narration of their day-to-day struggles, the concessions they made for the sake of staying alive, and their departures from their own moral standards may, at first glance, seem to have nothing heroic about them and to be far removed from scenes of massacre and armed resistance. Sadly, this fact has helped shape decisions about whether diaries and, more generally, personal testimonials are made available to the public. The economic factor has also had an impact: many authors who would like to see their self-narrative texts published have lacked the funds needed to realize this wish. The result is that, to the present day, family attics and institutional archives are bulging with countless works that are still waiting to see the light.

This book is divided into five chapters. The first introduces the two diarists, Der Nerses and Krikor Bogharian. It also provides a description of the surroundings in which these two deportees lived and information regarding their families. The focus here tends to be on the first phase of deportation, in which families and relatives were still mostly together. Many Ayntab residents lived together in exile. Family savings were not yet depleted. But how long could family and community mutual support—a primary means of survival—last in such extreme conditions?

The second chapter examines the general situation in Bilad al-Sham. The Armenians deported to this region were not subjected to mass slaughter. How, then, should we describe this environment, in which the deportees often ran a pitiless race against time at a murderous pace? The chapter focuses on the nationalist-colonialist policies of Ahmed Jemal Pasha, commander of the Ottoman Fourth Army, whose field of operations was Bilad al-Sham. It is primarily based on testimony by our two diarists. This chapter also examines the presence in Salamiyya of Ayntab residents and deportees from other regions. The narrator here is mainly Bogharian, who describes the surroundings and the local populace. Early on, local conditions were relatively encouraging. But the life of an Armenian deportee depended mostly on outside factors. Deportees and their families were far removed from the minimum conditions necessary to create a stable life and to ensure ways of surviving. Thus Salamiyya, while initially promising some modicum of protection, would soon become an unbearable place for many.

The third chapter examines each of the three links in a "money-food-connections" chain that defined the context in which these Armenians carried out their struggle for survival. Demonstrably, all three links represented means of survival. Each was closely bound to the others, and elimination of any one of them could bring the whole process of adaptation and survival to a halt, with fatal consequences for the deportees. Under the conditions that prevailed in the Hama-Salamiyya region, exemplified by the experiences of Der Nerses's and Krikor Bogharian's own families, all three links were progressively weakened as time went on, making the effort required for survival more onerous. This situation harbored the obvious threat of an irreversible decline that hung over the heads of every last deportee in the region, Der Nerses and Krikor Bogharian included.

In the fourth chapter I follow the diarists' path, introducing failed attempts to survive as the specter of death loomed ever larger within Hama-Salamiyya. Der Nerses in particular writes of the period beyond this stage—more precisely, the period that began in 1917—and thus becomes a witness to moral decline. Hunger and epidemic diseases pushed the death rate to merciless levels, and the deportees attempting to cope with this state of affairs had become, generally speaking, weak, spent creatures. Der Nerses often says of the deportees at this stage that they had "become animals," meaning that their whole social structure had collapsed, obliterating the normal human relations on which it was founded.

The fifth and final chapter highlights how the deportees were now ready to make all sorts of compromises for the sake of surviving, engaging in behavior they would have abhorred under normal conditions. Here I describe the forced collective Islamization of Armenians in Hama-Salamiyya—which, however, was not salvation, but just one of several steps taken in order to survive. Deportees' struggles to survive in such extreme conditions continued, many times proving fatal. In Krikor Bogharian's family, a fortunate transformation due to initiative taken by his mother, Santukhd, would ensure the family's survival. At the same time, however, Der Nerses's family, like the majority of deportee families, experienced a period of mortal agony. This is how things continued until the end of World War I.

Notes

1. Andrea Löw, *Juden im Getto Litzmannstadt. Lebensbedingungen, Selbstwahrnehmung, Verhalten* (Göttingen: Wallstein, 2006), p. 45.
2. Annette Wieviorka, *L'ère du témoin* (Paris: Hachette littératures, 1998), p. 13.
3. Philippe Lejeune, *On Diary*, ed. Jeremy Popkin and Julie Rak (Honolulu: University of Hawai'i Press, 2009), p. 20.
4. Marc Nichanian, *The Historiographic Perversion*, trans. Gil Anidjar (New York: Columbia University Press, 2009), pp. 93–94.
5. Carlo Ginzburg, *The Cheese and the Worms: The Cosmos of a Sixteenth-Century Miller*, trans. John and Anne Tedeschi (Baltimore: Johns Hopkins University Press, 1992).
6. See Elke Hartmann and Gabriele Jancke, "Roupens 'Erinnerungen eines armenischen Revolutionärs' (1921/51) im transepochalen Dialog – Konzepte und Kategorien der Selbstzeugnis-Forschung zwischen Universalität und Partikularität," in Claudia Ulbrich, Angelika Schaser, and Hans Medick, eds., *Selbstzeugnis und Person – Transkulturelle Perspektiven* (Vienna: Böhlau, 2012), pp. 31–71; "Rupeni

'Hay heghapokhagani me hishadagnere,' inknavgayutyan arargay yev badmakragan aghpyur" [Rupen's "Memoirs of an Armenian Revolutionary" as self-presentation and historical source], in National Archives of Armenia, ed., *Rupen Der Minasian: Pasdatghteri yev nyuteri zhoghovadzu* [Rupen Der Minasian: Documents and materials] (Yerevan: National Archives of Armenia, 2011), pp. 39–48.
7. See Carlo Ginzburg, "Microhistory: Two or Three Things That I Know about It," *Critical Inquiry* 20, no. 1 (Autumn 1993): 21–24.
8. "Hadvadzner Der Nerses Kahana Tavukjiani orakiren" [Selections from Father Nerses Tavukjian's diary] *Hay Anteb* 6, no. 3 (1965): 66–67.
9. Philippe Lejeune and Catherine Bogaert, *Le journal intime. Histoire et anthologie* (Paris: Textuel, 2006), pp. 23–24.
10. Hayg A. Aramian, *Hayots Danteagan: Medz yegherni badkam. Kavaran yev hrashali Harutyun* [The Armenian *Purgatorio*: The message of the great tragedy; Purgatory and miraculous resurrection] (Beirut: Donigian, 1970).
11. Vahram Dadrian, *To the Desert: Pages from My Diary*, trans. Agop Hacikyan (London: Gomidas Institute, 2006).
12. Krikor Beledian, "Traduire un témoignage écrit dans la langue des *autres*," in Vahram and Janine Altounian, eds., *Mémoires du génocide arménien. Héritage traumatique et travail analytique* (Paris: Presses universitaires de France, 2009), p. 98.
13. Vahram Mavian, *Ampoghchagan yerger* [Complete works] (Antelias: Catholicossate of Cilicia, 1993), pp. 235–242.
14. Yehuda Bauer, *Rethinking the Holocaust* (New Haven and London: Yale University Press, 2002), p. 149.
15. Ibid.

Selected Bibliography

Published Material

Altounian, Vahram and Janine, eds., *Mémoires du génocide arménien. Héritage traumatique et travail analytique*. Paris, 2009.
Aramian, Hayg A. Հայոց Տանթէական. Մեծ եղեռնի պատգամ. Քաւարան եւ հրաշալի Յարութիւն [Hayots Danteagan: Medz yegherni badkam. Kavaran yev hrashali Harutyun] [The Armenian *Purgatorio*: The message of the great tragedy; Purgatory and miraculous resurrection]. Beirut, 1970.
Bauer, Yehuda. *Rethinking the Holocaust*. New Haven and London, 2002.
Dadrian, Vahram. *To the Desert: Pages from My Diary*, trans. Agop Hacikyan. London, 2006.
Ginzburg, Carlo. *The Cheese and the Worms: The Cosmos of a Sixteenth-Century Miller*, trans. John and Anne Tedeschi. Baltimore, 1992.
"Microhistory: Two or Three Things That I Know about It," *Critical Inquiry* 20, no. 1 (Autumn 1993): 10–35.
Lejeune, Philippe and Bogaert, Catherine. *Le journal intime. Histoire et anthologie*. Paris, 2006.
Löw, Andrea. *Juden im Getto Litzmannstadt. Lebensbedingungen, Selbstwahrnehmung, Verhalten*. Wallstein, 2006.
Mavian, Vahram. Ամբողջական երկեր [Ampoghchagan yerger] [Complete works]. Antelias, 1993.
Nichanian, Marc. *The Historiographic Perversion*, trans. Gil Anidjar. New York, 2009.

Popkin, Jeremy and Rak, Julie, eds. *On Diary*. Honolulu, 2009.
Ulbrich, Claudia, Schaser, Angelika and Medick, Hans, eds. *Selbstzeugnis und Person – Transkulturelle Perspektiven*. Vienna, 2012.
Wieviorka, Annette. *L'ère du témoin*. Paris, 1998.
Ռուբեն Տէր Մինասյան. փաստաթղթերի եւ նյութերի ժողովածու [Rupen Der Minasian: Pasdatghteri yev nyuteri zhoghovadzu] [Rupen Der Minasian: Documents and materials]. Yerevan, 2011.
"Հատուածներ Տէր Ներսէս Քհնյ. Թավուգճեանի օրագիրէն" [Hadvadzner Der Nerses Kahana Tavukjiani orakiren] [Selections from Father Nerses Tavukjian's diary] *Hay Anteb* 6, no. 3 (1965): 66–67.

Chapter 1

The Diarist, his Environment and the Reasons for Keeping a Diary

Keeping a Diary: An Ordinary Virtue in Extreme Conditions

Why keep a diary? That classical question is prioritized for the simple reason that it presents an occasion to enter the inner worlds of our two diarists during the deportation, to examine them and study them in depth. Theirs were, naturally, unusual inner worlds; but the same holds for the hundreds of thousands of other Armenians subjected to the same fate. The cases of Der Nerses and Bogharian differ from those of the great majority of their countrymen precisely because each of the former left behind an indispensable instrument, his diary, that allows us to see and understand the experience of those times as reflected in people's inner worlds and spiritual suffering. Der Nerses's and Bogharian's diaries also give expression to the shifts taking place in the outside world, both in their surroundings and in society. In this respect, each diarist's inner environment substantially reflects transformations in his outer environment, to borrow Alain Girard's phrase.[1] Thus these diaries also provide us with a means of examining, assessing, and interpreting both particular incidents and larger developments.

To be sure, we have to do here with two different individuals, two different personalities, whose differences are naturally reflected in their diaries: the diarist is directly rooted in his context, and there is a reciprocal relationship between diarist and environment.[2] When we read the two diaries in this perspective, we come closer to their social surroundings and can better understand the shifts and transformations taking place there.

In Bogharian's case, all indications are that this was his first experience of keeping a diary. His daily observations and jottings went into a small notebook that he kept in his pocket.[3] However anodyne the subjects he wrote about, taking notes on his experiences in the unusual conditions of the deportation was not completely risk-free. Bogharian would later learn of the sad fate of sixteen-year-old Hagop Der Melkonian from Ayntab, who likewise kept a diary. When Hagop was being deported to Der Zor with his family, the police discovered the young man's diary on his person. After an investigation, charges were brought against him on the basis of some of his entries. The authorities brought him before a court martial, after which Der Melkonian was hanged in Marash (present-day Kahraman Maraş).[4] The case of Yervant Odian[5] offers another example of the dangers involved. Once he reached Hama, Odian considered himself to be in relative security, and he, too, began to keep a diary. By 1916, he had filled three small notebooks. Later, however, he was arrested on false charges. Luckily, he found a way to have his diaries destroyed to avoid further complications.[6] Chavarche Missakian was arrested in 1916 in Istanbul, jailed, and subjected to severe torture. Diary notes found on his person served as the main basis of the charges brought against him.[7] Despite the general atmosphere of uncertainty, Bogharian never faced this kind of direct persecution by the authorities and continued writing in his diary to the very end of 1916, ignoring the probable risks involved.

Der Nerses was a relatively experienced diarist. His diary, in the state in which it has come down to us, opens in May 1909. It is noteworthy that its first sections were written during the years in which he served on a relief committee representing Armenians from Ayntab; its mission was to distribute moneys collected in Ayntab to victims of the 1909 massacres of Armenians in Cilicia.[8] To this end, Der Nerses traveled with the other committee members through the Armenian villages of the Antioch district. What likely motivated him to keep a diary was the desire to make a record of the mass killing and testify to its consequences. Der Nerses was on the same mission in mid-1915, when caravans of Armenians being deported from the inner Anatolian provinces to Syria began passing through Ayntab. This priest's diary was now not only a means of testifying to his experience, but also the place in which he carried on a conversation with himself and God. It was likewise in these pages that, struggling with himself, he tried to reaffirm his will to survive when everything around him grew dark as difficulties piled up or members of his family died—in a word, when his personal world began to fall apart.

Keeping a diary also represented, for both Der Nerses and Bogharian, an "intellectual and aesthetic experience" to borrow Todorov's description of some people's way of reacting to extreme situations.⁹ At a time when Krikor Bogharian, Der Nerses, and their countrymen were living under uncertain, humiliating conditions, keeping a diary and occupying oneself with the written word and things literary could be considered "ordinary virtues."¹⁰ Such activities are mental exercises that lift individuals above a predominantly inhuman, extreme environment: making daily entries in a diary is one way of attaining the spiritual satisfaction brought by resisting dark tyranny and injustice, while simultaneously forging a symbolic, abstract bond with one's earlier, normal life. Yet such situations are in constant flux, which means that keeping a diary does not affect the diarist in the same way at all times. Indeed, to the same extent that catastrophic conditions grow still more dismal and hopes of extricating oneself from a terrible predicament gradually dwindle, keeping a diary can become torture, or at least a spiritually draining exercise for many. In such circumstances, keeping a diary no longer helps the diarist flee the present; quite the contrary, the diary is then transformed into a kind of mirror that bitterly reflects the hopelessness of its author's situation. Alexandra Garbarini, whose *Numbered Days* is a magisterial study of this theme, observes that under such extreme conditions, keeping a diary can simply throw the crumbling of the diarist's personal world and the hopelessness of the present situation into sharper relief before his or her own eyes.¹¹ Garbarini points out that many of the Jewish diarists who were confined in ghettos proved unable to continue keeping a diary from the latter half of World War II on, that is, from the moment the mass killing was sharply accelerated.¹²

We find evidence for Garbarini's thesis in Der Nerses's diary as well. In the years of exile, the regularity with which the priest from Ayntab kept his diary was twice interrupted. The first major interruption dates to 1916–1917, when Der Nerses, deported for a second time along with the rest of the clergy, spent eight months in exile in Tafile. The second dates to the period from April to October 1918. In both periods, as we shall see, Der Nerses was despondent. In Tafile, he was cut off from his family, and his loneliness and helplessness stand out the more sharply as a result. As for the second of these two periods, the priest's family was with him throughout it, but misery, famine, and epidemic had invaded his home and the situation seemed hopeless, the more so as death had begun to mow down members of his own household. In both periods, keeping a diary would have been a painful task for Der Nerses; this, no doubt, is why we find no entries in the diary for days at a time or, often, only hasty jottings. Moreover, all the entries in these two periods reflect fear, anxiety, despondency, and a sense of abandonment.

Krikor Bogharian: The Thirst for Knowledge during a Deportation, and the Intellectual Alternatives

Krikor Bogharian was a studious, diligent youth of eighteen when he reached Hama on 17 October 1915.[13] Born in Ayntab in 1897, he was the son of Karekin Bogharian, a priest, and Santukhd Bogharian-Tahtajian. He entered Ayntab's local Vartanian school at an early age, graduating in 1912. The diploma preserved in his personal archives shows that he was an outstanding pupil. Admittedly he showed little aptitude for drawing or music, he had exceptionally high grades in Armenian, Ottoman Turkish, French, and English, the four languages taught in the school, as well as penmanship (Armenian, Ottoman, French) and all other subjects.[14] In 1912, he began his secondary education at Cilicia High School, which had been founded in Ayntab that very year. As Bogharian later noted in another text, the children in the schools he attended as a boy learned Ottoman Turkish as their "mother tongue."[15] In other words, Turkish was the dominant language in Ayntab's Armenian schools. As an adolescent, Bogharian drew up an inventory of the manuscripts in Ayntab and also authored a study of the city's Armenian dialect.[16]

He was within one year of graduating when the deportation forced him to leave school. This was naturally a big disappointment for him, especially because his main preoccupation as a young man was his plan to finish his secondary-school education and pursue further study. In his diary, Bogharian often evokes his school in Ayntab, his teachers and their lessons, and his classmates. On 9 September, he wittily notes that whereas he would have been studying astronomy for the first time had he been present for the new school year, he had instead become a master at backgammon, which he played all day long with compatriots in his new neighborhood in Hama.[17] From the very first days of his circumstances in exile, we see him engaged in a struggle against the constraints of the times and his new life—an attempt to compensate, through independent study, for the fact that he could no longer go to school.

His father's library proved one of the best available means to that end. Though unable to bring all of it from Ayntab, the family had nonetheless brought a rather impressive number of books with them. Krikor's father, the priest Karekin Bogharian, had been a well-known bookseller in Ayntab and, at the same time, the local representative of a daily newspaper published in Istanbul, *Byuzantion* (Byzantium).[18] Thus Krikor Bogharian grew up in the world of books, an environment he had clearly loved as a child. When the hour of the deportation struck, the family took to the road with seventeen large parcels and various trunks, a load requiring eight mules to carry it; one of the trunks was filled with nothing but books.[19] Among them, Bogharian writes, were "fourteen literary and historical books, ten dictionaries, thirteen books on religion and the church...one yearbook...and ten schoolbooks."[20]

Only a few days after the deportees had reached their place of exile, Bogharian embarked on a reading program that he would pursue almost without interruption until the end of the period covered by his extant diary. He promptly found other compatriots from Ayntab who had likewise managed to bring part of their libraries with them to Hama. He borrowed the first book he read there, Charles Seignobos's *History of Civilization*, from Dr. Kilejian, finishing it in about two weeks.[21] The next book he read was Teotig's 1908 *Yearbook*, one of the books owned by his family,[22] followed by the Bible.[23] A few weeks later, he bought an Assyrian grammar from Hama's Assyrian school and began studying it.[24] Still later, he began learning literary Arabic.[25] He also read Kevork-Mesrob's *Armenian Church History*,[26] Frederic William Farrar's *Sermons*,[27] Smpad Tavtian's *Armenian Literature Reader*, Ghevont Alishan's *Ancient Armenian Religion*,[28] Ernest Renan's *Vie de Jésus*,[29] Leo's *History of Armenian Literature*[30] and *Armenian Printing*,[31] Daniel Varuzhan's *The Heart of the Race*,[32] Tevfik Fikret's *Halûk'un defteri*,[33] Moses of Khoren's *History of the Armenians*, Archbishop Malachia Ormanian's *National History*,[34] the journal *Keghuni* (published by the Armenian Catholic Mkhitarist monastery in Venice),[35] and two books that he had borrowed from Movses Kazanjian, J. Chaumeil's *Manuel de pédagogie psychologique*[36] and Irénée Carré's and Roger Liquier's *Traité de pédagogie scolaire*.[37]

Krikor did more than just read; he also set about translating, in their entirety, some of the books he read. Over the space of some two months, he first translated Frank Wilson Blackmar's *Outlines of Sociology*,[38] and then went on to translate a book he had read before the deportation, Seignobos's *Histoire de la civilisation*.[39] Krikor writes that one of his teachers from Ayntab, Krikor Sarafian, as well as his friend Kevork Baboyan, likewise translated Thomas Harwood Pattison's *The Making of the Sermon*, followed by John Lubbock's *Le Bonheur de vivre*.[40] In this respect, Bogharian was fortunate: thanks to his intellectual efforts, he was able to create "a space in which he could breathe freely amid the reigning sadness," as Todorov puts it.[41]

He also had an opportunity to share his newly acquired knowledge with classmates and teachers, first in Hama and then in Salamiyya. This was surely an encouraging circumstance, one that would help sustain hope in anyone who was suddenly thrust into an extreme situation. In other words, if Primo Levi in his Nazi concentration camp had Piccolo by his side, a man to whom he could recite passages from Dante, thereby

Figure 1.1. Ayntab, Vartanian school. Graduating diploma given in 1912 to Krikor Bogharian. (Source: Haigazian University Library, Beirut)

experiencing moments of boundless spiritual and intellectual satisfaction,[42] Bogharian, for his part, was flanked by more than one Piccolo, and these companions lent a new and brighter tinge to his otherwise gloomy life. Bogharian arranged to have the paper he needed for his translations brought from Hama. He had no desk. Rather, "I would sit," he writes, "on a sofa, with a gasoline jerrycan that served me as a desk in front of me. I would make the ink myself, thinning the purple crystal paint with water."[43] Another way of satisfying his thirst for reading materialized when his father, on 18 November 1915, once again began receiving—albeit quite irregularly—the daily *Byuzantion*.[44] In addition to all this, Bogharian also carried out a census of the Armenians in Salamiyya while he was there.[45]

Thanks to these various intellectual five-finger exercises, the young man from Ayntab managed to maintain a certain continuity with the studies that he had been forced to break off and the natural life that had once been his. Reading, translating, and intellectual discussion were all activities that could occasionally breathe new life and new spirit into his gloomy, oppressive daily round. For Bogharian, these were surely moments that allowed him to forget his and all the other deportees' uncertain situation; in a way, they distanced him from his extreme life conditions. We can put his decision to keep a diary in this general context: the undertaking brought him into daily contact with the written word and literature, the life of the mind and his unfinished education, his hometown and the ordinary boy's life that he had led there. Yet it remains true that, as discussed above, keeping a diary could also have the opposite effect by holding the diarist at a distance from the worlds he is seeking to rejoin and thus precipitating a fatal rupture between him and his past. In Bogharian's case, however, it may be presumed that writing a diary was a salutary way of forging a symbolic link with his past life and the classmates from whom he had been forcibly separated.

Der Nerses: Commun(icat)ing with God by Way of a Diary

Reverend Nerses Tavukjian, as a representative of a generation older than Bogharian's, was a man of a different mold. He, too, hailed from Ayntab. Born in 1870, he was christened Krikor. Thus, by an odd coincidence, this first name is a commanding presence in both of our diarists' personal worlds. It was also the given name of Krikor Bogharian's father, who, after being ordained and taking a new name in accordance with Armenian church custom, baptized his eldest son Krikor. Der Nerses's brother's son, who was born in exile and died in infancy, was likewise christened Krikor.

Krikor, the future Der Nerses, attended Ayntab's Nersesian Armenian elementary school (founded in 1856)[46] and, later, a school just opened by the Franciscans. In 1885, he left school to take up the weaver's trade. When he lost his father at an early age, the burden of providing for the family fell mainly on his shoulders. Thus life's exigencies prevented the young Krikor from continuing his schooling. He clearly enjoyed learning and tried to make up for his deficient education in a number of different ways. In a big town such as Ayntab, where Armenians and Turks lived side by side, a good command of Turkish was plainly one key to success. This did not represent any particular problem for Ayntab's Armenians, who were preponderantly Turkish speakers—only a minority used Armenian on a daily basis. This was undoubtedly the environment in which young Krikor Tavukjian grew up. Then, while pursuing his career as a craftsman, he decided he should learn to read and write Ottoman Turkish as well, and for several years studied written Turkish in evening courses at the Vartanian school. Krikor Bogharian's father was one of his classmates there.[47]

In 1896, Tavukjian added a new fillip to his education by entering Turkey's Central College, an American missionary establishment located in Ayntab, while also taking a teaching post in the Vartanian school. He then became a candidate for the priesthood, leaving Ayntab in 1901 to prepare for the celibate priesthood in the seminary in Armash (present-day Akmeşe). The novice returned to Ayntab in 1903, where he married Anitsa Syulahian and, in 1904, was ordained and consecrated a priest. He was subordinate to the Catholicosate in Sis (present-day Kozan). Karekin Bogharian was among those ordained with him, and both men served in Ayntab until the deportation.[48] The largely self-taught Der Nerses was plainly one of the town's Armenian notables. Deported, he reached Hama on 1 August 1915, having been put on a wagon with his family and taken from Ayntab to a rail transit station southeast of Aghja Koyu (present-day Akçaköy, to the west of Karkemish); from there they made the journey to Hama by rail.[49]

Our two diarists, then, knew each other: Der Nerses and Krikor Bogharian's father had become friends in Ayntab. Moreover, Krikor Bogharian himself must have been well acquainted with Der Nerses, since the older man had been one of his teachers in Cilicia High School, which Der Nerses had helped found and on whose school board he served.[50] In other words, the present work involves two mutually acquainted authors whose nevertheless quite different daily lives explained their different inner worlds and often differing day-to-day concerns. This constellation would have been still more interesting if we had had the diary of the third "Krikor," Rev. Karekin Bogharian, at our disposal. We know from his son's testimony that he kept one: Krikor Bogharian's father jotted down a record of his daily life in the available free space in Teotig's 1908 *Yearbook*.[51] This diary, however, has not been published and is believed to be lost.

In Krikor Bogharian's case, reading, translating, and keeping a diary comprise the three factors thanks to which he maintained, throughout the years far from home, a link with his studies and earlier life in Ayntab. In a way, the same factors also detached him from the uncertainty and humiliations that were his daily lot, fueled the hope that he would one day resume the life he loved, and in the process reinforced his will to survive. Matters were very different in Der Nerses's case. He never alludes to his reading, although we know that he, too, had a sizable library at his disposal, inasmuch as Krikor Bogharian often borrowed books from him. It must be added that Der Nerses's spiritual life, sermons, and daily relations with his flock may also have helped sustain this devout clergyman's hopes, providing him with a source of inspiration. In the conditions imposed by the deportation, however, insurmountable barriers to spiritual activity were soon to make their appearance. Here too, Der Nerses' diary proved to be the place in which, liberated from the manifold constraints imposed by the outside world, he could enter into communication with God, express wishes, and solicit divine intercession, but also tacitly voice protest.

In his diary, Der Nerses indicates that he feels God's presence more strongly every time his and his family's situation takes a turn for the worse. In such periods, almost all the entries in his diary culminate in supplications addressed to God, such as "Lord have mercy," "Lord preserve us," "Lord help us," and "May the Lord bring things to a happy end." (Interestingly, the formulas used are never the same.) But the clergyman's relationship to God is sometimes also marked by moments of exasperation. At such times, his style becomes extremely sober and his criticism takes an indirect form. On 9 October 1916, he writes, bitterly, "Can it be that the sons and daughters of the Armenian Church, after worshiping Christ for fifteen hundred years, are destined to perish in Arabia's depths? Enough."[52] One has the impression that this is an outburst against God; yet Der Nerses immediately adds, cautiously: "God is great and his providential dispositions are inscrutable. He will undoubtedly transform this great evil into a blessing; but he who sees that divine blessing may consider himself fortunate indeed."[53] In the last phrase, a protest against the Lord's slowness to intercede is again detectable.

Sometimes politics and utopian aspirations enter into Der Nerses's conversations with God, giving rise to imagery that affords us glimpses of his optimism about the future. The best example is found in his diary entry for 31 October 1916, which was in fact written in one of the most difficult periods of the priest's exile. Here he states his opinion that the prolonged war will eventually bring the European Great Powers' haughtiness and pride to a fall. The peoples will suffer greatly; but their suffering will be the prelude to the creation of a "new heaven" and "new earth." "The map of the world will be drawn in a way that the governments never expected. And, from this pandemonium, God will bring forth blessings for mankind. May the Lord hasten that day; if He does not, few will be the sons and daughters of the Armenian nation who live to see it."[54] In these lines, a pointer to the idea of international social revolution is discernible. Here, however, it is above all important to note how Der Nerses uses his diary to keep his hope for the future alive and, simply, to survive.

"They Say Something Has Happened in the Vicinity of Der Zor"

Manifestly, when Der Nerses and Krikor Bogharian were deported from Ayntab in 1915, they still had no clear idea of the fate in store for them, or more generally of the murderous crime being perpetrated against the Armenians of the Ottoman Empire. Their daily jottings faithfully reflect their initial ignorance of what was happening and, later, the diarists' dawning awareness of the unspeakable crimes that in time became their own reality as well. In the historiography of the Armenian Genocide, it is by now an established fact that there were certain differences in the fates meted out to distinct groups of deportees. The first salient point is that the Armenians of the Armenian High Plateau, who as a rule were deported from their towns and villages in June–July 1915, were subjected to collective massacres on the road to exile; indeed, these groups were repeatedly decimated before reaching the Syrian steppes. The second salient point is that after crossing the Taurus Mountain chain and entering the empire's Arab provinces, the caravans of deportees were forced to follow one of two different routes.

One of these routes ran through the northern reaches of Arab Mesopotamia (Jazira), an area into which many thousands of deportees were driven. The majority of people in this group were subjected to massacres. The relevant geographical zone comprised the steppes stretching from the Euphrates to the Tigris, with the Khabur River valley at the center of this region. The names of the towns and villages in this region, such as Der Zor, Ras el-Ain, Margada, Mosul, Shedadiye, and Marat, have become symbols evoking all the horror and dread of the genocide. This is the region that saw what Raymond H. Kévorkian has termed "the second phase of the Genocide," that is, the slaughter of the Armenians who had been concentrated in Mesopotamia.[55] Whereas in Ras el-Ain, for example, the mass murder began in March 1916, it reached its peak elsewhere, with a massacre of Armenians concentrated in the region of Der Zor, where two hundred thousand Armenians were exterminated between July and December 1916.[56]

But there was, as noted, another deportation route, corresponding roughly to the inland regions of Bilad al-Sham or the eastern regions of the *vilayet* of Suriyye. It included, principally, the *sanjak*s of Hama, Sham, Kerek, and Hauran. In other words, the deportees were resettled along a route that ran parallel to the Mediterranean and extended southward from Aleppo to the boundaries of the Sinai Peninsula. This geographical zone roughly corresponds to the region traversed by the railway from Aleppo to Damascus, which also served Homs and Hama. In the case of this second deportation route, the deportees' resettlement areas stretched southward from Damascus, extending through Hauran, Dera'a, Amman, and Kerek and as far south as Ma'an. This route partially coincides with the string of towns and villages along the Hijaz railroad. Although famine and epidemics led to massive human losses in these places, it bears emphasizing that no massacres took place here. It is true that survival came at the price of a daily struggle, and that life here was ruled by uncertainty. Yet whenever it proved possible to adapt to the environment, start up a commercial enterprise, go to work in a trade, and succeed in making money, the deportees' chances of survival were significantly higher.

That account of matters, however, is one made with benefit of hindsight. Let us now see how our two diarists experienced these realities from day to day. More precisely, let us see the extent to which the Armenian exiles in Bilad al-Sham were aware of this difference in the destinies of the two groups of Armenian deportees.

Krikor Bogharian's diary leaves one with the impression that, in the first few weeks of the deportation, he was on an ordinary journey. To be sure, uncertainty and fear were constant presences; however, the fact remains that Bogharian and his family made the journey from Ayntab to Hama without suffering any hardships of note. Accompanied by hundreds of other Ayntab natives, the Bogharians remained together throughout the trip and managed to take nearly all their household goods with them. Traveling exclusively by train, they reached Hama in some six days. Initially, the family preferred to believe that they were involved, as the authorities had indicated, in a provisional measure and would be returning to Ayntab after three months.[57] But as month followed month with no sign of an impending return, the Bogharians' experience of the realities of their deportation very quickly undid this initial conviction.

Compatriots of the Bogharians who had been deported before them were already living in Hama, as were other Armenians from Marash, Kilis, Fendejak (present-day Dönüklü), Antioch, Kesab, and the Musa Dagh or Mt. Moses region. Thus the majority of deportees in Hama were from Cilicia or the area just to its east. In the first stage of their deportation, according to Bogharian, ten thousand people were settled in tents on a hill near Hama's rail transit station. The number of deportees living there would have fluctuated constantly, as various epidemics swept away large numbers of victims in short order, whereupon other deportees were resettled there in their turn; still other groups of people were sent further south on orders of the *sevkıyat*.[58] For the first few days, Krikor Bogharian and his family were also resettled there. They evidently had to live in a tent at first, but four days later, like some of their compatriots, they rented a room in a house near the train station. As a rule, several families from the same city lived together in these houses, one family to a room. Krikor Bogharian and his family later moved frequently, first within Hama and then to Salamiyya, but, generally speaking, these deportees did not live in tents. The deportees could circulate freely in Hama and make purchases in the local stores. Bogharian often took advantage of this circumstance to visit the city's ancient remains, the open and closed markets, and the Assyrian school. Every Sunday, he attended Armenian mass, which was celebrated in the Assyrian church.[59]

Krikor's father continued to serve as a priest. More exactly, under the conditions of exile, his work consisted primarily in officiating at burial services. As a result, the family had a modest income. But this large family lived, for the most part, on its savings and the proceeds of the sales of certain household objects (rugs, copperware, woolens, covers, and bedsheets).[60] Obviously, this state of affairs could not continue for long. Moreover, the threat of being deported elsewhere hung constantly over the family's head: "Although we are comfortable in our new house," Bogharian writes, "we are left constantly wondering whether we are to remain in Hama or whether we, too, will be sent further south."[61] It was surely because of their terror before this uncertainty that many deportees, rather than be relocated to other, still more unfamiliar places, preferred to remain in Hama, waiting and surviving in this city until the end of the war, that is, until they could return to their homes. Hama's

Armenians went so far as to petition the Ottoman authorities to let them stay put, and some fifteen hundred people signed the petition.[62] In both Hama and Salamiyya, the Armenians were plainly aware that they enjoyed relatively favorable conditions. Thus, while Bogharian wrote a sad entry in his diary on the first anniversary of his deportation from Ayntab, he nevertheless concluded with the words: "Praise the Lord that we ended up in a hospitable district and that many of us were able to save our skins. Seeing the wretched widows and orphans who have come from Anatolia or the area around Sepasdia/Sivas, we praise the Lord a thousand times over for our situation."[63] Elsewhere, the diarist notes that he and his fellow deportees in Hama are "grateful to Jemal Pasha" for their relatively fortunate situation.[64]

In fact, one observes a state of total helplessness in the face of unfolding events. The Bogharians were manifestly impotent actors: decisions came from the authorities, while the Bogharian family lived in a waiting posture, incapable of anticipating even the short term, the more so as they were ignorant of both general developments and events taking place around them. Evidently, this situation disturbed the diarists. "Stuck in an isolated spot, we do not know what is going on in the world and are ignorant of the course of the war," Bogharian writes on 6 September 1915.[65] Of course, this does not mean that they were utterly unaware that something extraordinary was happening to Armenians, as scarcely a month after their arrival in the city, the Armenians in Hama began to witness the pitiful, wretched, helpless condition of their compatriots arriving from Anatolia's inner provinces. "It seems that Armenians are condemned to disappear as a nation," was Bogharian's conclusion.[66] This was, however, mere supposition, made without benefit of an overall view of things or a clear conception and characterization of the genocide. In the first months, the deportees' official sources of news were the Istanbul Armenian newspaper *Byuzantion*, already mentioned, which began to arrive in Hama in September 1915,[67] as well as Ottoman Turkish newspapers and official declarations. Yervant Odian, who spent some time in Hama in 1916, points to the example of the newsroom that the German army had set up in the city: it was frequented by deportees like Odian, who could read various German or Ottoman newspapers there.[68] In these information sources, however, they primarily found news reports about the course of the war that were, as might be expected, incomplete and one-sided.

The new deportees who continued to arrive in Hama were major sources of information. For example, Armenians there learned from deportees from Suedia (present-day Samandağı) that some of the Armenians of the Mt. Moses district had taken up positions on the mountain and were resisting there.[69] The most important sources of news, however, seem to have been the rail transit station and personal letters that went from hand to hand. Our two diarists make no allusion to these two sources of information, probably to avoid unnecessary risk. Yervant Odian, however, does mention them in his deportation memoirs. Thus we learn that every day, Armenian settlers took turns waiting for the arrival of the troop transport train that ran from Aleppo southward. This train stopped in the city for a few hours, which gave the deportees an opportunity to go looking for people with news. An Armenian professional (e.g., doctor, pharmacist, dentist) could usually be found among the passengers and would be discreetly drawn aside by settlers and peppered with questions.[70] As for personal letters, those containing important information about unfolding events were written in a kind of code involving metaphors that the letter writer would use in descriptions.[71]

This and such information transmitted by word of mouth were not of much help in forming a general picture of the mass murder or discovering its real scope. In the case of Bogharian's diary, entries about Armenians being driven toward the deserts around Der Zor do not appear until July 1916. In this particular instance, the information came from members of a nomadic Arab tribe known as the Aneze who, in line with their summer custom, were migrating from their desert toward the cities. "As they tell it," Bogharian writes, "the Armenians in the Der Zor district are in a very sorry state. [The Arabs] had purchased hundreds of Armenian girls and women at a price of from one to three mejidieh each and had abducted many others."[72] Some of these Armenians later turned up in villages in the vicinity. "[Their] faces [are] tattooed, and hundreds of others have been abducted or bought," Bogharian writes.[73] Such information, however, was still not sufficient to permit the diarist to form a clear idea of what had happened—unless he was reluctant to admit the reality of the matter or too cautious to refer directly to it. Bogharian contents himself with writing: "It is clear that something has happened in the vicinity of Der Zor."[74] Only in October 1916, that is, more than a year after he and his family were deported, does the full impact of the mass killing make itself felt in the pages of his diary. "Very bad news is arriving from Der Zor; they've driven the people further on and carried out a collective massacre. In certain localities, they've left only the tradesmen alive."[75] At the end of the diary is one further such reference, in an entry made in December 1916. This time, Bogharian's information came from Armenians who had fled Der Zor. "They say that approximately 600,000 Armenians have been wiped out there by massacre, disease, or starvation."[76] By a telling coincidence, Bogharian stopped keeping a diary a few days after making this entry.

People Crushed like Ants: Der Nerses on the Armenians Arriving in Hama

Der Nerses, for his part, often engages in analysis in his diary, and his interpretations are frequently penetrating. This makes it easier for us to understand his environment and the impact it had on him. Until his own deportation from Ayntab, he was apparently unaware that a general plan to evacuate Armenians from their native regions had been put into practice. In these months, ominous news began arriving about deportations of Armenians from other provinces, and reports were also circulating to the effect that Armenian soldiers serving in the Ottoman army were being slain by their own commanding officers; meanwhile Armenians were also being taken into custody in Ayntab.[77] Furthermore, Der Nerses witnessed the passage of Armenian deportees through Ayntab; they came, as a rule, from towns and villages nearby.[78] In other words, these deportees represented the population of Cilicia and neighboring districts. The priest from Ayntab writes: "From the beginning, I have thought that the relocation of the people of Cilicia resulted from strategic considerations. More exactly, perhaps, its causes are complex; there is not just one reason for it. It may even be that mixing the Christian populace with the Arab element will prove to have its uses in future."[79] These lines—written early, in June 1915—clearly reveal Der Nerses's incomprehension of the Ittihadist faction's general plan. Regardless, he is remarkably prophetic as far as the fate of Cilicia's Armenians is concerned.

Der Nerses and his big family took up residence in a *han* on their very first day in Hama. Shortly thereafter, they rented a house. Like the Bogharians, the whole family made the journey to Hama together, along with hundreds of other natives of Ayntab. When they arrived, some twelve thousand Armenian deportees from Kghi/Kiği, Ayntab, Marash, Gürün, Fendejak, Kilis, Kesab, Hajin (present-day Saimbeyli), and the Mt. Moses area were already in the city and its environs. Between eighty and one hundred of these families—the number would gradually grow—had already found shelter in houses in the city; all the others were living in tents pitched on the hill.[80]

As a priest, Der Nerses was better acquainted than others with the deportees' condition. In his line of duties, he was in almost daily contact with deportees, especially the most wretched and helpless among them. Analyses and descriptions of the exile abound in the pages of his diary. In Der Nerses's view, the Armenians suffering worst were those who had arrived in Hama from localities in more remote provinces like Cesaerea/Kayseri, Tokat, Amasya, Sivas, Samson/Samsun, and Kghi.

In these groups adult males were rare, as the men, generally speaking, had been exterminated on the deportation routes. The others—women and children in particular—had been pillaged, and many had lost everything they had. When they finally set foot in Hama, these people were exhausted and demoralized. Hunger and disease swept dozens of lives from their ranks every day. In September 1915, Der Nerses and other priests in Hama buried more than eighty Armenian corpses on some days;[81] as Bogharian puts it, "the unsettled terrain in Hama has become a boundless graveyard."[82] The contemporaneous correspondence of ranking Ottoman officials also referred to this alarming mortality rate.[83] Depicting the condition of one of these ravaged groups, deportees from Kghi, Der Nerses writes: "All of them are walking graves, and do not even have time to bury their dead."[84] The high number of deaths left Der Nerses in a state of consternation. In September, the priests were constantly busy burying the dead.

> The dying are those who have come from Anatolia naked and hungry and have already fallen ill on the way. They are women and young boys and girls. These are people who sleep on the hill with the ground for a mattress and the air for a blanket; at night they are drenched in dew and they suffer from sunstroke by day. They keep dying because they have arrived here as physical and moral corpses as a result of exhaustion and months of unrelieved suffering.... Many have become so apathetic that they do not even go to the trouble of reporting their dead.[85]

Der Nerses concludes his entry for the same day with these lines:

> Alas for the Armenian nation, which is so wretched and has no one but God to defend it and watch over it. If God does not make a blanket of his love and a mattress of his pity for these people living out in the open, the Armenian nation will be destroyed for no reason and Syria shall be the Armenians' grave. O, Lord God, take pity on this long-suffering nation.[86]

Later, Der Nerses wrote in his autobiography that he and his colleagues had buried around eight thousand Armenian deportees on the hill in Hama.[87]

Especially in view of the condition of the Armenians arriving from the interior, Der Nerses thought it crucial that the deportees from Ayntab and Marash, who had arrived together as a group without suffering great hardship en route, not be sent elsewhere. For a nuclear or extended family that has been deported, continuing to live together, or in a community with compatriots from the same city, is evidently a favorable condition for survival. However, Hama was simply a transit station for the many Armenians who were deported again and driven further south, in directions that thus far were unfamiliar. The resulting state of affairs, as we have already seen in Bogharian's case, left the Armenians incapable of anticipating even the short-time future and prey to the feeling that their lives were not at all either certain or secure. With this in mind, Der Nerses compares the Armenians concentrated in Hama to ants; they "are targets of persecution, and it is clear that domesticated animals command more respect from the police than they do."[88] This grim metaphor depicts all the deportees as animals; in fact, in calling them "ants," the diarist reduces them to weak, insignificant insects that human beings can grind underfoot at will.

Deportations from Hama to regions further south on the way to Damascus and Hauran generally took place by camel but were sometimes carried out by rail. The beasts of burden would be loaded with the deportees' possessions while the people themselves usually accompanied the caravans on foot.[89] Sometimes groups of up to four thousand deportees left Hama en masse.[90] Der Nerses was horrified by the disorderliness of these caravans, caused by the local authorities' disregard of the exiles' pleas to be deported together with the other members of their families or other people from their native towns or villages. The authorities, aiming simply to keep new settlers from thronging Hama, were reducing the number of Armenians pouring into the city by driving them further south. "No townsman travels together with his fellow townsman; constant chaos reigns. Things are done in such a way that brother is separated from sister, and fathers and mothers, from their children," Der Nerses writes.[91] Immediately afterward, he adds: "What a bane for people who are ill, like me, and for families teeming with children."[92] Transfers of this sort deprived the deportees of the mutual aid and cooperation that people could expect from their families or other people from their native town or village. It seems that all these resettled people clearly understood that the presence of their loved ones and acquaintances was an important factor in enduring and surviving. That was why Der Nerses was convinced that remaining in Hama was, for his townsmen from Ayntab, tantamount to salvation. "We will be thankful if they let us natives of Ayntab remain in the city, since that will spare us the hardships involved in being sent here and there—especially because the city of Hama, its drawbacks notwithstanding, has positive features as well."[93]

In Der Nerses's diary, unlike in Bogharian's, there are no direct allusions to the mass murders perpetrated in the areas to the east of Hama and the Euphrates River. Is this merely evidence of an experienced individual's prudence? In any case, as mentioned earlier, of the two diaries at our disposal, the published version of Der Nerses's is without doubt the more faithful to the original manuscript and is convincingly free of traces of subsequent editorial intrusion. This is pointed out for the simple reason that the rare allusions to the genocide in Bogharian's diary leave the impression of having been incorporated later into the original text. The most conspicuous of these addenda is the entry for 15 February 1916. On that date, the young Bogharian learned from a townsman who had arrived in Salamiyya from Ayntab that the Turkish authorities had taken over the Armenian school and other educational institutions in Ayntab that he dearly loved, and were now using these buildings for military purposes. Disturbed by the news, he wrote in his diary (published years later):

> The Turkish beast's claws and ravenous maw have annihilated everything. Nothing is sacred and there is no honor left. An entire nation has been consumed by the holocaust. But woe unto you! You, too, will one day be meted out divine punishment. Blessed are those who will live to see that day, blessed are those who will demand retribution for the blood of one million innocents and take vengeance!"[94]

This excerpt's terse, solemn, accusatory style and the historical information given suggest that it is a later interpolation. The passage does not much resemble the other entries in Bogharian's diary, in which the diarist generally strikes us as sober and circumspect. Its vocabulary, however, is the firmest reason for suspicion of the paragraph: Words such as "holocaust" or "vengeance," and especially the figure of "one million" victims, are more reminiscent of the Armenian rhetoric of the post-Catastrophe period. It is highly improbable that such wording would have been used during the deportation itself, especially as the deportees had no access to the Armenian press outside the Ottoman Empire, where the first traces of such rhetoric were already beginning to appear. Of course it remains unclear whether the passage was only partially rewritten, or later added in its entirety to the diary.

However that may be, let us return to Der Nerses's diary and its references to mass violence. Here there is no direct mention of massacres such as might indicate that the diarist had well understood the unprecedented, terrifying nature of the events. Yet Der Nerses's status remained that of a community representative in Hama and, thereafter, in Salamiyya. He went on pastoral visits to Homs and later ventured as far as Tafile, a town south of Jerusalem in the vicinity of Ma'an (in the *sanjak* of Kerek-Ma'an), passing en route through various other localities, where he encountered and spoke with many people. Under these circumstances, this priest from Ayntab, who had already been an eyewitness to other human catastrophes that had befallen the Armenians, was plainly aware of what had happened and understood the unprecedented character of the event. Only a few weeks after arriving in Hama, he wrote: "Grief and suffering are increasing daily. We think that the suffering has reached its limit; yet we see it mounting day by day. It follows that the suffering is infinite and knows no limit."[95] In such conditions it seems the question is not whether, but, rather just *when* allusions to the genocidal plan begin to crop up in Der Nerses's diary. The first interesting entry in this regard appears perhaps as early as 3 September 1915, when a train brought new deportees to Hama, among them people who had come from as far away as Samson. It is clear that Der Nerses spoke with these displaced people, who were in a lamentable state, before writing: "Officials in those regions have received an order to wreak utter destruction; but [we] do not know to what end God has miraculously preserved the lives of a number of women and children and brought them as far as this place."[96] On the very next day, Hama again took in new deportees: "famished, completely naked women and small children."[97] "Even in the lexicon of this long-suffering nation," Der Nerses adds, "it is impossible to find words to describe their misery; we have to invent new ones."[98] In the months and years ahead, until he was liberated by the Allied forces, Der Nerses avoided making general allusions to the mass murder. Instead he described, in the greatest possible detail, the altered mode of life that his community and compatriots led in the conditions of exile—including their moral condition, in which Der Nerses saw proof of alienation and degradation, backsliding, and moral bankruptcy. It was the lot of the priest from Ayntab to observe this picture day after day, to live and survive in this environment, to feel its effects and be influenced and moved by it. Presumably, someone who could not know when the war would end or people would be allowed to go back home in peace and resume their former lives, at a time when all

Figure 1.2. A view from Hama in the 1920s.
(Source: AGBU, Nubarian Library, Paris)

the answers to all these questions were draped in uncertainty, would regard the deportees' extraordinary mode of life as a catastrophe. Der Nerses's diary is replete with descriptions of this mode of life and information about it to be discussed later.

The Mainstays of Survival: Community and Family

Scrutiny of the memoirs of survivors from Bilad al-Sham—in this case, our two survivors' diaries—reveals two different categories of groups of deportees. First there were the Armenians who had been driven from the interior provinces of Anatolia and the Armenian homeland and reached these regions of Syria already decimated, exhausted, pillaged, and despondent. Though deportees in this category may have set out in more or less orderly groups, they were subjected to hardship, violence, and massacres on the road to involuntary exile. Consequently, groups and families had been broken up and lost their initial unity and homogeneity. By the time they set foot in Bilad al-Sham, these deportees—women and children, as a rule—could no longer rely on a social fabric that might have helped them survive.

The second group of deportees comprised exiles who had been driven from areas bordering or relatively close to Bilad al-Sham. These deportees had for the most part come from Cilicia. The shorter distance involved was the main reason that people in the second group suffered less while being displaced from their homes to Bilad al-Sham. These deportees crossed the Taurus Mountains and immediately found themselves in the Arab world, a place that, however foreign and however conducive to a sense of uncertainty and insecurity, was nevertheless exempt from—or, more precisely, had only rarely been the theater of—the traditional conflicts that pitted Armenians against Kurds, Circassians, or Turks, which in the past had been the source of numerous massacres repeatedly instigated or organized by the authorities. In a word, this area was free of, or marked only by the embryonic presence of any "imaginary construct" (to use Jacques Sémelin's term) that could, in times of severe crisis, be exploited by the antagonistic force that created it in order to bring a situation to a boiling point or provide an occasion for major massacres.[99]

It must of course be borne in mind that in 1915 there were also caravans of deportees who, after leaving their native Cilicia or localities to the east (including Ayntab), were not driven toward the region south of Cilicia, Bilad al-Sham but were, rather, led south and east into the area known as the Syrian Jazira, where most were massacred. This constitutes a separate episode that our diarists did not directly witness and will not be considered here.

Of interest here are the deportees who came to Bilad al-Sham from Cilicia and the area just east of it. Generally speaking, during the forced relocation these people succeeded in preserving intact their family units and, often, their community structures and those of their native town or village as well. True, in the three years and more spent in exile, the efforts of family members or people from the same town or village to stay together were often foiled: relatives were driven in different directions and different groups of people from the same locality were scattered across different cities or districts. Nevertheless—and this seems to be the crucial consideration here—the core of the family, that is, parents, children, and other very close relatives, usually remained intact. Moreover, so many people from the same district could find themselves in a single place of deportation that the life they continued to live there was similar to the one they had led in their original community, albeit in a new geographical locale. In other words, the deportees were mainly able to preserve their city's or village's community structure and way of life. In fact, the same community notables who had represented them to the local authorities in their places of origin continued to do so in their places of deportation as well.

My thesis is that the reproduction of family and community life took on vital significance here, under the conditions of the deportation, in which each and every new day brought a struggle to survive. Admittedly, a community structure is essentially conservative and can even be retrograde: it encourages self-containment and self-imposed isolation and sometimes acts as a barrier to modernization and tolerance of outsiders. Yet it may be observed that in those fateful days of the deportation, the preservation of such social structures and organic units strengthened cooperation and mutual assistance among people from the same locale. It is clear that in catastrophic conditions, this mutual help and support could become a crucial factor in survival.

The situation among the prisoners in Nazi concentration camps (*Lager*) was similar. There, groups were formed on the basis of nationality and party affiliation or between long-time internees on the one hand and newer arrivals on the other. The "community" life created by Communist prisoners is a case in point. The powerful collective feeling of belonging to the party and the considerable number of Communists in the camps soon led interned Communist Party members to isolate themselves from the others to the point that an internal demarcation sprang up between Communist and non-Communist prisoners. The collective internment of Communists, however, also gave their partisan dynamism and spirit of unity in action a new lease on life, bolstering every Party member's chances of survival. By virtue of these factors, the Communists in the camps were able to create both supply networks and their own communications networks with the outside world; and the condition for benefiting from them was Communist Party membership. Writings by survivors attest that mutual aid of this sort amounted to a guarantee of survival for large numbers of Communist prisoners.[100] Shalamov, too, shows how prisoners cooperated and assisted each other in his description of the common criminals interned in the Soviet camps, who also attempted to re-create the thieves' (*urkis'*) world from which they had come.[101]

Primo Levi explains this phenomenon as an outgrowth of the kind of relationship between an "us" and a "them" that prevails under extreme conditions.[102] As we will see, an image of such an "us" also came into being in Hama and thence among the Armenians from Ayntab who lived together in Salamiyya. Here it is essential to keep in mind that this was a group that had maintained a very strong sense of local belonging. The Ottoman Empire's Armenians, especially those who lived in the interior provinces, would be called a *proto*-national rather than a national collectivity. Their native towns and, in the best of cases, their regions were powerful sources of identity that often took precedence over feelings of national collective belonging. Each of these settlements was, in fact, a *Heimat* distinguished by its peculiar features and characteristics. It was thanks to these local traits that, as Archbishop Torkom Kushagian writes, "they recognized each other and were, in general, recognized by everyone."[103]

Thus, in conditions of catastrophe, the feeling of local belonging becomes still more dominant, and the feeling of solidarity within the community—in this case, among the people of Ayntab—becomes a mainstay of survival. This can be called the stage of *intra-community mutual assistance*, in which solidarity exists simultaneously between compatriots belonging to the same group and between members of the same family. Here the community is an organic unit whose existence facilitates the struggle for survival. In such a context, individuals can display an intolerant attitude toward those who are not members of their local community, even if these outsiders belong to the same ethnic-national group. One example illustrating this phenomenon in Rakka during the years of the Great Tragedy is attested in the eyewitness account of Garabed Kapigian (1867–1925), an intellectual nearing fifty who, at the time of the events he witnessed, was a publicist and teacher in Sivas's Armenian secondary school.

Like most Armenians of his generation, Kapigian had undoubtedly been educated to believe in the idea of a single, homogeneous Armenian nation. Traces of this education are strikingly apparent in his narration of an episode that began when the caravan of deportees in which Kapigian found himself reached the gates of Rakka, where the gendarmes strictly forbade Armenians to set foot in the city. Thus, after a pause, the caravan was forced to continue marching toward Der Zor. Meanwhile, Armenian notables from Erzurum/Garin had succeeded in bribing their guards and entering the city; there they immediately sent a telegram expressing their gratitude to the *mutasarrıf* of Urfa, within whose jurisdiction Rakka lay, requesting that he grant them permission to settle in Rakka. They went to see the local *kaymakam* for the same purpose, conducting negotiations with him on behalf of their townsmen from Erzurum. In the end, they were asked to pay a bribe of five hundred Ottoman lira in exchange for the right to circulate freely in Rakka, and they took up a collection among themselves to raise the money.

Of course the Armenians who were not from Erzurum took note of what was happening, and many of them, Garabed Kapigian included, went to see the Erzurum notables, begging them not to ignore or abandon them. The natives of Erzurum, however, proved unwilling to make the least concession. In fact, when the moment to enter the city came, they used every means at their disposal to keep those who were not from Erzurum from joining their ranks. Kapigian, who in the end somehow managed to enter Rakka himself, was embittered by the Erzurum natives' attitude and wrote that they lacked all "national and social spirit and feeling, and moral fiber as well."[104] Elsewhere, he remarked: "What an appalling betrayal of the great name and reputation that has put the Armenians of Erzurum in the forefront of the Armenian provinces! What a terrible pity when one thinks of the respect and consideration that Armenians have conceived for their elder brothers from the Armenian Plateau!"[105]

Meanwhile, it should be noted that the existence of intra-community mutual assistance depended heavily on the conditions of survival. The further the situation deteriorated and the harder it became for the deportees to secure their daily bread, the more this mutual assistance among natives of the same town or village was jeopardized and the narrower its limits became. Once such a situation had developed, people could rely only on the solidarity of their immediate family or relatives. This began the stage of *intra-familial mutual assistance*, a restricted solidarity that could be reduced still further, until the stage of the smallest possible unit had been reached and the individual was abandoned to his or her fate. Moral bankruptcy and all kinds of infringements of the social order were the hallmarks of this last stage in particular. (Of course this does not mean the complete extinction of anything remotely resembling mutual assistance or the disappearance of humane behavior without a trace.) At this most extreme stage, solicitude for others' welfare and willingness to help others—now rare—acquired new value and scope, becoming virtues or even audacious moral acts that proceeded from an effort to remain human. We need to keep these circumstances in mind while examining the way the lives of deportees from Ayntab unfolded in Hama and Salamiyya.

Separating Relatives and Townspeople: How to Make Survival Impossible

The personal circumstances of our two diarists show how the nucleus of the family was preserved in Hama and Salamiyya. They also show how the Ayntab Armenians' communal-compatriotic structures—the nuclear family's natural extension, as it were—were maintained in those two cities.

Krikor Bogharian's family had been one of a caravan of about 120 Armenian families deported from Ayntab.[106] Apart from Krikor himself, the Bogharian family included Krikor's father, the priest Karekin Bogharian (age 48); Krikor's mother, Santukhd (38); his sister, Hripsime (9); and his brothers, Khachig (16), Atam-Norayr (11), and Nubar (four and a half).[107] In Hama, the family found the Armenians who had been deported in the caravans that had set out from Ayntab before their own. Other caravans of deportees from their hometown reached Hama in the weeks after their own arrival. Natives of Ayntab very soon came to represent the biggest group of deportees in the Syrian city. Later, many of the Ayntab families who had been resettled in Hama were forced to resettle again further south. Other caravans arriving from Ayntab by rail were transported further south in their turn, but directly, with no stopover in Hama.

It is clear that in the first few weeks after being deported, all the members of Krikor Bogharian's extended family remained in Hama. Yet the good fortune of being regrouped in a single place did not last long. The first blow came on 3 September 1915, when the authorities ordered the family of Krikor's paternal uncle, together with another eighty Ayntab households, to leave for a destination still further south, the *sanjak* known as Hauran.[108] Eventually the Ayntab Armenians would lead a collective existence in Hauran, too, in the *kaza* of Ajlun and, in particular its seat, the town of Irbid.

Krikor Bogharian, like many other Ayntab natives, was to spend only a short time in Hama. In October 1915, two months after being resettled there, the majority of the Ayntab Armenians in the city were transported to a small town nearby, Salamiyya. The Bogharians' extended family was not significantly dispersed as a result of this move. Indeed, Krikor writes in connection with the transport: "My grandfather, maternal uncle, my maternal aunt's husband Rupen Boshgezenian, and the families of many of our neighbors will be going with us."[109] The picture of the Ayntab Armenians' places of deportation, and their concentration in a number of different towns, becomes clearer when we consider the geographical distribution of Bogharian's classmates. Just before the forced relocation, they numbered more than forty. Bogharian frequently refers to his classmates in his daily diary entries. On 16 April 1916, he drew up a list of their places of residence: fifteen were in Homs and Hama, seven in Salamiyya, seven or eight in Ayntab, six in Irbid, five in Der Zor, one in Aleppo, and one in Birejig/Birecik.[110] The fact that not only his classmates but several of his teachers as well were living in the same place was a piece of good fortune for Bogharian. He spent time with his friends and went on walks with them, and he conversed with his teachers and showed them his translations. Bogharian managed to continue this shared existence with relatives and friends more or less until the end of the war.

By comparison, Der Nerses is more sparing with information about his family. He arrived in Hama with all the members of his immediate family, who would accompany him to Salamiyya as well. Yet it is not at all clear which members of his extended family were with him in Hama and which were not. We know only that Der Nerses's brother Hagop was living there with his family, as were his wife Anitsa's mother, Mariam (Zantur) Syulahian, and another of her daughters, and that daughter's family. Der Nerses and his brother lived with their respective families under the same roof.

In these extreme conditions, the fact that family members lived together could mean above all that they provided each other with moral support, pooled their efforts to earn a living, and organized and facilitated their battle for existence by assigning distinct tasks to each member of the family. All these things may appear to be ordinary acts of the kind that have generally characterized the daily life of families or broader communities in times of peace as well as in extreme conditions. Indeed, the vital importance of the family unit is a theme that philanthropic organizations concerned with problems of relocation have repeatedly emphasized: in their view, preserving the unity of the family is so crucial that reuniting scattered families becomes a high priority—this, they are convinced, is the best way to guarantee the family members' physical and moral self-defense and ensure the preconditions for a normal existence. For the same reason, Article 16 of the Universal Declaration of Human Rights clearly stipulates that "the family is the natural and fundamental group unit of society and is entitled to protection by society and the State."[111] Terrence des Pres affirms that the family, as "the most narrow but intense social unit," was what made it possible to establish human relations among the prisoners in the Nazi camps—that is, in those cases in which a few family members were fortunate enough to continue to live together.[112]

In our two diarists' daily entries as well, this spirit of mutual assistance and their sense of its importance emphatically make themselves felt. In Bogharian's case, for example, when he first went to work for a carpenter from Ayntab to earn money, he came down with malaria and was treated by a doctor from Ayntab whom he had had as a teacher for a year. His brother, Khachig, was likewise apprenticed to a tradesman from Ayntab, a tinsmith. When the family first arrived in Salamiyya, they stayed with two families from their hometown before renting an apartment of their own. One of Bogharian's duties was collecting brush for the family to use as firewood. The members of his immediate family and his aunt boiled cracked wheat together, made tomato paste, and dried eggplant and peppers for the winter.

But in the case of Krikor Bogharian's family, this spirit of unity in the face of the ordeals of the deportation was dealt a heavy blow when Krikor's father was exiled and forced to leave his loved ones behind. On the decision of the authorities, twenty-one priests and three Protestant ministers who had been deported to various localities in Bilad al-Sham were banished to the Tafile district. Although the young man from Ayntab rarely complains about the consequences of his father's absence, it is quite clear that this banishment plunged him and his family into a spiritual crisis. Krikor was obviously more worried and agitated thereafter. A few weeks after his father's departure, he wrote in his diary: "To forget my sad thoughts, I visit Sarafian and Kevork Baboyan; we take walks together. No news at all of my father to the present day."[113] After this separation, Krikor Bogharian more noticeably remarks on waiting impatiently for the postman, who came from Hama. He also expresses the feelings and concerns of his mother after she was forcibly separated from her husband: "Who can sound the depths of her sorrow and suffering? She is the mother of five children and, now, is their father as well."[114]

Der Nerses's family, too, had the good fortune to be able to stay together. In 1915, the 45-year-old priest from Ayntab was living with his wife, Anitsa; their two sons, Nerses (11) and Kevork (3); and their three daughters, Mariam, Tshkhuyn (known as Dudu), and Shoghagat. In the pages of Der Nerses's diary, one of the best expressions of the mutual assistance that the family members gave each other is undoubtedly the descriptions of the care that Der Nerses and his relatives received when they were ill. Many pages of the diary are given over to this subject. Der Nerses writes in great detail about the illnesses that afflicted him, his wife, and their children. Often very private in nature, the descriptions were most certainly not intended for publication and therefore were not included in the published version of the diary. Important for our purposes in the entries in question is the mutual tenderness that appears in them, the noble spirit of moral and material assistance, the human sympathy and indissoluble familial bond. In conditions like those endured by this family, in which it was often impossible to find medicine, a doctor, or even a pharmacist, the Tavukjians were united by a single will in the struggle against sickness. One cannot but be deeply moved by the pages in which the priest describes his wife's grave illness, the solicitude he showed her, and his frantic race through the streets of Hama in search of a doctor for his wife, already in her death throes.[115]

The entries in Der Nerses's diary are often a somber mirror reflecting the disintegration of the deportees' humanity in scenes attesting to his compatriots' demoralization and the slow disappearance of a spirit of mutual assistance. Yet they also contain descriptions of opposite behaviors: every time the priest's material situation approaches the precipice and despair threatens to overwhelm him, an affluent, devout compatriot from Ayntab appears and helps him out with a gift of cash or a large quantity of wheat or flour. As we shall see, there was more than one such beautiful moment of mutual assistance among compatriots in Der Nerses's day-to-day existence as a deportee.

The priest's exile to Tafile is a turning point in his diary. In these months when he was far from his family and friends, the entries are undeniably at their gloomiest and most despondent. They are also hastily written and reflect new levels of mental anguish. In the conditions of this resettlement, Der Nerses's will to stay alive plummeted. For the first few weeks, he had no news at all of his family. Dejectedly, he writes: "Everything has already come to an end; all we think about is how to survive."[116] In this same period he begins to relate his dreams, something he does not do earlier. His family members often appear in these dreams, particularly his children. "Insomnia, anxiety, less and less food"—in a way, this is the sum and substance of the sad, nightmarish daily exertions that followed his second deportation.[117] His new situation is so distressing that he begins to recall even his days in Salamiyya with nostalgia. Thus, when suffering from insomnia, he recalls his summer nights there, when he and his family "slept comfortably on the roof."[118]

As for the preservation of community structures, it went beyond the internal factor of mutual assistance to also allow the notables who represented the community to approach the authorities and negotiate questions bearing on their compatriots' destiny on firmer grounds than would otherwise have been possible (even if power relations were radically altered in the conditions of exile). The continued existence of this representative body could multiply the ties between deportees and local authorities, opening up new possibilities for survival. It is especially noteworthy that the authorities in Hama and Salamiyya sometimes accorded a degree of respect to the deportees' representatives, even though the latter found themselves in the role of victim. Their meeting with the authorities and conferring with them, presenting them with requests, being received in their offices and sometimes even being treated to their hospitality—all this has to be seen from the standpoint of the mass of Armenians, stripped of their rights in the humiliating conditions of their exile. In reality, these relations with the authorities restored, at least in part, the notables' diminished credit and thereby, perhaps, that of the whole community. Evidently, this is an instance of a social phenomenon in which, Martine Hovhanessian explains, a group of deportees reestablishes the community's guiding principles and in so doing also seeks to win back its self-respect.[119] It seems that in conditions of forced relocation as well as violence, meetings between the community's notables and representatives of the side exercising that violence helped the Armenians regain a certain self-respect and sense of honor. To be sure, such feelings could be of short duration, but that would have had a completely different meaning for a group that was, from the moment it was deported and sent south, constantly subject to insult and injustice.

This community and its compatriotic structure were mobilized in places frequented by our diarists when, for example, the Ottoman authorities levied troops and demanded that the deportees, too, furnish the army with conscripts. In the extraordinary conditions of the exile, as we shall see in greater detail, conscription could deprive a family of its most capable worker, leaving it defenseless and confronted with increasingly severe hunger and the likelihood of death. For precisely this reason, the community's leading members spared no effort to keep deportees from being drafted. Der Nerses and other notables from Ayntab first conferred with on this question with the military commander of Hama, Osman Bey, in April 1916.[120] Ayntab's representatives also sent Ahmed Jemal Pasha a petition bearing on the question of conscription.[121] When the question came up again in 1917, the community's representatives mobilized once more. Further meetings were held with

Osman Bey, and telegrams were drawn up and sent to the "*sadaret*,[122] the *harbiye* command,[123] the *vali* of Sham, and the commandant of the Fourth Army."[124]

All this manifestly involved the fundamental issues of keeping families together while reinforcing the community and its internal dynamism. Being surrounded with relatives and acquaintances from one's immediate family, extended family, and community was a basic precondition of physical, material, and moral support. It is very often factors like these that make survival in extreme conditions possible. Conversely, measures adopted at the state level to separate family members, other relatives, or people from the same town or village attest to the state's desire to make it impossible for the targeted group to survive, or at least its desire to put an end to its collective existence as a community.

From the same standpoint, one can examine various wartime decisions the Ottoman authorities made regarding the numbers of deported Armenians in their new places of residence. Thus, according to the first such decision handed down by the authorities, the number of Armenians deported to the Jazira region of Syria was not to exceed 10 percent of the local population.[125] The following months saw new decisions relevant to this issue; all of them clearly intended to diminish the proportion of Armenians. On the other hand, the few fortunate Armenians who had been granted permission to continue living in their native town were not to form more than 5 percent of its total population and could in no circumstances comprise more than twenty families.[126] A subsequent decision concerning Aleppo lowered the share of Armenians from localities whose Armenians had been deported to 2 percent of that city's population.[127]

At least in Aleppo and a number of other towns in Bilad al-Sham, these decisions proved impossible to put into practice. It is nevertheless important to examine them, since such steps are excellent indexes of the authorities' intentions. Fuad Dündar explains these state decisions in two ways. First, he says, there was a military reason for them: the imbalance between the Armenian and non-Armenian population had to be big enough that the local inhabitants could always keep the deported Armenians under their control, forestalling any attempt at rebellion. Second, the authorities had embarked on a policy of assimilation and Turkification.[128]

To these explanations must be added another, quite as important: the overriding objective was to weaken the deported Armenians as a collectivity and a community and leave them defenseless. In the conditions defined by these pre-programmed population figures, it would be impossible to revive community life or reanimate mutual assistance at the family or community level. These population targets generally meant that the deportees would be settled in their places of residence in extremely scattered fashion, and that it would be impossible for them to maintain community solidarity or even family unity there. This could by itself increase the vulnerability of the deportees living in extreme conditions and very quickly transform it into a mortal threat.

Figure 1.3. The Bogharian family, early 1920s. Seated (from left): Santukhd Bogharian (née Tahtajian), Father Karekin Bogharian. Standing (from left): Hripsime, Khachig, Krikor, Atam-Norayr, Nubar. (Source: Annie Kambourian family collection, Paris)

Notes

1. Alain Girard, *Le journal intime* (Paris: Presses Universitaires de France, 1986), p. xvi.
2. Gabriele Jancke and Claudia Ulbrich, "Von Individuum zur Person: Neue Konzepte im Spannungsfeld von Autobiographietheorie und Selbstzeugnisforschung," in Gabriele Jancke and Claudia Ulbrich, eds., *Von Individuum zur Person: Neue Konzepte im Spannungsfeld von Autobiographietheorie und Selbstzeugnisforschung*, special issue, *Querelles: Jahrbuch für Frauenforschung* 10 (2005), p. 19.
3. "Harutyun Kahana Der Melkonian (1866–1916)" [Father Harutyun Der Melkonian (1866–1916)], in *Ayntabiana*, vol. 2, *Mahardzan: Mahakrutyunner, tampanaganner yev gensakragan noter* [Funeral monument: Necrologies, funeral orations and biographical notes] (Beirut: Atlas, 1974), p. 505.
4. Ibid.
5. Istanbul Armenian writer and publicist (Istanbul, b. 1869–Cairo, d. 1926).
6. Yervant Odian, *Accursed Years: My Exile and Return from Der Zor, 1914–1919*, trans. Ara Melkonian (London: Gomidas, 2009), pp. 123, 128.
7. Chavarche Missakian, *Face à l'innomable Avril 1915*, trans. Arpik Missakian (Marseilles: Editions Parenthèses, 2015).
8. The team charged with this philanthropic mission was active from 25 May to 19 July 1909. Approximately one year later, Der Nerses was sent on another mission to the Antioch/Antakya region, this time to distribute Ottoman state aid to massacre victims. His second mission lasted from 15 June to 4 October. In these four months, the priest from Ayntab reconstructed the Armenian parish councils that had been dissolved as a result of the catastrophe in the city of Antakya and the Armenian villages of the Mt. Moses (Musa Dagh) district. Nerses Kahana Tavukjian, (Inknagensakragan noter)" ["Father Nerses Tavukjian (Autobiographical Notes)"], *Shirag: Kraganutyan u arvesdi amsakir* [*Shirag:* Monthly for literature and the arts] 51, no. 8 (August 1987): 55.
9. Tzvetan Todorov, *Facing the Extreme: Moral Life in the Concentration Camps*, trans. Arthur Denner and Abigail Pollack (London: Weidenfeld & Nicolson, 1999), p. 91.
10. Ibid., pp. 107–110.
11. Alexandra Garbarini, *Numbered Days: Diaries and the Holocaust* (Ann Arbor, MI: Yale University Press, 2006), p. 152.
12. Ibid., pp. 143–144.
13. All the dates in Krikor Bogharian's diary, given according to the old calendar, have in the present book been brought into conformity with the new calendar. Der Nerses used the new calendar, except in a number of 1916 entries extending over a period of several months.
14. Haigazian University Library archives, "Krikor Bogharian's Archives," "Vartanian grtaran. Vgayagan" [Vartanian School diploma], 21 June 1912, Ayntab.
15. "Armen Muradian (1895–1957)", *Ayntabiana*, vol. 2, p. 97.
16. Haigazian University Library archives, "Krikor Bogharian's Archives," "Gensakragan noter" [Biographical notes], manuscript, 8 May 1950, pp. 1–9.
17. Krikor Bogharian, "Orakrutyun darakiri gyankis" [Diary of my life in deportation], in *Tseghasban Turke. Vgayutyunner kaghadz hrashkov prgvadzneru zruytsneren* [The genocidal Turk: Eyewitness accounts from the narratives of people who were miraculously saved] (hereafter "Diary"). (Beirut: Shirag, 1973), p. 134.

18. Father Karekin Bogharian, "Inknagensakrutyun" [Autobiography], *Yeprad* (Aleppo), nos. 2862–2864 (1947); "Verabradz, Der Karekin Avak Kahana Bogharian (1867–1946)" [Survivor, Father Karekin Bogharian, senior priest (1867–1946)], *Ayntabiana*, p. 14.
19. Bogharian, "Diary," pp. 126, 129.
20. Ibid., p. 165.
21. Ibid., pp. 130–131.
22. Ibid., p. 133.
23. Ibid., p. 134.
24. Ibid., p. 138.
25. Ibid., p. 171.
26. Ibid., p. 140.
27. Ibid., p. 148.
28. Ibid., p. 151.
29. Ibid., p. 154.
30. Ibid., p. 164.
31. Ibid., p. 171.
32. Ibid., p. 166.
33. Ibid., p. 167.
34. Ibid., p. 173.
35. Ibid., p. 184.
36. Ibid., p. 187.
37. Ibid., p. 196.
38. Ibid., p. 154. We have had to guess the title of this book, since Bogharian gives the title as simply *Sociology*. Blackmar is the author of two other books bearing that word in their title: *The Elements of Sociology* and *The Study of History and Sociology*.
39. Ibid., p. 165.
40. Ibid., p. 163. See also "Krikor A. Sarafian" in *Ayntabiana*, p. 208.
41. Todorov, *Facing the Extreme*, p. 93.
42. Primo Levi, *If This Is a Man*, trans. Stuart Woolf (New York: Orion Press, 1959), pp. 131–134.
43. Bogharian, "Diary," p. 196.
44. Ibid., p. 147.
45. Ibid., p. 148.
46. "Grtagan gyanke Ayntabi mech yev badmutyun Ayntabi hay tbrotsnerun" ["Education in Ayntab and a history of Ayntab's schools"] in Kevork A. Sarafian, ed., *Badmutyun Antebi Hayots* [History of the Armenians of Ayntab], vol. 1 (Los Angeles: Amerigapnag Antebtsineru miutyun [Association of the natives of Ayntab living in the United States], 1953), p. 653.
47. Krikor Bogharian, "Der Nerses avak kahana Tavukjian" [Der Nerses, senior priest], in K. Sarafian, ed., *History of the Armenians of Ayntab*, vol. 1, p. 469; Karekin Bogharian, "Autobiography," p. 11; Tavukjian, "Autobiographical notes," p. 54.
48. Bogharian, "Der Nerses," pp. 469–472.
49. Father Nerses Tavukjian, *Darabanki orakrutyun* [Diary of days of suffering], ed. Toros Toramanian (Beirut: High Type Compugraph—Technopresse, 1991), pp. 72–73.
50. Krikor Bogharian, "Giligian Jemaran (1912–1915)" [Giligian secondary school (1912–1915)], in *History of the Armenians of Ayntab*, vol. 1, pp. 781, 783.
51. Bogharian, "Diary," p. 133.
52. Tavukjian, *Diary*, p. 123.
53. Ibid.

54. Ibid., p. 125.
55. Raymond Kévorkian, *The Armenian Genocide: A Complete History*, trans. anon. (London: I.B. Tauris, 2011), p. 691.
56. Ibid., pp. 651-652, 668.
57. Bogharian, "Diary," pp. 126-129.
58. *Sevkıyat* is, here, a military term meaning dispatch. The word is also used to designate the transport of freight.
59. Bogharian, "Diary," pp. 129-138.
60. Ibid., p. 131.
61. Ibid., p. 131.
62. Ibid., p. 137.
63. Ibid., pp. 187-189.
64. Ibid., p. 182. At the beginning of World War I, Ahmed Jemal Pasha (1872-1922) took command of the Ottoman Fourth Army, based in Bilad al-Sham and the neighboring districts.
65. Ibid., p. 134.
66. Ibid., p. 135.
67. Ibid., p. 138.
68. Odian, *Accursed Years*, pp. 109-110.
69. Bogharian, "Diary," p. 131.
70. Odian, *Accursed Years*, p. 110.
71. Ibid., p. 110.
72. Bogharian, "Diary," p. 182.
73. Ibid., p. 195.
74. Ibid.
75. Ibid., p. 199.
76. Ibid., p. 206.
77. V. N. Gyuleserian, "Dasn yev meg yegheragan dariner Ayntabi mech, 1908-1919" [Eleven tragic years in Ayntab, 1908-1919], in *History of Ayntab's Armenians*, pp. 1019-1020.
78. Tavukjian, *Diary*, pp. 65-66.
79. Ibid., p. 68.
80. Ibid., p. 73.
81. Ibid., p. 83.
82. Bogharian, "Diary," p. 138.
83. BOA. DH. ŞFR (Başbakanlık Osmanlı Arşivi Dahiliye Nezareti Şifre Kalemi [BOA Primeministerial Archive, Office of the Cipher in the Ottoman Interior Ministry]), nr. 57/71, Bâb-ı Âlî, Dâhiliye Nezâreti, Emniyyet-i Umûmiyye Müdîriyyeti, 54, Sûriye Vilâyeti'ne, 8 Z. 1333, 17 October 1915, in *Armenians in Ottoman Documents (1915-1920)* (Ankara: Başbakanlık Devlet Arşivleri Genel Müdürlüğü, 1995), p. 116.
84. Tavukjian, *Diary*, p. 75.
85. Ibid., p. 83.
86. Ibid.
87. Tavukjian, "Autobiographical Notes," p. 56.
88. Tavukjian, *Diary*, p. 75.
89. Ibid., p. 77.
90. Ibid., p. 75.
91. Ibid., p. 77.
92. Ibid., p. 78.
93. Ibid., p. 80.
94. Bogharian, "Diary," p. 156.

95. Tavukjian, *Diary*, p. 77.
96. Ibid, p. 82.
97. Ibid.
98. Ibid.
99. Jacques Sémelin, *Purify and Destroy: The Political Use of Massacre and Genocide*, trans. Cynthia Schoch, CERI Series in Comparative Politics and International Studies (New York: Columbia University Press, 2009), pp. 49–50.
100. See David Rousset, *Les jours de notre mort* (Paris: Ramsay, 1988); Margarete Buber-Neumann, *Milena: The Tragic Story of Kafka's Great Love* (New York: Arcade Publishing, 1997).
101. Varlam Chalamov, *Récits de la Kolyma*, trans. Sophie Benech, Catherine Fournier, Luba Jurgenson, (Lagrasse (France): Verdier, 2006), pp. 217–226. Partially translated as *Kolyma Tales*, trans. John Glad (Harmondsworth: Penguin, 1994).
102. Primo Levi, *The Drowned and the Saved*, trans. Raymond Rosenthal (New York: Summit Books, 1988), pp. 36–39.
103. Archbishop Torkom Kushagian, "Mudki khosk" [Introduction], in Arshag A. Alboyajian, *Badmutyun Hay Gesario* [*History of Armenian Caesarea*], vol. 1 (Cairo: Papazian, 1937), p. ii. In the mentality of people from the same town or village, the Armenian equivalent of *Heimat* was a polyvalent word: depending on the circumstances, it could designate—interchangeably, as Alon Confino points out in a related context—the local, regional, or national level. See Alon Confino, *The Nation as a Local Metaphor: Württemberg, Imperial Germany, and National Memory, 1871–1918* (Chapel Hill and London: University of North Carolina Press, 1997), pp. 184–185.
104. Archives of the AGBU's Nubarian Library, "Aram Andoniani tseghasbanutyan nyuteru havakadzo" [Aram Andonian's collection of materials bearing on the genocide], File Garabed Kapigian, "Rakkayi archev" [Before Rakka], p. 106.
105. Ibid, pp. 105–106. Raymond Kévorkian, basing what he says on this report by Garabed Kapigian, likewise castigates these Erzurum Armenians for their "lack of solidarity" and "extreme parochialism" (Kévorkian, *Armenian Genocide*, p. 659).
106. Bogharian, "Diary," p. 124.
107. Ibid., p. 127.
108. Ibid., p. 133.
109. Ibid., p. 141.
110. Ibid., pp. 169–170.
111. The Universal Declaration of Human Rights, adopted by the United Nations General Assembly on 10 December 1948 (http://www.un.org/en/documents/udhr/) [last consulted on 24 April 2012]). The same disposition has been ratified in the declarations of many other international organizations.
112. Terrence des Pres, *The Survivor: An Anatomy of Life in the Death Camps* (New York: Oxford University Press, 1976), p. 122.
113. Bogharian, "Diary," p. 187.
114. Ibid., p. 203.
115. Der Nerses Tavukjian, "Orakrutyun mekenakrvadz pnakir" [Typescript of the diary] (hereafter "Ms. Diary"), pp. 141–143.
116. Tavukjian, *Diary*, p. 117.
117. Ibid., p. 126.
118. Ibid., p. 121.
119. Martine Hovanessian, *Le lien communautaire. Trois générations d'Arméniens* (Paris: Armand Colin, 1992), p. 44.
120. Tavukjian, *Diary*, p. 109.
121. Ibid.

122. *Sadaret*, the grand vizier's office.
123. *Harbiye kumandanı*, the military command.
124. Tavukjian, *Diary*, p. 139.
125. Fuat Dündar, *Modern Türkiye'nin Şifresi: Ittihat ve Terakki'nin Etnisite Mühendisliği (1913-1918)* (Istanbul: Iletişim Yayınlar, 2008), pp. 316-319.
126. Ibid., pp. 314-321; Fuat Dündar, *L'ingénierie ethnique du Comité Union et Progrès et la Turcisation de l'Anatolie*, doctoral thesis (Paris: EHESS, 2006), p. 409; Taner Akçam, *The Young Turks' Crime against Humanity: The Armenian Genocide and Ethnic Cleansing in the Ottoman Empire* (Princeton, NJ: Princeton University Press, 2012), pp. 242-263
127. Dündar, *Modern Türkiye'nin Şifresi*, pp. 316, 319.
128. Dündar, *L'ingénierie ethnique*, pp. 258, 408.

Selected Bibliography

Published Material

Akçam, Taner. *The Young Turks' Crime against Humanity: The Armenian Genocide and Ethnic Cleansing in the Ottoman Empire*. Princeton, NJ, 2012.

Armenians in Ottoman Documents (1915-1920). Ankara, 1995.

Bogharian, Krikor. Ցեղասպան Թուրքը, վկայութիւններ քաղուած՝ հրաշքով փրկուածներու զրոյցներէն [Tseghasban Turke. Vgayutyunner kaghvadz hrashkov prgvadzneru zruytsneren] [The genocidal Turk: Eyewitness accounts from the narratives of people who were miraculously saved]. Beirut, 1973.

———, ed. Այնթապականք / *Ayntabiana*, vol. 2. Մահարձան: մահագրութիւններ, դամբանականներ եւ կենսագրական նօթեր [Funeral monument: necrologies, funeral orations and biographical notes]. Beirut, 1974.

Chalamov, Varlam. *Récits de la Kolyma*, trans. Sophie Benech, Catherine Fournier, and Luba Jurgenson. Lagrasse (France), 2006.

Confino, Alon. *The Nation as a Local Metaphor: Württemberg, Imperial Germany, and National Memory, 1871-1918*. Chapel Hill and London, 1997.

Des Pres, Terrence. *The Survivor: An Anatomy of Life in the Death Camps*. New York, 1976.

Dündar, Fuat. *L'ingénierie ethnique du Comité Union et Progrès et la Turcisation de l'Anatolie*, doctoral thesis. Paris, 2006.

———. *Modern Türkiye'nin Şifresi: Ittihat ve Terakki'nin Etnisite Mühendisliği (1913-1918)*. Istanbul, 2008.

Garbarini, Alexandra. *Numbered Days: Diaries and the Holocaust*. Ann Arbor, 2006.

Girard, Alain. *Le journal intime*. Paris, 1986.

Hovanessian, Martine. *Le lien communautaire. Trois générations d'Arméniens*. Paris, 1992.

Jancke, Gabriele, and Claudia Ulbrich, eds. *Von Individuum zur Person: Neue Konzepte im Spannungsfeld von Autobiographietheorie und Selbstzeugnisforschung*. Göttingen, 2005.

Kévorkian, Raymond. *The Armenian Genocide: A Complete History*, trans. anon. London, 2011.

Levi, Primo, *The Drowned and the Saved*, trans. Raymond Rosenthal. New York, 1988.

———. *If This Is a Man*, trans. Stuart Woolf. New York, 1959.

Missakian, Chavarche, *Face à l'innomable Avril 1915*, trans. Arpik Missakian. Marseilles, 2015.

Odian, Yervant. *Accursed Years: My Exile and Return from Der Zor, 1914–1919*, trans. Ara Melkonian. London, 2009.
Rousset, David. *Les jours de notre mort*. Paris, 1988.
Sarafian, Kevork A., ed. Պատմութիւն Անթէպի Հայոց [Badmutyun Antebi Hayots] [History of the Armenians of Ayntab], vol. 1. Los Angeles, 1953.
Sémelin, Jacques. *Purify and Destroy: The Political Use of Massacre and Genocide*, trans. Cynthia Schoch. New York, 2009.
Tavukjian, Father Nerses. Տառապանքի օրագրութիւն [Darabanki orakrutyun] [Diary of days of suffering]. Beirut, 1991.
———."Օրագրութեան Մեքենագրուած Բնագիր" [Orakrutyan mekenakrvadz pnakir] [Typescript of the diary] (Ms. Diary).
———. "Ներսէս Քհնյ. Թաւուգճեան (Ինքնակենսագրական նօթեր)" [Nerses Kahana Tavukjian (Inknagensakragan noter)] ["Father Nerses Tavukjian (Autobiographical Notes)"], *Shirag* 51, no. 8 (August 1987): 53–59.
Todorov, Tzvetan. *Facing the Extreme: Moral Life in the Concentration Camps*, trans. Arthur Denner and Abigail Pollack. London, 1999.

Primary Sources

Haigazian University Library Archives, "Krikor Bogharian's Archives"
Archives of the Armenian General Benevolent Union's (AGBU) Nubarian Library

CHAPTER 2

THE DEPORTEES IN THE REGION OF BILAD AL-SHAM
A RACE AGAINST TIME AT BREAKNECK SPEED

The Struggle for Survival in Bilad al-Sham

Primo Levi describes his life in the Nazi camps as "cut off from the world and outside time."[1] Conditions in Hama and Salamiyya or, more generally, Bilad al-Sham were no different. Some of those who settled here were human wrecks who had escaped the horror of massacres; the rest were to learn about the massacres perpetrated on the banks of the Euphrates and the Khabur, not far from their own native towns and villages. The deportees in Bilad al-Sham would not themselves face such mass killings, but they were constantly anguished over the eventuality of being transferred elsewhere or even collectively put to death. Some local populations and local officials treated them with extreme brutality, targeting deportees for various excesses. Yet all this was far from resembling the appalling events that had unfolded in the inner Anatolian provinces, the Armenians' historical homeland. Unlike the Armenians there, the deportees in Bilad al-Sham were in many respects the masters of their fate, albeit in a hellish environment: misery and disease had begun to spread death everywhere. Consequently, the deportees in this place were engaged in a pitiless race against time throughout the war. The pace was unbearable for many Armenians, and it was often mortal.

The region of Bilad al-Sham was part of the zone under the command of the Ottoman Fourth Army. It is no secret to historians that these troops' supreme commander, Ahmed Jemal Pasha, had serious differences of opinion with the Ittihad's other ranking leaders over questions involving the fate of the empire's Armenians.[2] If it is true that Jemal Pasha opposed the extermination of the Armenians, can it also be said that he was opposed to deporting the Armenians from Anatolia and the Armenian homeland? One thing is clear: when Jemal was in Bilad al-Sham during the war years, his policy toward the deported Armenians was sui generis and in many respects differed radically from the activity of the Ittihadist leaders of other provinces. To implement the policy, Jemal Pasha relied on a broad network of close friends and comrades-in-arms extending throughout Bilad al-Sham. This network's activities sometimes even contradicted measures put in place by the same region's local civil authorities, who took their orders from Interior Minister Talaat.[3] The essential issue is the absence of massacres in the far-flung territories under the Fourth Army's command and the relative security enjoyed by the Armenian deportees there. The question can accordingly be formulated this way: In this environment, what was the Armenian deportees' life like? What were the conditions in which many died while others tried to adapt to the situation? Answers to these questions are found in Bogharian's and Der Nerses's diaries.

Jemal Pasha's Policies in Bilad al-Sham from the Deportees' Point of View

Jemal Pasha affirms in his memoirs that it was on his initiative that tens of thousands of Armenians were settled in Bilad al-Sham instead of being sent to the Mesopotamian steppes, and adds that only after complex negotiations with the central government authorities did it become possible to implement this policy successfully.[4] The commander of the Fourth Army, who was at the same time a member of the triumvirate that exercised absolute power over the empire, tried to create the impression that he had purely humanitarian motives for taking the deported Armenians into his protection.[5] When all is said and done, the three years of their exile (May 1915 to October 1918) are but a short lapse of time when it comes to determining, examining, and drawing definite conclusions about all the many facets of the position adopted by Jemal Pasha and his followers. It is likewise a short lapse of time with respect to identifying the concrete steps that followed from this stance and the projects that it presumably spawned. Not just Jemal, but all of his close companions from these years wrote about this subject, and they occasionally provide crucial, illuminating information about the forced resettlement of the Armenians in Bilad al-Sham. For instance, Falih Rıfkı Atay, one of Jemal's closest comrades-in-arms in the Fourth Army, reveals in his memoirs that there was a plan to settle the Armenians in the Arab regions. The purpose, he adds, was to use the Armenians, as the Circassians and Kurds had been used, as a force to counter the ethnic Arab population.[6]

It is not my aim here to reopen the vast debate about Jemal Pasha's activity in Bilad al-Sham or to re-examine the entire correspondence between this military commander and the Ittihad's other ranking leaders. The purpose of the present work is to reconstruct the daily life of the Armenian deportees in Hama and Salamiyya. Here, therefore, the floor is ceded to the Armenian deportees in Bilad al-Sham—that is, the Armenian deportees who were the main object of the conflict between Jemal Pasha and his comrades and co-thinkers, are now to relate their own day-to-day lives.

Having adopted this perspective, one's first impression is that throughout the war, Armenians were indeed spared massacres in the extensive areas in the Fourth Army's zone of control. The Armenians deported to these places were given the opportunity to restore a number of different facets of their community life. Nonetheless, they never perceived themselves as living in a zone of freedom. In these years of forced resettlement, though the Armenians may have managed to revive the social and economic aspects of community life, they were never allowed to resuscitate the two institutions that were most fundamental to their national and religious identity: the Armenian national schools and Church. It might be objected that children's school education was not a particularly high priority for deported parents facing the multiple problems involved in obtaining their daily bread under wartime conditions. That is, generally speaking, true; indeed, like Krikor Bogharian and his brothers, many schoolchildren went into trades and took on all sorts of work so that they might contribute to alleviating their family's desperate struggle to obtain means of subsistence.

That said, however, we also know of situations in which Armenian deportees founded orphanages, especially after 1917, at a time when living conditions had become exceptionally harsh and the number of starving Armenian orphans in the streets of Bilad al-Sham's cities had increased many times over. In several places, with the consent of local authorities and sometimes in collaboration with them, orphanages were founded and staffed primarily by Armenians. Various accounts of these orphanages in Hama, Damascus, and Aleppo all confirm that the language used in them was Turkish.[7] Armenian language instruction, which under normal conditions might have been an Armenian school's or Armenian orphanage's raison d'être, was prohibited in these institutions.[8] Furthermore, by a decision of the central authorities, these orphans could be adopted only by demonstrably non-Armenian inhabitants of the area. None but these non-Armenians, Hilmar Kaiser writes, were allowed to provide for and educate the orphans.[9] Taner Akçam's position is more categorical: the "religious conversion and assimilation" of Armenian children, he writes, were "two of the most significant structural components" of the genocidal process.[10] In short, the manifest aim was to ensure that the Armenian orphans were estranged from their religious and community identity.[11]

We are also familiar with the situation in Damascus's Armenian school, which had been founded before the war by the city's small Armenian community. In the years of the deportation, when thousands of Armenians had arrived in Damascus, instruction was suspended and the school was closed.[12] From this standpoint, the case of Jerusalem's Zharankavorats School is also interesting. This religious and educational Armenian institution had been in operation before the war. At the time of the deportation, fifteen to twenty Armenians who had been studying at the seminary in Armash (present-day Akmeşe), near Izmit, were deported to Jerusalem, where they began taking classes at Zharankavorats. This did not last long: on Jemal Pasha's orders, all these former seminarists were conscripted, and the school was forced to close its doors until the end of the war.[13]

In considering the linguistic question, it is also important to bear in mind that most of the deportees who arrived in Bilad al-Sham were, as already noted, Armenians from Cilicia and the area immediately to the east. Most Armenians from this geographical zone were Turkish-speaking. Jemal Pasha knew these Armenians well, as he had served as the *vali* of Adana province in 1909–1910 and cultivated close relations with the local Armenians. Adana's Turks had, as a result, even given him the nickname "Garabed,"[14] which, it seems safe to say, was by no means intended positively from the Turkish standpoint. Precisely this component of the population, which was familiar to Jemal, was resettled in various towns and villages in Bilad al-Sham on his initiative. While residing in Bilad al-Sham, Jemal maintained his relationship with Adana's deported notables and even interceded personally to improve the situations of some of them. In a word, under different circumstances and in a different environment, he was again willing to enter into relations with this element, turn its abilities to account, and incorporate it as an element of his strategic plans.

Presumably, the fact that these deportees were, overall, Turkish-speaking helped them earn Jemal Pasha's protection. Moreover, even those who were able to write in Armenian did not, at least in their correspondence, because letters that Armenians sent each other by official post in the war years had to be written in Ottoman Turkish.[15] In addition to this linguistic factor, a religious factor also came into play in the case of Bilad al-Sham's Armenian deportees: obviously under pressure from the local authorities, all these Armenians were required to convert to Islam in the space of a few weeks. Developments like these can be justified as a stratagem devised by Jemal Pasha to ensure the Armenians' survival in his zone of influence.[16] There is, however, another side to the coin—a less flattering one that raises fundamental questions. It is quite improbable that any high-ranking Ittihadist leader would, at war's end, have agreed to let the surviving Armenian deportees return to their native towns and villages. The Ittihadist administrative apparatus's decision to deport the Armenians from Anatolia and the eastern provinces was inextricably bound up with ideology. Where such racist, criminal plans are concerned, it strains credulity that even personalities such as Jemal Pasha could have disagreed with the decision. On this point of basic principle, the ruling party was a monolithic collective that spoke with one voice. The difference of opinion that separated Jemal from his comrades consisted chiefly in resistance to the plan to physically eliminate the Armenians: as Kaiser writes, "differences were about the methods used and not the final objective."[17] It was for this reason that he opened Bilad al-Sham's gates to the deported Armenians.[18]

Moreover, once the resettlement stage was over, the measures Jemal adopted vis-à-vis the Armenians may be supposed to have been, rather, reflections of a long-term plan. A miniature version of these plans is perhaps discernible in educational activities carried out in this region at the time by two close associates of Jemal's, Halidé Edib (Adıvar) and Hasan Amja. Both Edib and Amja rounded up Armenian or Kurdish orphans, cared for them, gave them Islamic names, and provided them with Ottoman Turkish education in orphanages in Lebanon or Damascus, with the intention of one day making them model citizens of the empire. Edib's memoirs leave the impression that this activity was largely inspired by the example of missionaries, or even that of French colonialism; in a sense, it represented a Turkish reaction to these missionaries' work, which had been very influential in Bilad al-Sham. It is thus no accident that the Beirut and Ayntura orphanages that Edib chose to work in—the future foundation stones of her educational activity—were confiscated missionary schools. Taking up Jemal's invitation to come to Syria and direct a network of educational institutions there, the Turkish intellectual presents her mission as follows: "He [Jemal Pasha] had seen the strong inclination of the Arabs towards the French, based on the educational efforts of the French, and he was desirous of copying their methods in a less religious and more liberal sense."[19]

There is a certain resemblance between Halidé Edib's or Hasan Amja's[20] educational work, on the one hand, and, more broadly, Jemal Pasha's Armenian policy. The only difference, I submit, resides in the dimensions of their activity. The purpose was the same: gradually to strip the Armenian component of the population of central features of Armenian identity—in this case, the Armenian language and the Christian religion—forcibly replacing them with Turkish and Islam. Pushing this thesis, we may say that Jemal Pasha believed that the Armenian element in the Arab environment of Bilad al-Sham, cut off as it was from its natural habitat, could become a faithful tool of Ottoman policy, counterbalancing foreign influences in the region. Moreover, with their enterprising commercial spirit and knowledge of many different trades, the Armenians could become an important factor in developing the region's economy. These ideas are to some extent reflected in the recommendations that Hasan Amja gave Jemal Pasha when Jemal asked him to resettle the deported Armenians under the Fourth Army's jurisdiction in places where conditions would make it easy for them to take up some kind of economic activity.[21]

In the same years, and especially in 1916, the Mount Lebanon region suffered from a terrible famine that eventually wiped out almost one-third of the local population, primarily Christian Maronites, whose elite had adopted positions that served French interests. Jemal Pasha was very much aware of the catastrophe that had befallen the Lebanese; it is even supposed that he was involved in planning the measures that created conditions of famine in Lebanon. This is an indispensable angle from which to examine Jemal Pasha's relatively tolerant position vis-à-vis the Armenian deportees and the measures he took in the same period with regard to Mount Lebanon's population.

All this smacks of a colonialist approach to politics—an approach in which nationalism and modernization traverse the same scene hand in hand. Ussama Makdisi captures the essence of this conception of things with the apt label "modern Ottoman imperialism."[22] This policy more often found expression in the outer reaches of the empire—in this case, the Arab provinces. In this sense, the Arab provinces appear to have been a field in which Jemal Pasha and his followers had a free hand to experiment with population strategies by deporting some peoples and enfeebling or resettling others, or endeavoring to alter their religious and ethnic identities. In a word, Jemal and his associates were guided primarily by the political cynicism and delirious logic typical of rulers who implement imperialist, colonialist policies of this kind. After all, what Jemal Pasha failed to achieve in Bilad al-Sham in the three years he was active there would later, under different conditions and with a different approach, be realized by the French occupation forces destined to become the ruling element in Syria, Lebanon, and Cilicia after the war's end. In these regions, the French, too, would carry out an occupation policy that was essentially imperialist-colonialist in nature: settling or resettling local peoples and then using those same peoples to gain leverage with which to strengthen and perpetuate the French presence in these countries.[23]

In my view, Jemal Pasha was not merely the nationalist colonialist official just portrayed. He embodied another figure as well: that of the pragmatic military man prepared to utilize all of the many different means at his disposal to succeed in the military operations he was leading against the Allied forces on the Egyptian front. In this respect, he differed little from the Nazi German officials during World War II who ran the ghettos in which captive Jewish populations were concentrated. Because of their Jewish labor force, the ghettos located in the regions of the East—the Lodz (Litzmannstadt) Ghetto being the one most often discussed—became important elements in the framework of the Nazi war effort. Motivated by strategic considerations, these Nazi officials postponed implementation of the plan to exterminate the Jewish captives under their jurisdiction. Thus the Jews in the ghettos, like the Jews in the camps in the final years of the war, became forced laborers

Figure 2.1. A view from Hama in the 1920s.
(Source: AGBU, Nubarian Library, Paris)

utilized by various factories belonging to the Wehrmacht.[24] Their disappearance would, quite simply, have dealt a serious blow to the war effort. At the same time, these Nazi officials in all probability still regarded the extermination of the Jews under their jurisdiction as the "Final Solution"; in this regard, they did not differ from their Nazi co-thinkers. Nevertheless, the officials' strategic interests helped prolong the lives of the Jewish captives who managed to survive despite their extreme working conditions. Was Jemal Pasha not motivated by the same strategic concerns when he integrated thousands of Armenian deportees, men and women alike, into army factories in Bilad al-Sham, especially from 1917 on? A majority of them worked in conditions of semi-slavery. Yet their labor guaranteed them their means of subsistence, and sometimes also a negligible wage. Most important, the deportees received military *vesikas*, and thus assurance that they would not be sent elsewhere.

Life in Exile in Salamiyya: Diary Observations of the Local Ismailis

> *Salamiyya...*
> *City whose gates are always open*
> *And call out, like mouths come out to greet you.*
> *On every handful of soil*
> *Is a butterfly's wing, a captive's chains,*
> *A letter of Mutanabbi's or Hajjaj's whip,*
> *Or a tooth of Khalif's or an orphan's tear.*
> —Muhammed al-Maghut (1934–2006), "Salamiyya"
> Translated from an Armenian translation
> of the Arabic by Mihran Minassian

> I went walking through Salamiyya today. It must have been built on the ruins of a Byzantine, and perhaps also a Roman, city. On the black stones of the ruins are, besides engraved crosses, inscriptions in the Greek alphabet; here and there, a few meters below ground level, one sees conduits for water.[25]

A few days later, the same amateur archeologist quoted above writes:

> Together with a few friends, I visited some of the antiquities in Salamiyya, the fortress, and the Ziyaret [a shrine], located about an hour northwest of the city. The fortress stands on a man-made hill thirty meters high and, is known as "Shamiramis." Between the hill and the fortress are ditches some eight meters deep. There are ruins at the highest point of the fortress. The ramparts and a few walls are intact….The Ziyaret is located to the east of the fortress, a little higher, on a hill that may be the peak of an extinct volcano, because there are still rather big black boulders there.[26]

At first glance, one might suppose these lines were penned by a Western traveler visiting the many-splendored East and noting, in the peculiar style of the day, his impressions of the various stops on his itinerary and the native inhabitants and their way of life. In fact, the writer was an Armenian deportee, the eighteen-year-old Krikor Bogharian, who had been forcibly resettled in Salamiyya along with his family and thousands of his compatriots. Armenians from Ayntab were deported en masse beginning in October 1915 (the details will be examined in the next section). They were free to circulate in and around the city. Bogharian availed himself of this opportunity, which explains why his diary includes observations about places he has visited.

What is more, the young man from Ayntab had an inquisitive mind; he was alert to what was going on around him and observed the life and customs of Salamiyya's native inhabitants with unflagging interest. About the city's houses, he writes:

> They have one story, as a rule; there are only five two-story houses in the whole town. They are damp, because they are ground-floor buildings. The doors and windows face north or west. Instead of wooden beams, the roofs are made of reeds; only new houses have beams. The stone houses use the black stone that seems to have been abundant here. Public buildings are constructed with rectangular bricks made of a mixture of earth and straw, with the result that they are not resistant and can collapse during storms. These public buildings display one of two "architectural styles." One, the old style, has a cowl-shaped dome sitting atop a square or rectangular room; the other is merely a square or rectangular room with a roof over it.[27]

Bogharian also attentively followed the local women's day-to-day occupations, recording his observations:

> Generally speaking, the men are lazy. The women plow; rake the fields; help out at harvest-time; plaster the walls of the houses; mind the cattle and the flocks; do the milking and use the milk to make yoghurt and butter; carry very heavy loads on their heads; transport the manure they collect in the course of the day in *tepir*s [trays made of interwoven reeds] that they carry, again, on their heads, in order to dump it on the public manure-pile; knead and bake bread in the *tonirs*; and do the usual domestic chores as well (washing, cooking meals, nursing children, and the like). It is shameful for a man to carry a "load." Girls and young married women are good-looking and graceful, as a rule, but the old women are ugly.[28]

Krikor and his family would continue to live and, like everyone else, wage a daily struggle for survival in this city. In contrast to the depictions of Bilad al-Sham's various ethnic groups generally found in Armenian survivors' accounts, Bogharian's remarks about Salamiyya are characterized by their lack of stereotyped depictions of the local populace and even testify to a certain sympathy for these inhabitants. Colored predominantly by Orientalist notions, most Armenian descriptions of the local Arabs depict them as uncivilized and backward. Such prejudiced characterizations were widespread among the various peoples living in Anatolia and the Armenians' homeland, and Armenians were no exception in this regard. The pejorative characterization of Arabs was especially current among Ottoman elites, who often took a colonialist attitude toward the inhabitants of the empire's Arab provinces. It must be borne in mind that the Taurus mountain chain, especially as seen from Istanbul, constituted the frontier of "civilization"; in the regions to the south lay the desert and the nomadic Arabs' homelands. All indications are that this mindset was common to the Turkish and non-Turkish Istanbul elites. As Ziya Gökalp saw it, the line of demarcation running between the "Turko-Kurds" (that is, between Anatolia) and the Arabs constituted the frontier of civilization. The Young Turk ideologue very probably meant to imply that the Arabs occupied the lowest level of the civilization in question.[29]

A personal incident related by Yervant Odian is highly symptomatic here. It dates from his days in exile near the end of World War I, when the Armenian author from Istanbul was forcibly relocated, after a succession of long, draining moves from one place to another, in Sultaniye (present-day Karapinar), a village east of Konya. The incident took place while the Ottoman army stationed in the empire's Arab provinces was retreating before the Allied forces, which had already taken Damascus and Aleppo. The Turks of Sultaniye were filled with dread at the thought of armed Arab detachments arriving in their district together with the advancing Allied forces, convinced as they were that the Arabs would commit acts of brute violence of all sorts. Haunted, as it were, by the specter of an invasion of "barbaric" Arabs, the local Turks were all fearfully awaiting it. Eventually, ten or fifteen Arab cavalrymen did indeed appear, advancing toward Sultaniye with *keffiye*s wrapped around their heads. Terrible panic seized the village. The local Turks recovered their calm only after persuading themselves that these Arabs were loyal troops retreating with the rest of the Ottoman army.[30]

Although Odian mocked such Turkish prejudices, but it must be said that like the accounts of other Armenian deportees then in Sultaniye, his memoirs contain stereotypical remarks about Arabs. For example, he describes the loathing that a Turkish major on duty in Der Zor felt for Arabs; at the time of this observation, the Istanbul Armenian writer was himself leading a deportee's existence in that Mesopotamian city. As if intending to justify and ground the Turkish officer's attitude, Odian begins to detail his impressions of Arabs in turn: "Indeed, I don't think that there's a race on earth like the Arabs, so lacking in cleanliness. Lice abound on them, even in relatively well-to-do families. They don't even have a basic idea of cleanliness."[31] It is ironic that in these years a Turkish major and, in the person of Yervant Odian, a deported Armenian intellectual both continued to cultivate the very same attitude toward the Arabs, and that Odian managed to maintain his anti-Arab Anatolian prejudices intact despite the breakdown of trust between Armenians and Turks and the appalling events that had taken place during the war.

The memoirs of another deportee, Vahram Dadrian, describe Arabs in terms at least as pejorative. Feeling no need to engage in long analyses, Dadrian contents himself with dividing the Bedouin Arabs into two groups, "savages and semi-savages."[32] In his view the fellahin, the sedentary Arabs, were simply "more civilized in comparison with Bedouins," although when it came to hygiene "they remain quite as backward as their nomadic compatriots."[33] Der Nerses also uses the adjective "semi-savage," with reference to the people of Salamiyya.[34] In his case, however, this seems to be an instance of unreflective use of a cliché that prevailed among Anatolians or more generally the peoples living to the north of the Taurus Mountains—the more so as Tavukjian's remark was not made after a characteristic incident involving the local populace and had no obvious motivation. On the contrary, it was meant to underscore his impression that the district's native inhabitants now appeared morally superior to the Armenian deportees making a living as merchants in Salamiyya's market. Apparently the epithet "semi-savage" had simply become a reflex for people of this generation. Catholicos Sahag II provides another example. When he informed the Patriarch of the Istanbul Armenians that the first caravans of deportees had begun moving south, he was unsure precisely in which direction these Armenians were being led. "We do not know where they are bound," he wrote. "The most probable destination is Mesopotamia, the land of sand-storms and half-savage Bedouins."[35]

In this general context, the absence of negative descriptions of Salamiyya's native inhabitants in Bogharian's diary takes on greater significance. Not only does he not speak pejoratively of them, but he also occasionally depicts in glowing terms the hospitality of Salamiyya's inhabitants, as well as the tolerance with which they accepted the resettlement of many thousands of Armenians in their town. These phenomena lend Bogharian's account its particularity and quite likely distinguish it from many other examples of autobiographical narrative by Bilad al-Sham survivors. In the main, his remarks to this effect consist of extremely brief asides, yet their presence is surely evidence of a feeling of relative security among Salamiyya's Armenian deportees. "The local inhabitants are not unsympathetic toward us Armenians,"[36] Bogharian writes. The attitude of Salamiyya's notables reinforced the young diarist's impression. "Salamiyya's renowned *masters* [princes] are Armenophiles, especially the two brothers Emir Tamir and Emir Mirza."[37] Another local dignitary, Emir Suleiman, put his own home at the disposition of an Armenian family from Ayntab, the Kharajejians, who had made a name for themselves as merchants.[38] The young Bogharian's sentence —"Praise the Lord that we've ended up on hospitable soil!"[39] which was written upon his resettlement in Salamiyya, attests his relative comfort and peace of mind.

Let us consider Bogharian's explanations for this singular situation before essaying one of our own. "Because the people of Salamiyya are not Sunni Muslims, they do not count in the central government's eyes. There are many deserters from the army; those who are caught are punished with the gallows."[40] In another passage, he provides general information about Salamiyya and its inhabitants:

> The village has grown to the size of a small town, with a population of around six thousand. The people belong to the Ismaili sect; there are only a few Sunnis, who are principally government officials. There is no *cami-minare* [mosque-minaret]. From time to time, a voice reciting *ezan* [prayers] can be heard in one corner of the market. There were no young men left among the city's inhabitants; many had been drafted, and some had migrated earlier to America.[41]

This was Bogharian's "hospitable" Salamiyya. A big village (today a city) lying thirty-two kilometers southeast of Hama, it was the product of a peculiar history. It was mentioned even in the Byzantine period as a prosperous transit station on the edge of the desert, a crossroads of various trade routes. Beginning in the ninth century, in the period of Abbasid rule, Salamiyya gradually acquired its Ismaili identity as adherents of the Ismaili faith became increasingly concentrated in the village. From here, Ismaili preachers were dispatched to other places to propagate their creed. Salamiyya was also the birthplace of Ubayd Allah, the celebrated Ismaili who founded the Fatimid Caliphate in Northern Africa, and whose successors would capture Salamiyya as well.[42]

Under the Ottomans, however, the city of Salamiyya lost its leading position, saw its former splendor fade, was deserted by its inhabitants, and remained uninhabited for centuries. Not until the mid-nineteenth century did the deserted city undergo a thoroughgoing transformation. In these years the central Ottoman authorities were striving to extend their control over the territories lying along the Euphrates, especially the trade route between Baghdad and Aleppo that ran through them, which they wished to protect from Bedouin attacks. An important dimension of this Ottoman central government policy consisted in inducing nomads to take up a sedentary existence while settling new populations in zones fringing the desert. This settlement policy mandated the founding of new villages and small towns.

It was under such circumstances that Salamiyya, too, experienced a renaissance, this one pioneered by Ismailis. They came mainly from villages lying in the Khawabi River valley (in the Alawi Mountains), but also from the nearby towns of Kadmus and Misyaf. In these districts, conflicts frequently broke out between the Ismailis and the Alawis, who formed a relative majority there; they were generally caused by disputes over ownership of the arable land. There were also internal conflicts among the Ismaili princes (emirs), which often culminated in bloodshed. In the wake of a killing of this kind, one of the community's emirs, Ismail ibn Mohammed, became a fugitive. The Ottoman authorities sought to arrest and banish him, but eventually granted Ismail an opportunity to extricate himself from his predicament in the form of an offer to go settle with his followers on the eastern banks of the Orontes (al-Asi) River, an area in which the Sublime Porte was implementing its resettlement and land reclamation policies. A *firman* promulgated by the Sultan in 1849 further stipulated that all settlers in the region would be exempt from state taxes and the draft.[43]

For the Ismailis, this presented an opportunity to resettle in ruined, abandoned Salamiyya, a place that seems to have retained the character of a homeland, in their eyes. The first settlers did in fact establish their homes in the ruins of the old city's fortress. Later, as they fanned out, the foundations of the present-day town were laid. The new settlement was initially given the name Mejidabad in honor of the then reigning Sultan, Abdülmejid (1839–1861). Gradually, however, the name Salamiyya came to replace this official name.[44] The movement to repopulate the village was supervised by Ismaili emirs, the community's leaders. It was the emirs who, in this period, conducted negotiations with the chieftains of the nomadic tribes who also lived in this region, with an eye to ensuring peaceful coexistence between neighbors.[45] The new settlers were farmers and as such had the skills required to restore the former reputation of the district's soil, famed for its fertility from the Byzantine period on. Ismailis, although they made up the great majority of these colonists, were by no means the only element in the population; they were accompanied by Circassian and Alawi farmers who for the most part settled in the countryside.[46] These groups were later joined by local Bedouin families who had adopted a sedentary way of life.[47]

The Ottoman authorities' de facto penetration of the Salamiyya district dates from 1884, when Salamiyya was accorded the administrative status of a *kaza* attached to the *sanjak* of Hama. Troops and gendarmes were stationed there that year, and the local population began to pay state taxes and was subjected for the first time to the law on conscription.[48] Early in the twentieth century, Salamiyya, with a population of nearly six thousand,[49] ranked as the biggest Ismaili population center in the Ottoman Empire. But the community life that sprang up thanks to the district's privileged status underwent rapid, drastic change under Sultan Abdülhamid II. Beginning in this period, Istanbul came to regard the Ismailis as heretics and also as agents of foreign powers, especially Great Britain. Among the reasons for the emergence of this attitude were the upheavals that rocked the Salamiyya community late in the nineteenth century when, the Ismailis began to show fealty to Agha Khan, whom they now looked to as their spiritual leader. Agha Khan, however, resided in Sind and later Bombay (Mumbai), cities located in India, then part of the British Empire; this circumstance heightened the Ottoman administration's suspicions.

Plainly, this population group was generally considered a minority by its Sunni or Alawi neighbors, with whom it frequently clashed. The glory, power, and triumphs of remote centuries held an important place in the group's collective memory and, in a way, took on a more pronounced character as a result of the vulnerable situation in which the Ismailis found themselves, now that Istanbul often regarded them as adversaries of the ruling Ottoman authorities. Can the Ismailis' historical destiny be said to resemble the Armenians? Was it this similarity that motivated their sympathy for the deportees, confirmed in a number of personal accounts by Armenian survivors?

True, the stock figure of the "hospitable," "life-saving" Arab appears frequently in the Armenian historiography of the years following the genocide. It is basically an ex post facto construction shaped by the continuing co-existence of Arabs and Armenians in Arab countries. In various memoirs, this topos stands in sharp contrast to the narrative of actual events. Nevertheless, Salamiyya would seem to constitute an exception in this regard. "The people of Salamiyya, the Armenians' Good Samaritans": thus were the townspeople described by Robert Jebejian, a native of Ayntab who later lived in Aleppo, as he recalled the attitude of the people of Salamiyya toward the Armenians in the years of the genocide.[50] Here, too, of course, one might suppose this is a reconstructed narrative composed under the influence of subsequent developments. However, Jebejian's thinking and writing about the people of Salamiyya flows directly from his personal memories as a deportee and reflects an attitude sui generis toward the city. He himself never resided there; he was in Aleppo during the mass violence. But that little boy then around nine years old would later remember very well how, in the last year of the war, his maternal and paternal uncles' families, who had initially been deported to Salamiyya, settled in the city where he and his family were living. He first heard descriptions of the townspeople's "decent treatment" of the Armenian deportees from these relatives. So profound an impression did this leave on him that, much later, after Jebejian had become a well-known physician in Aleppo, he attempted to express his gratitude by reciprocating the kindness of Salamiyya's natives. "I have tried," he writes, "to repay my patients from the town with free medical services."[51] This feeling of gratitude is also conspicuous in the case of another survivor from Ayntab, Hovhannes Zarigian, who spent his years as a deportee in Salamiyya and later became an enterprising, accomplished automobile mechanic (he was also active as a writer and publicist). Zarigian, too, notes that he did not charge customers from Salamiyya for his services.[52]

The main narrator of events in Salamiyya is Bogharian, for it is his diary that holds the most noteworthy account of Salamiyya, especially with regard to the local populace, the town, and prevailing conditions. But to a large extent, the life of the Armenian deportees in this region was shaped by external factors. Deportees and their families had nothing even remotely resembling the minimal conditions for creating a stable environment and thus securing their means of survival. Though Salamiyya initially seemed to foster hope that the deportees' situation could be stabilized, it soon became an unbearable place for many who, like Der Nerses, would be forced to leave the town in search of other means of survival.

Figure 2.2. Krikor Bogharian (Source: Krikoris Bogharian family collection)

Deportees Transform Salamiyya and Breathe New Life into the Local Market

"The weather is good," Der Nerses writes; "the water is drawn from wells, but is abundant; albeit clean, it is a little salty. The roads are dirt roads, yet they are cleaner than Aleppo's streets. The market is full of deported craftsmen. All who learn that they are to be allowed to stay here are content and cheerful."[53] Thus, from October 1915 on, began a new life for deportees in Salamiyya. The process of repopulating the district, set in motion on the initiative of the *kaymakam*, Nejmeddin Bey, proceeded at a brisk pace in the following weeks and months. In November of the same year, Der Nerses notes in this connection that five to six hundred Armenian families had been relocated in Salamiyya.[54] In other words, there was at least one Armenian deportee for every two natives of the town. The Armenians' numbers would continue to swell, even though a policy of dispatching groups of deportees to the surrounding villages was gradually put in place to prevent overcrowding.[55] Bogharian appears to have been scrupulously precise when citing figures in connection with the deportees, the more so as he was responsible for preparing lists of Armenians eligible for state aid. According to him, Salamiyya's Armenian population had increased markedly by July 1916, reaching 4,020 individuals or 670 families.[56] By June 1916, a total of 7,500 Armenians had been resettled in the *kaza* of Salamiyya (i.e., the town and surrounding villages).[57]

Krikor Bogharian's diary entry of 5 July (22 June) 1916 records census results containing miscellaneous information about the Armenians relocated in the villages near Salamiyya. Scattered among twenty-five different villages, the deportees numbered 3,047 in all, although Bogharian observes that the figure cited in this census should be reduced by around one thousand to account for the people who had, in the meantime, either died or been sent to the town of Salamiyya. Generally speaking, the quantitative distribution of the population, broken down village by village, displays great internal disparities: the highest concentration of deportees in a single village was four hundred thirty-seven, whereas in some villages barely ten Armenians could be found. We further learn from Bogharian that the Armenians were distributed among these villages according to their place of origin. At the same time, observations about the forcibly relocated Armenians often included elsewhere in his and Der Nerses' diaries are repeated by way of these statistics. They clearly show that the majority of Armenians here were from localities just north of the Taurus mountains (Ayntab, Marash, Sereg/Siverek, Dörtyol, Jihan/Ceyhan, Beylan/Belen) and that some of them, as we have already seen in considering the example of the natives of Ayntab, had sustained minimal losses before reaching these villages. Alongside them, however, were natives of Sivas and Agn/ Eğin (present-day Kemaliye) who had likewise been resettled in one or another isolated village, but had reached this region after suffering the dire consequences of a terrible journey. It has been observed that children comprised as much as ninety per cent of some of these groups of deportees.[58] That is grounds for the supposition that these groups of Armenians hailing from regions beyond the Taurus mountains, that is, from the inner Anatolian provinces, were predominantly made up of human wrecks—women, children, and orphans—and that the adult men in these groups had been put to death.

It is obvious that a majority of the Armenians who had been relocated in the *kaza* of Salamiyya, particularly those in the district's administrative seat, came from urban centers—a circumstance that was inevitably fraught with consequences in this primarily rural area. What occurred in the town of Salamiyya in the following months would appear not to have been a unique phenomenon, inasmuch as similar developments were observable in the same period in other cities and towns in Bilad al-Sham faced with a heavy influx of Armenian deportees. Indeed, at a time when these cities and towns had been largely emptied of their adult male populations as a result of conscription (whether the men had been inducted or gone into hiding), while the war situation gradually took a heavy toll on trade and the market, the Armenians' arrival had had unprecedented repercussions in many localities. The fact is that the new arrivals were not just experienced merchants; they were also "condemned to succeed" in order to ensure their survival in their new surroundings. If they did not—we have already had occasion to observe the profound instability of the daily lives of these deportees cut off from their native soil—they could very quickly find themselves in dire straits, deprived of any and all sources of income. Officially, the newly arrived Armenians were *muhacir* [settlers], yet they were for the most part forced to go without any state aid: they were not provided with living quarters and only sporadically received a dole.

In the aggregate, these circumstances led to a far-reaching transformation of local markets. From one day to the next, the arrival of thousands of Armenian deportees and the fact that many of them immediately took up a craft or began working in commerce breathed new life into local economies. Salamiyya, Hama, Jarash, Rakka, Damascus—in these cities and towns, all of which are described in survivors' personal narratives, Armenians threw themselves body and soul into the world of work, determined to succeed at any price. In that sense, these localities were marked by the mass violence in a peculiar way: they became places in which the deportees were afforded a chance—even if, in certain localities, it proved to be only a temporary one—to earn their living by the sweat of their brow. Salamiyya, as we shall see, exemplified the result: a headlong rush to take up any form of activity, to accept a job of any kind, sometimes to go to work with all the other members of one's family and, very often, to take over certain branches of the economy, even if this meant incurring the hostility of the local groups that had to put up with the consequences. In a word, the Armenians completely transformed Bilad al-Sham's economy. Salamiyya would not be left untouched by this phenomenon.

> It is as if Salamiyya has become an 'Armeniantown.' The man who fires the cannon to announce the end of the daily Ramadan fast is an Armenian; the tavern-keepers are Armenians; a *çavuş* in the town hall is an Armenian; nine out of ten shopkeepers are Armenians, the bakers (there are now four of them) are Armenians, two or three Armenian secretaries have found work in municipal offices.

Thus does Bogharian presents the state of affairs in the town in his entry for 15 July (2 July).[59] He further notes that there were abundant employment opportunities for construction workers in Salamiyya, as in this period houses were being built for the *kaymakam* and *kadı* (judge) and work on the construction of a school and a state agricultural institute was ongoing.[60] According to the information available for 1916, Salamiyya's Armenians worked primarily in the trades: they were bakers, goldsmiths, weavers, wool spinners, carpet-makers, *manusa*-makers,[61] and tailors. Others were grocers, saddle-merchants, *bastaci*,[62] and peddlers. The Armenians who arrived in Salamiyya with substantial capital generally traded in flour and also goods imported from Homs and Hama. Finally, there was a group of deportees who had no trade at all and had already exhausted their savings. To secure an income, they performed unskilled labor, collecting brushwood, disposing of rubbish, sweeping houses, carrying loads, or making bricks.[63] Employment opportunities multiplied for such laborers with the coming of spring or harvest-time, for Salamiyya suffered from a labor shortage in the war years: men and women went out together to bring in the harvest in exchange for a daily wage (from six to fifteen piasters in May 1916) as well as their daily sustenance, provided by the landowner.[64] Men who had been Bogharian's teachers in Ayntab fell into this group: the majority of them had no trade and were forced to take up one occupation or another simply in order to support themselves and their families. Such men often worked as gardeners, night watchmen, or peddlers.[65] The same Bogharian, whose diary often mentions the presence of Armenian beggars in Salamiyya, notes also in fall 1916 that beggars had generally disappeared from the town; this was, in his estimation, evidence of relative prosperity. The beggars—mostly Armenian women from Sivas who had no one to support them—had found employment spinning wool,[66] a trade that was on its way to becoming one of the main occupations of Salamiyya's Armenians.

There were also certain opportunities for employment in the civil service in Salamiyya. For instance, Hovhannes Efendi Levonian,[67] who had been the *mal müdir* [municipal treasurer] in Ayntab, assumed the same civil service post in this Ismaili town and accordingly took a hand in the distribution of state aid.[68] Armenians who could read and write Ottoman Turkish were appointed to posts as secretaries in the Bureau of Trades [*sınaî*] and the Office of Food and Supplies [*iaşe*].[69] Garabed Babigian, a native of Ayntab, assumed the post of *muhtar/mukhtar*.[70]

All these descriptions have certain points in common with accounts by other Armenian survivors who found themselves in various cities or towns in Bilad al-Sham. The impact of Armenian deportees on Hama's economic situation, for example, did not escape Yervant Odian's attention:

> Almost half the shops in the market were in the hands of Armenians. The majority of the Arab shops had been forced to close due to the military call up. There were Armenian grocers, Armenian butchers, vegetable sellers, haberdashers and cloth sellers, as well as many barbers, shoemakers, carpenters, dentists, photographers, pharmacists, bakers, tailors, ironsmiths, and so on. It was the Armenians who opened the first photography shops in Hama. The Armenians also opened, for the first time, two restaurants.[71]

What Vahram Dadrian relates about Jarash is in many respects identical, although Dadrian falls back on the usual clichés when describing the local Arabs:

> Despite the fact that water runs abundantly through the village, the local people had never come up with the idea of making garden or a water mill, which is so indispensable for farmers....Immediately after their arrival, the Armenians built eight mills along the river. Then they created and planted around fifty vegetable gardens, where they grow all sorts of vegetables, according to the season. The skilled workers have opened about forty shops, where they make their livings as cobblers, gun smiths, comb-makers, felt-makers, farriers, iron-mongers, butchers, etc. Because of the shops, water mills, and vegetable gardens, the little village of Jeresh has become a profitable business town. Every day hundreds of Fellahs and Bedouins come from afar to have their wheat ground or their broken rifles repaired, their pots mended or their horses shod.[72]

Manase Sevag spent the war years in Damascus, where tens of thousands of Armenian deportees had settled. Sevag's account of his experiences during the war is also replete with information of this kind:

> Armenian merchants' and shopkeepers' business methods were a novelty in Damascus' markets. The local merchants and shopkeepers were not slow to express their heartfelt admiration, laced with a touch of jealousy, with the expression *"ermen shater"* [industrious Armenian]. Armenians from Caesarea living in Damascus produced sausages [*sucuk*] and salted and dried meat [*basturma*], selling considerable quantities of both. Before the Armenian deportees' arrival, the inhabitants of Damascus had never seen preserved meat or the Macedonian cheese that Armenian exiles from Macedonia made for the whole city. The Armenians opened shoemaker's shops, where they put a score of people to work under their supervision; most of the people of Damascus wore shoes made by Armenians, and the Arabs would often say that, if it hadn't been for the Armenians, they would be walking around barefoot. The Armenians tried their hand at every kind of job that paid, but was also difficult, and they made a go of it every time. The Armenians sold wheat. They opened shops in Saman Pazar and went into the flour business, selling large quantities at lower prices than the local merchants. There was an Armenian pharmacy in Damascus. Of all the city's photographers, Mihran Hadikozian, a photographer from Rodosto, had the greatest success; he was to become the photographer whose work came closest to Jemal Pasha's, the provincial governor's, the army commanders', and the ordinary people's idea of beauty. Apkar Balekjian, a native of Rodosto, was responsible for producing weapons for the [Ottoman] Fourth Army. Since no coal whatsoever was to be had, trains were fueled with wood; an Armenian deportee from Adana was charged with furnishing it.[73]

Accounts of this kind hold a note of national chauvinism, particularly when their authors identify the Armenians' diligence and enterprising spirit as the cause of these sweeping socioeconomic changes. Often forgotten or underestimated are the prevailing wartime conditions—especially the draft, which carried off a substantial segment of these cities' and towns' labor supply, or simply made fugitives of potential workers. At any rate, many different eyewitness accounts confirm that the Armenian deportees were very quickly integrated into the economic life of Bilad al-Sham's cities and towns and, in short order, came to dominate various trades and certain sectors of the local markets.

All this, however, is just one side of the coin. The war wore on, and in the whirlpool of battle and extermination, Armenian deportees constituted the most vulnerable element. This holds for the region of Bilad al-Sham as well, even if it was considered relatively secure. True, the Armenians were integrated into the economic life of these places of deportation; yet in the final analysis the stability of local markets depended heavily on the course of the war and particularly the extent of military requisitions. The unparalleled inflation that set in in 1917 paints a very revealing picture that goes a long way toward explaining the crisis into which ordinary deportees were plunged. So severe was their predicament that, from this time on, many Armenians left "hospitable" Salamiyya, a town that gave them a sense of security, in a migratory movement to bigger cities nearby, such as Hama and Homs. What explains this collective migration? The Armenians who took part in this population movement were primarily those who, unable to find a permanent source of income in Salamiyya, had kept body and soul together by doing odd jobs. When economic crisis struck, the existing means of survival began to disappear and the specter of starvation loomed before the deportees. It was this situation that compelled them to abandon hospitable, comparatively secure Salamiyya and try their luck in the neighboring urban centers, where they glimpsed the possibility of finding employment, even if equally secure living conditions were not to be had here.

This migratory wave also points to the local authorities' relaxation of restrictions on the deportees' freedom of movement in 1917. We know, for example, that Der Nerses was arrested in November 1915 by the Ottoman police and subjected to sharp questioning for having traveled from Salamiyya to Hama without a *vesika*.[74] In 1917, however, the deportees enjoyed greater freedom of movement, albeit within a restricted area; we see them moving from Salamiyya to Hama, from Hama to Homs and even distant Aleppo. In the conditions precipitated by the extraordinary economic crisis of the final war years, this relative freedom of movement was without a doubt a major advantage for the thousands of deportees looking for work, and enabled them to subsist. A great many of those on the move were women who had set out in quest of employment in *imalat hane*s in the big cities.[75] "Some of those in the poor class of the population, spurred by hunger and misery, have scattered here and there in the big towns in the hope of finding a way to earn a living; every day, new itinerants take to the road."[76]

It should here be emphasized that knowing a trade or possessing a small amount of capital did not guarantee success. In Bilad al-Sham, it did not even necessarily guarantee a family of deportees a minimal subsistence. Der Nerses's own example shows that even if a deportee mastered a trade, worked hard at it, and put his young children to work as well, the extreme conditions of these years had the last word. Market prices were constantly rising and modest capital investments could not hold up under the pressure, so many new businesses were condemned to a quick demise. In other words, the deported Armenians were defenseless and ravaged, without land or houses, vulnerable in a thousand ways, at the mercy of fate.

Many of the Armenian craftsmen who had found work making cloth in the war years suffered the same fate. We learn from the priest from Ayntab, for example, that from 1917 on, Armenian deportees in the Hama-Homs-Salamiyya region, those from Ayntab in particular, had begun to revive what was once the most widely practiced crafts in their native town: weaving *manusa* on a loom. Der Nerses calls this craft simply "*manusa*-making."[77] Many had the impression that by engaging in cloth-making again, they were resurrecting a fundamental dimension of everyday existence in Ayntab. This development inspired countless deportees with hope and a sense of security.

Before the war broke out, textile production is estimated to have provided some 21,000 inhabitants of urban Ayntab with a source of income. This figure includes people who spun wool or cotton, loom-makers, those who laid the warp, dyers, workers responsible for constructing the wooden frames of the looms [*tezgah* or *tezgeah*], merchants who imported spun fiber, and so on, as well as their families.[78] The source from which we take this information further notes that the textile industry provided an estimated 1,500 Turkish families in Ayntab—that is, around 7,500 people—with a livelihood. It follows that 14,000 of the 21,000 people mentioned above were Armenians; this represents about half of Ayntab's Armenian population.[79] In our view, in the resettlement zone stretching from Hama to Salamiyya, where Ayntab's Armenian deportees were forcibly relocated, the revival of cloth-making must also be deemed a factor favoring the preservation of community structures in an unfamiliar environment under extremely difficult conditions. After all, this undertaking was essentially a resurrection of a form of manufacture that presupposes the existence of various labor networks. If one group engages in importing and selling fiber, a second has to prepare the *direzin*,[80] a third has to work the looms and weave the cloth, and a fourth has to dye the cloth thus produced. Cloth production thus required a whole network of merchants, craftsmen, and laborers working in coordinated fashion. Evidently, it proved possible to recreate this network in circles of deportees from Ayntab living in the Hama-Salamiyya region.

In Salamiyya, Der Nerses found himself turning to this craft, with which he had been familiar since his youth. Let us follow the priest turned cloth-maker to see why this trade, like a wide variety of other means of survival, ultimately proved to be quite unreliable. In the constantly changing world of the deportees, the priesthood had ceased to be a means of earning a living. The Armenians around Der Nerses had already been producing cloth for months, and he, in his turn, tried to adapt to the new circumstances. In September 1917, with capital of five hundred piasters at his disposal (three hundred of which had been a present from compatriots of his who had settled in Hama), he had someone make him a *direzin*, purchased eight *top* (skeins) of local fiber, and went to work.[81] He completed his task in twenty-two days. In a place like Salamiyya, however, it was not particularly easy to take up such a trade: all the required materials had to be obtained at markets in Hama or Homs, so Der Nerses was forced to incur additional expense by making a voyage each time they needed materials. Many of the Ayntab cloth-makers in Salamiyya had already had to leave the town and settle in other cities nearby for reasons of this kind. Der Nerses's brother Hagop had done so in his turn, taking his family with him. Yet Der Nerses's own example shows that moving was anything but easy. One had to move with one's entire family and establish oneself in a new city and a new home—at a higher rent, obviously, than in Salamiyya. By October 1917, Der Nerses's capital amounted to no more than three or four hundred piasters.[82]

At this point Armenian compatriots of Der Nerses's from Ayntab who were living in Hama rushed to his aid. Among them was Sahag Efendi Sahagian, who made him a present of five Turkish gold pounds.[83] Late in October, Der Nerses, too, finally moved with his family to Hama, where a few weeks later he was still turning out cloth with a *tezgah* and *direzin*, this time together with his brother.[84] Despite working day in and day out at this trade for months, the *manusa* produced netted him no profit and brought no improvement at all to his family's dismal economic situation. "Making a living has become so hard that even someone who works without pause cannot buy so much as a crust of bread, if he lives by the fruit of his labor alone."[85] The intensifying economic crisis was also clearly taking its toll on the textile trade, as the number of customers decreased, driving the price of cloth down.[86] This spelled the end of the *manusa* business, which, Der Nerses notes, had assured the survival of both ordinary people and the rich. In the face of this uncertain situation, the priest from Ayntab writes: "If things keep on going this way and, one day, grind to a complete halt, unemployment will deal another heavy blow to those who are already suffering from hunger; in that case, whole families will be found lying unconscious in their little huts or, to put it more accurately, will be found dead there. May the Lord deliver us, and have mercy on us all."[87] Finally, an incident occurred that, so to speak, put the last touch on this crushing situation: a pouring rain and a storm brought the roof of the room in which Der Nerses had set up his *tezgah* crashing down, smashing the loom and *direzin* to pieces and burying them beneath stone and dirt.[88] One after the next, the known means of survival were crumbling before the exhausted Der Nerses's eyes.

Figure 2.3. A view from Hama in the 1920s
(Source: AGBU, Nubarian Library, Paris)

Notes

1. Levi, *If This Is a Man*, p. 185.
2. See, e.g., Talha Çiçek, *War and State Formation in Syria: Cemal Pasha's Governorate during World War I, 1914–17* (New York: Routledge, 2014), pp. 107–124; Taner Akçam, *A Shameful Act: The Armenian Genocide and the Question of Turkish Responsibilty* (New York: Holt Paperback, 2007), pp. 184–189; Hilmar Kaiser, "The Armenians in Lebanon during the Armenian Genocide", in Aïda Boudjikanian, ed., *Armenians of Lebanon: From Past Princesses and Refugees to Present-Day Community* (Beirut: Haigazian University, 2009), pp. 31–56; H. Kaiser, "Regional Resistance to Central Government Policies: Ahmed Djemal Pasha, the Governors of Aleppo, and Armenian Deportees in the Spring and Summer of 1915," *Journal of Genocide Research* 12, no. 3–4 (September–December 2010): 173–218; Dündar, *L'ingénierie ethnique du Comité Union et Progrès*, pp. 324–328.
3. Kaiser, "Regional Resistance," pp. 189–207.
4. Djemal Pasha, *Memories of a Turkish Statesman, 1913–1919* (New York: George H. Doran, Harvard University, 1922), p. 279.
5. Ibid.
6. Falih Rıfkı Atay, *Zeytindağı* (Istanbul: Bateş Atatürk Dizisi, 2003), p. 66.
7. AGBU Central Archives, Cairo, File no. 23, ALEPPO (April 1910–December 1919), "Bulletin of the Orphanage," ed. Rev. Aharon Shirajian, 7 June 1919, Aleppo.
8. Kaiser, "Regional Resistance," pp. 193–194.
9. Ibid., p. 194.

10. Akçam, *The Young Turks' Crime against Humanity*, p. 290.
11. See Ronald Grigor Suny, *The History of the Armenian Genocide* (Princeton, Oxford: Princeton University Press, 2015), pp. 285–286, 321.
12. "Deghakragan pazhin—Haik I Tamasgos" [Geographical section: Armenians in Damascus], *Portsank* (mimeographed biannual) 1, no. 13 (15 February 1917); 1, no. 19 (15 May 1917).
13. Chilingirian, *Descriptions*, p. 11; Kurken Der Vartanian, "Karekin ark. Khachadurian pusher (Husher yev nisher)" [Archbishop Karekin Kachadurian: Thorns (Memoirs and marks], *Hayrenik* 40, no. 9–10 (438) (September–October 1962): 61–62. Akçam cites a 23 June 1915 cable that the Interior Ministry sent to the regions of Mosul and Der Zor stating that "no space or permission is to be given for the opening of Armenian schools in their areas of settlement." Similar cables were later sent to the local authorities in Urfa, Aleppo, and Damascus. Akçam, *The Young Turks' Crime against Humanity*, pp. 301–302.
14. Sdepan Shahbaz, "Abril 24—Hisnamyagin artiv jshmardutyunner" [April 24— Truths on the occasion of the fiftieth anniversary] in *Hushamadyan medz yegherni*, 3rd ed. (Beirut: Zartonk, 1987), p. 98.
15. Bogharian, "Diary," p. 204; Kaiser, "Regional Resistance," p. 193. Akçam, for his part, cites a 1 July 1915 telegram sent by the Interior Ministry to the interior provinces ordering that Armenians be prevented from publishing newspapers in Armenian in their places of exile (Akçam, *The Young Turks' Crime against Humanity*, p. 302).
16. Talha Çiçek defends this standpoint in *War and State Formation in Syria*, pp. 106–133.
17. Kaiser, "The Armenians in Lebanon," p. 56. In another extremely interesting essay, however, Kaiser attempts to defend Jemal's policy toward the Armenians in World War I. The historian here deems the Ittihadist chief's stance toward the Armenian deportees to have been, not merely in contradiction with that of the other Ittihadist rulers, but also a basic alibi clearing him of the charge of participation in the genocide (Kaiser, "Regional resistance," pp. 209–210).
18. A number of historians believe that during the war, Jemal Pasha was attempting to conclude a secret agreement with the Allied governments that would allow him to become the sultan of a vast zone encompassing Syria, Mesopotamia, and the *vilayet*s inhabited by Armenians and Kurds. David Fromkin, *A Peace to End all Peaces* (Henry Holt, New York, 2009), pp. 214–215. Raymond Kévorkian sees a connection between the absence of anti-Armenian massacres in Bilad al-Sham and Jemal's hopes of reaching an agreement with the Allies: the thousands of Armenians living in these areas could have served as a kind of bargaining chip for Jemal, according to Kévorkian (*Armenian Genocide*, pp. 683–685). Secret negotiations between the commander of the Fourth Army and the Allies may indeed have taken place. I am not, however, inclined to think that Jemal was sincere in his attempts to draw a connection between this issue and the condition of Bilad al-Sham's Armenians. Jemal's aim might simply have been to spread disinformation. It should not be forgotten that at the same time, the Allied forces were conducting secret negotiations with Arab circles in the Ottoman Empire in hopes of fomenting an uprising against the state. The leaders in Istanbul were most probably aware of this ferment, and one might equally well suppose that they were seeking, by way of Jemal's secret negotiations, to buy time by preventing the Allies from pursuing their project.
19. Halidé Edib, *Memoirs* (New York: Century, 1926), p. 400.
20. Hasan Amja was in charge of shelters for over 1,700 Armenian orphans and widows in Damascus (Edib, *Memoirs*, p. 406; Chilingarian, *Descriptions*, p. 26; Ormanian, *Reflections*, p. 354).

21. "Faits et documents: Les dessous des déportations, Souvenirs de Tcherkess Hassan bey," in *Renaissance* 1, no. 198 (22 July 1919).
22. Ussama Makdisi, "Rethinking Ottoman Imperialism: Modernity, Violence and the Cultural Logic of Ottoman Reform," in Jens Hanssen, Thomas Philipp, and Stefan Weber, eds., *The Empire in the City: Arab Provincial Capitals in the Late Ottoman Empire* (Beirut: Orient-Institut, 2002), p. 30.
23. To a certain extent, this point of view coincides with ideas put forward by Talha Çiçek in *War and State Formation*. According to Çiçek, Jemal Pasha's ultimate aim was "to integrate [the Armenians] into Syrian society, dispersing them in various districts as 'harmless minorities'" (Çiçek, *War and State Formation in Syria*, p. 133). Çiçek adds, however, that as a result Armenians would become "ideal citizens of the Ottoman state and would not endanger the formation of a unitary and fully authorized governmental apparatus in the Ottoman realm." It is unclear whether this thesis is intended as a justification of the policies pursued by Jemal. Çiçek considers the radical steps undertaken by Jemal Pasha in connection with Armenians as well as other groups in Bilad al-Sham (leaders of the Arab movement, Lebanese Christians, Jews) to be measures tending to promote "Ottomanization." Resorting to this euphemism makes it impossible to understand the totalitarian methods and aspirations to one-party rule embraced by the CUP, of which Jemal Pasha was a partisan. Çiçek often makes facile use of the phrase "subject to foreign influences" to qualify groups who became the focus of Jemal's policy. This is the same terminology used by the CUP itself, whereby the party's leaders sought to silence all dissenting voices in the Empire, often by eliminating them physically. In other words, absent a critical approach, the use of such language is misleading; it cannot adequately depict the context of ideological intolerance in which the CUP's leaders operated. Jemal Pasha's case is clearly that of a typical local tyrant convinced that his activity promoted state interests. The pretext of "Ottomanization" served as cover for his attempt to weaken local groups, eliminate their leaders, and thus render the groups "governable" so that, like any other colonialist potentate, he could construct a new order corresponding to his vision of things.
24. Yehuda Bauer, *Rethinking the Holocaust* (New Haven: Yale University Press, 2002), pp. 90–91; Ulrich Herbert, *A History of Foreign Labor in Germany, 1880–1980*, trans. William Templer (Ann Arbor, MI: University of Michigan Press, 1990), pp. 172–179.
25. Bogharian, "Diary," p. 143.
26. Ibid., p. 146. The name of the fortress in question is in fact Šaīmīmīs or Shumaymis. Repeatedly reduced to ruins over the centuries, it was entirely reconstructed under the Ayubians in the thirteenth century. It stands on an small, ancient cone-shaped hill of volcanic origin.
27. Ibid., p. 158.
28. Ibid., pp. 163–164.
29. Dündar, "L'ingénierie ethnique," p. 402.
30. Odian, *Accursed Years*, pp. 288–299.
31. Ibid., p. 214.
32. Dadrian, *To the Desert*, p. 107.
33. Ibid., p. 109.
34. Tavukjian, *Diary*, p. 113.
35. Archives of the Catholicosate of Cilicia (ACC), File Sahag II 100-1, Letter no. 4980/86 of 10 May 1915, from Catholicos Sahag II to Zaven, the Patriarch of Istanbul, Adana, folio 278.
36. Bogharian, "Diary," p. 155.
37. Ibid., p. 157.
38. "Barkev H. Kharajejian (1894–1964)," in Bogharian, *Ayntabiana*, pp. 604–605.

39. Bogharian, "Diary," p. 187.
40. Ibid., pp. 154–155.
41. Ibid.
42. J. H. Kramers and F. Daftary, "Salamiyya," in *The Encyclopedia of Islam*, CD-Rom Edition (Leiden: Brill, 1999).
43. Ibid.; Mohamed al-Dbiyat and Ronald Jaubert, "Le Repeuplement sédentaire des marges arides à l'époque contemporaine (1849–1960)," in Ronald Jaubert and Bernard Geyer, eds., *Les marges arides du Croissant Fertile. Peuplement, exploitation et contrôle des ressources en Syrie du Nord* (Lyon: Maison de l'Orient et de la Méditerranée, 2006), pp. 72–73; Norman N. Lewis, *Nomads and Settlers in Syria and Jordan, 1800–1980* (Cambridge: Cambridge University Press, 1987), pp. 58–67; Dick Douwes and Norman N. Lewis, "The Trials of Syrian Ismailis in the First Decade of the 20th Century," *International Journal of Middle East Studies* 21, no. 2 (May 1989): 216–217.
44. Lewis, *Nomads and Settlers*, pp. 61–62.
45. al-Dbiyat and Jaubert, "Le Repeuplement," p. 73.
46. Lewis, *Nomads and Settlers*, pp. 64–65.
47. al-Dbiyat and Jaubert, "Le Repeuplement," p. 76.
48. Douwes and Lewis, "The Trials of Syrian Ismailis," pp. 218–219; Kramers and Daftary, *Encyclopedia of Islam*.
49. Kramers and Daftary, *Encyclopedia of Islam*.
50. Robert Jebejian, "Selimiyetsin, darakir hayu pari Samaratsin" [The people of Salamiyya, the Armenians' Good Samaritans]. *Keghart, Suriahay darekirk* [Keghart: Syrian-Armenian yearbook] 5 (1996): 310.
51. Robert Jebejian, *Inknagensakrutyun, husher yev kordzuneutyunner* [Autobiography: Memories and activities] (Aleppo: n.p., 1999), p. 49.
52. Muhammad al-Dālī Abū Qāsim, *Al-Arman fī Salamiīya* (http://www.salamieh4dev.sy/index.php?option=com_content &view=article&id=171:20). Retrieved 26 April 2012.
53. Tavukjian, *Diary*, p. 93.
54. Ibid., p. 96.
55. Bogharian, "Diary," p. 151.
56. Ibid., p. 179.
57. Ibid., p. 175.
58. Ibid., pp. 179–181.
59. Ibid., p. 182.
60. Ibid., p. 142.
61. *Manusa* is a type of cloth, with or without a pattern, used to make various garments.
62. A small vendor who spreads his wares out on the ground or on a table at market.
63. Bogharian, "Diary," p. 198.
64. Tavukjian, *Diary*, pp. 111.
65. Bogharian, "Diary," pp. 144, 155, 165.
66. Ibid., p. 201.
67. Hovhannes Efendi Levonian (Ayntab, 1852–Aleppo, 1922).
68. Tavukjian, *Diary*, p. 137.
69. "Armen Muradian (1895–1957)", in Bogharian, *Ayntabiana*, p. 97.
70. Tavukjian, *Diary*, p. 137.
71. Odian, *Accursed Years*, p. 106.
72. Dadrian, *To the Desert*, p. 111.
73. Manase Sevagian (Sevag), "Tamasgos yev Hayere kaghakin angumen yedk" [Damascus and the Armenians after the fall of the city], *Arev* 3 no. 77 (8 November 1918).

74. Tavukjian, *Diary*, p. 100.
75. Bogharian, "Diary," p. 203. An *imalat hane* is a workshop.
76. Tavukjian, *Diary*, p. 135.
77. Ibid., pp. 135, 137.
78. Hagop K. Kabbenjian, "Manusakordzutyune Ayntabi mech" [The production of *manusa* in Ayntab], in Sarafian, *History of the Armenians of Ayntab*, vol. 2, p. 301.
79. Ibid.
80. *Direzin* or *drezin*, the laid warp.
81. Tavukjian, *Diary*, p. 138.
82. Ibid., p. 141.
83. Ibid.
84. Ibid., p. 142.
85. Tavukjian, "Ms. Diary," p. 125.
86. Tavukjian, *Diary*, p. 144.
87. Ibid., p. 146.
88. Tavukjian, "Ms. Diary," p. 130.

Selected Bibliography

Published Material

Akçam, Taner. *The Young Turks' Crime against Humanity: The Armenian Genocide and Ethnic Cleansing in the Ottoman Empire*. Princeton, 2012.

Amja, Hasan, "Faits et documents: Les dessous des déportations, Souvenirs de Tcherkess Hassan bey," *Renaissance* 1, no. 198 (22 July 1919).

Atay, Falih Rıfkı. *Zeytindağı*. Istanbul, 2003.

Bauer, Yehuda. *Rethinking the Holocaust*. New Haven, 2002.

Bogharian, Krikor. Տեղասպան Թուրքը, "Orakrutyun darakiri gyankis" [Diary of my life in deportation] (hereafter "Diary"). In Վկայութիւններ բաղուած՝ հրաշքով փրկուածներու զրոյցներէն [Tseghasban Turke. Vgayutyunner kaghvadz hrashkov prgvadzneru zruytsneren] [The genocidal Turk: Eyewitness accounts from the narratives of people who were miraculously saved]. Beirut, 1973.

———, ed. Այնթապականք / *Ayntabiana*, vol. 2. Մահարձան: մահագրութիւններ, դամբանականներ եւ կենսագրական նօթեր [Funeral monument: Necrologies, funeral orations and biographical notes]. Beirut, 1974.

Boudjikanian, Aïda, ed. *Armenians of Lebanon: From Past Princesses and Refugees to Present-Day Community*. Beirut, 2009.

Çiçek, Talha. *War and State Formation in Syria: Cemal Pasha's Governorate during World War I, 1914–17*. New York, 2014.

Dadrian, Vahram. *To the Desert: Pages from my Diary*, trans. Agop Hacikyan. London, 2006.

Der Vartanian, Kurken. "Գարեգին Արք. Խաչատուրեան. փուշեր (յուշեր եւ նիշեր)" [Karekin ark. Khachadurian pusher (Husher yev nisher)] ["Archbishop Karekin Kachadurian: Thorns (memoirs and marks)," *Hayrenik* 40, no. 9–10 (438) (September–October 1962): 56–69.

Djemal Pasha. *Memories of a Turkish Statesman, 1913–1919*. New York, 1922.

Douwes, Dick, and Norman N. Lewis. "The Trials of Syrian Ismailis in the First Decade of the 20th Century." *International Journal of Middle East Studies* 21, no. 2 (May 1989): 215–232.

Dündar, Fuat. "L'ingénierie ethnique du Comité Union et Progrès et la Turcisation de l'Anatolie," doctoral thesis. Paris, 2006.
Edib, Halidé. *Memoirs.* New York, 1926.
The Encyclopedia of Islam. CD-Rom Edition. Leiden, 1999.
Fromkin, David. *A Peace to End all Peaces.* New York, 2009.
Hanssen, Jens, Philipp Thomas, and Stefan Weber, eds. *The Empire in the City: Arab Provincial Capitals in the Late Ottoman Empire.* Beirut, 2002.
Herbert, Ulrich. *A History of Foreign Labor in Germany, 1880–1980,* trans. William Templer. Ann Arbor, 1990.
Jaubert, Ronald, and Bernard Geyer, eds. *Les marges arides du Croissant Fertile. Peuplement, exploitation et contrôle des ressources en Syrie du Nord.* Lyon, 2006.
Jebejian, Robert. Ինքնակենսագրութիւն, յուշեր եւ գործունէութիւններ [Inknagensakrutyun, husher yev kordzuneutyunner] [Autobiography: Memories and activities]. Aleppo, 1999.
Kaiser, Hilmar. "Regional Resistance to Central Government Policies: Ahmed Djemal Pasha, the Governors of Aleppo, and Armenian Deportees in the Spring and Summer of 1915." *Journal of Genocide Research* 12, nos. 3–4 (September–December 2010): 173–218.
Kévorkian, Raymond. *The Armenian Genocide: A Complete History,* trans. anon., London, 2011.
Levi, Primo. *If This Is a Man,* trans. Stuart Woolf. New York, 1959.
Lewis, Norman N. *Nomads and Settlers in Syria and Jordan, 1800–1980.* Cambridge, 1987.
Odian, Yervant. *Accursed Years: My Exile and Return from Der Zor, 1914–1919,* trans. Ara Melkonian. London, 2009.
Ormanian, Archbishop Malachia. Խոհք եւ խօսք [Khohk yev khosk] [Reflections and remarks]. Jerusalem, 1929.
Sarafian, Kevork A., ed. Պատմութիւն Անթէպի Հայոց [Badmutyun Antebi Hayots] [History of the Armenians of Ayntab], vol. 1. Los Angeles, 1953.
Sevagian, Manase. "Դամասկոս եւ Հայերը քաղաքին անկումէն ետք" [Tamasgos yev Hayere kaghakin angumen yedk] [Damascus and the Armenians after the fall of the city], *Arev* 3 (77), 8 November 1918..
Suny, Ronald Grigor. *The History of the Armenian Genocide.* Princeton, Oxford, 2015.
Tavukjian, Father Nerses, Տառապանքի օրագրութիւն [Darabanki orakrutyun] [Diary of days of suffering]. Beirut, 1991.
———. "Օրագրութեան Մեքենագրուած Բնագիր" [Orakrutyan mekenakrvadz pnakir] [Typescript of the diary] (Ms. Diary).
Յուշամատեան Մեծ Եղեռնի / *Hushamadyan medz yegherni,* 3rd ed. Beirut, 1987.

Primary Sources

Archives of the Catholicosate of Cilicia (ACC)
AGBU Central Archives, Cairo

Chapter 3

The Circle of Salvation in Extreme Conditions
Money-Food-Connections

Mutual Assistance in Life-Threatening Conditions

What were the deportees' day-to-day means of survival? How were they to confront the unprecedented crisis? How would they meet their family's everyday needs? Their daily concerns clearly reflect the reality of the catastrophe and the steady intensification of these extreme conditions. The diary—in this case, Bogharian's and Der Nerses's jottings—brings us closer to the realities on the ground, making possible an authentic reconstruction of the environment in which survivors waged their life-and-death struggle. This chapter will present that battle to find something to eat and meet other immediate needs.

In the extreme conditions of the Armenian genocide, family and community often provided the best basic guarantee of survival. They offered protection to the individual and at the same time were insurance against moral decline. Family and community were by no means abstract concepts; rather, they became very real assets in the onerous conditions of the struggle for survival. It was in the narrow framework of the family and the broader framework of the community that the steps that determined whether or not an individual survived were taken, and it was also there that each member of the family or community contributed to the struggle to survive by earning income with which to buy necessities, securing food and fuel, or caring for the sick, among other things. All these simple acts of daily life took on their full significance in the extreme conditions of deportation and massacres of Armenians.

But while the family and community could create a secure space in this struggle for survival, money and food were the indispensable instruments for providing it—they made survival real. A family or community that was deprived of these material values could disintegrate in its turn, and the individuals comprising it find themselves abandoned to their fate. Then despair could gain the upper hand. Ultimately, these conditions gave rise to a group of degraded and dehumanized Armenians known as the "walking dead."[1]

This is why it is essential to examine these material assets in Bogharian's and Der Nerses's cases. Such an examination will allow us to understand and assess the day-to-day battle to survive that unfolded under the protection of the family and sometimes also the community until liberation in 1918, and also to identify the instruments available in this domain and the means used to obtain them. Der Nerses's and Bogharian's diaries are full of information that can help to answer these questions.

Let us start the discussion of this theme with the deportation of our two diarists from Ayntab. Their families, following the example of their compatriots from Ayntab, succeeded in bringing their savings with them, as well as various movable assets (jewelry, carpets, woolens, kitchen and laundry equipment, etc.). Drawing on their savings and occasionally selling household goods, Bogharian's and Der Nerses's large families were able to secure the food they needed in the first phase of their deportation. But this state of affairs could not last for long, the more so because in the prevailing wartime conditions, everything had become more expensive and state-imposed price controls were not respected. What is more, deportees who once had owned their homes now had to pay rent every month. Both Krikor Bogharian's father and Der Nerses continued to perform their priestly duties, but they received scant recompense in the situation created by the deportation. Times had plainly changed: in the conditions of their exile, the Armenians of Ayntab did not, in exchange for spiritual services, give the priests the material emolument (called the "priest's right" in Armenian) they had customarily allotted them in the past. Der Nerses often expresses the displeasure this caused him; he was of course well aware that his family's survival depended heavily on whether or not he received this recompense. "To date, it has occurred to none of the people to encourage the servant of the Word by giving him a gift of his or her own free will. This shows that there has been a spiritual decline among the people, who are shirking their duties, something that will not come to a good end."[2]

In a word, both families would be condemned to dire poverty and consequently starvation if they failed to find new sources of income. The gravity of the situation was accentuated in July–August 1916, when members of the priesthood were deported again. Nearly two weeks after the departure of Krikor Bogharian's father, the young man wrote in his diary: "When my father left, he left my mother with just 280 kurush (piasters). How are we supposed to get by on such a meager sum?"[3] A few months later, the Bogharians' predicament in Salamiyya worsened. "Because we are in dire economic straits, my brother Khachig, too, is going to work as a simple laborer. We have neither wheat nor bulgur for the winter."[4] Der Nerses was also confronted time and again with economic hardship, and with the gradual deterioration of his already critical situation.

How to obtain money, how to find nourishment, how to stay healthy: these were the most basic problems of survival, the ones that the diarists of Hama and Salamiyya found themselves confronting head-on day in, day out. Every deportee's agonizing preoccupation consisted in looking for solutions to these problems; it took up the better part of their daily lives. This phenomenon is well expressed in our two diarists' writings, which describe the search for sources of income, the fluctuating prices of food on the market, and the ups and downs of the Ottoman stock market as dominant concerns. These issues took on ever more vital significance for them as it increasingly became clear that their fate depended on resolving them. They accordingly found many different answers for these questions, opening up new horizons for us to explore. In a way, "money, food, and connections" represented three links in a chain, each linked to the others in such a way that the loss of any one of them could interrupt the normal course of things, with fateful consequences for a deportee. It is, moreover, hard to determine the limits of the influence of each of the three agents in this trinity. There obviously were circumstances in which money was the means needed to obtain nourishment or someone's intercession. Conversely, intercession could open the door to sources of nourishment and thereby to material income as well. The interconnection between these three factors will stand out still more sharply when we use living examples to examine them.

It is important that we succinctly discuss these matters in our attempt to reconstruct the daily life of Hama's and Salamiyya's deported Armenians, with their overwhelming concerns about money and food. Our task is facilitated by the fact that our two diarists provide us with an abundance of information here. What kind of food did the deportees find in local markets? How much food did our diarists and their families survive on? Where did they get money to buy food with? Having answered these questions, we will have a better appreciation of the environment in which the deported Armenians endeavored to survive in

Hama and Salamiyya, as well as in Bilad al-Sham more generally. In particular, we will have more clearly identified three basic ways, all of them vital, of coping with the grueling conditions in these places.

In reality, the deportees' dependence on these factors put them in an exceedingly uncertain, insecure position. The death or conscription of an economically active member of the family, the late arrival of an expected sum, or the failure of a commercial venture or arrangement to work in a trade could, in the space of one day, jeopardize the life of a whole family or irremediably upset its already extremely fragile social and economic equilibrium. The resulting predicament would of course set it on the path to decline, that is, to bankruptcy, illness, and the deaths those factors routinely caused. Likewise in these harsh conditions, meanwhile, various familial, economic, or cultural relations that could play a key role in ensuring the survival of a whole family took on new value: rudimentary craft skills, for example, or mastery of Ottoman Turkish. A mother might, in her husband's absence, take over as the head of the family and, thanks to her relations with her associates, establish more solid prospects for its survival and well-being. Under normal conditions, such capabilities might never have emerged or their value might never have made itself felt. Extraordinary situations invest such ties or skills with new significance and value.

The Ayntab Armenian Deportees' Diet: Never Running Short of Bulgur or Daily Bread

From a nutritional point of view, Hama and its rural environs, including Salamiyya, offered many advantages. Since the latter half of the nineteenth century, the central Ottoman authorities had implemented a regional settlement policy designed to augment the sedentary population and the area under cultivation (*ma' âmura*) at the expense of the *bâdiya*, the nomadic Bedouins and the uncultivated land that formed their habitat. Here it is important to note only that Hama and the surrounding countryside had long been an important agricultural center and that a profusion of locally cultivated crops were sold in the region's markets in the period described by our diarists. Grain, cotton, silk, and wool were the main agricultural products in the region, which was so fertile it was known in the Ottoman period as "Northern Syria's Granary."[5]

Wartime conditions, however, often made the stability of markets uncertain. Fluctuations in the value of currency or grain requisitions for the Ottoman army sometimes led shopkeepers or market traders to hoard stocks of basic foodstuffs, leaving ordinary buyers suddenly unable to obtain them. Such conditions never lasted long, however; basic necessities would soon be offered for sale again in local markets. In the Hama region, two major factors tended to prevent severe food supply crises: Hama was located in an agricultural zone in which various kinds of grains, and fruits, and vegetables were cultivated; and the Syrian steppes, where Bedouin nomads brought milk and yogurt to market, were in the immediate vicinity of the city. This picture contrasts with the situation in other Ottoman regions, where supply routes could be closed off, plunging whole towns and villages into extreme hardship or even subjecting them to famine. Bogharian relates how in October 1916 people came to Salamiyya from Hama, Homs, and even Lebanon—where the populace was dying of starvation—to buy wheat on the market there.[6]

Here, of course, it must be borne in mind that, local products aside, certain materials and goods had either disappeared altogether from the market or were sold at prices that put them beyond the reach of the majority of the population. These were essentially Ottoman exports; Bogharian talks about matches and sugar, whose prices had already soared sky-high by May 1916.[7]

In his entry for 3 December 1915, Bogharian gives a detailed description of his family's staple diet in Hama and, later, Salamiyya. In Hama, the family ate mainly eggplant, tomatoes, pepper, watermelons, pomegranates, grapes, yogurt, bulgur, and meat. After they settled in Salamiyya, their basic diet consisted of grapes, beets, potatoes, oranges, milk, tomatoes, peppers, turnips, radishes, and bulgur.[8] In this first phase of their exile to these places, they did not eat the pilaf of Ayntab, or its *chorba* (soup), *nivig* (a dish made with vegetables, chickpeas, garlic, and olive oil), "tasty grapes, of many colors and varieties," its delicious *cherez* (a mixture of raisins, walnuts, and pistachios), or *shireh* (grape molasses), about which the young diarist often writes with nostalgia.[9] But basic nutrition was to be had, even though prices were so unstable that from time to time, certain foodstuffs might be unavailable to ordinary people.

An entry in Der Nerses's diary is quite revelatory in this regard. Writing in October 1917, at a time when Salamiyya's economic situation was gradually deteriorating and Armenian deportees were trying to leave the town and settle in nearby Hama, Der Nerses notes: "We had to go without bread and live on vegetables alone for a few days early last week; for a few months now, we've been eating barley bread, and now we're even mixing the barley with millet. Although we occasionally try to put some strength in our bones by cooking the vegetables with oil and meat, living without bulgur and wheat bread is making us weaker."[10] This situation represents a departure from a traditional diet more than anything else—a situation in which people were suddenly deprived of the two staples of their daily diet, in this case, bulgur and wheat bread. The consequence was not inevitably illness, especially as the local market was comparatively rich in other foodstuffs providing basic nutrition.

Indeed, Der Nerses and Bogharian rarely complain about shortages of basic food products on the local market, let alone their total unavailability. For Bogharian, noting current prices was practically a daily chore. He makes constant mention of the cost of wheat, bread, flour, and bulgur in his diary, also frequently referring to the prices of many other foodstuffs: vegetables, greens, cereals, dairy products, eggs, olive oil, and meat. Alongside these abundant data on food, we also find information on Bogharian's weight. Thus we learn that, on 1 December 1915, around three and a half months after leaving Ayntab, he weighed 54 *okha*, the equivalent of about 69 kilograms.[11] This seems to be a very natural weight for someone who, according to his 1925 Lebanese identity card, was five feet nine inches (175 cm) tall.[12]

Here it is also important to know the average family's minimum nutritional requirements and what it cost to meet them. Bogharian and Der Nerses provide abundant information about food prices that allows us to reconstruct the prevailing state of affairs. Bogharian transmits perhaps the most characteristic piece of information in this connection when, worried about his family's diet, he declares that for one winter—that is, a period of three months—the family needs seventy *liders* (179.2 kg) of wheat. This figure does not differ very sharply from one found in another Armenian source, which reports that before the outbreak of World War I, the average inhabitant of a village in the Palu district consumed approximately three *olchag*s (92.1 kg) of bulgur annually, or 7.67 kilograms per month.[13] At the prices prevailing on Salamiyya's market at the end of 1916, this quantity of bulgur cost 29.1 piasters monthly per capita, whereas by March 1918, as we shall see in the tables below, it cost 155.2 piasters (1.22 Ottoman gold lira). In other words, a six-member household needed 174.6 piasters (1.37 Ottoman gold lira) monthly at the end of 1916, and 931.2 piasters (7.44 Ottoman gold lira) in March 1918.

Wheat, from which bulgur and bread were produced, was the basic foodstuff of a household in Ayntab. Judging from Bogharian's and Der Nerses's purchases, the average family of Ayntab Armenian deportees ate a meal made with bulgur almost daily. Meanwhile, a young man of Bogharian's physical constitution needed, on average, 2,400 to 2,700 calories daily. Bogharian would have needed at least that much, as he was

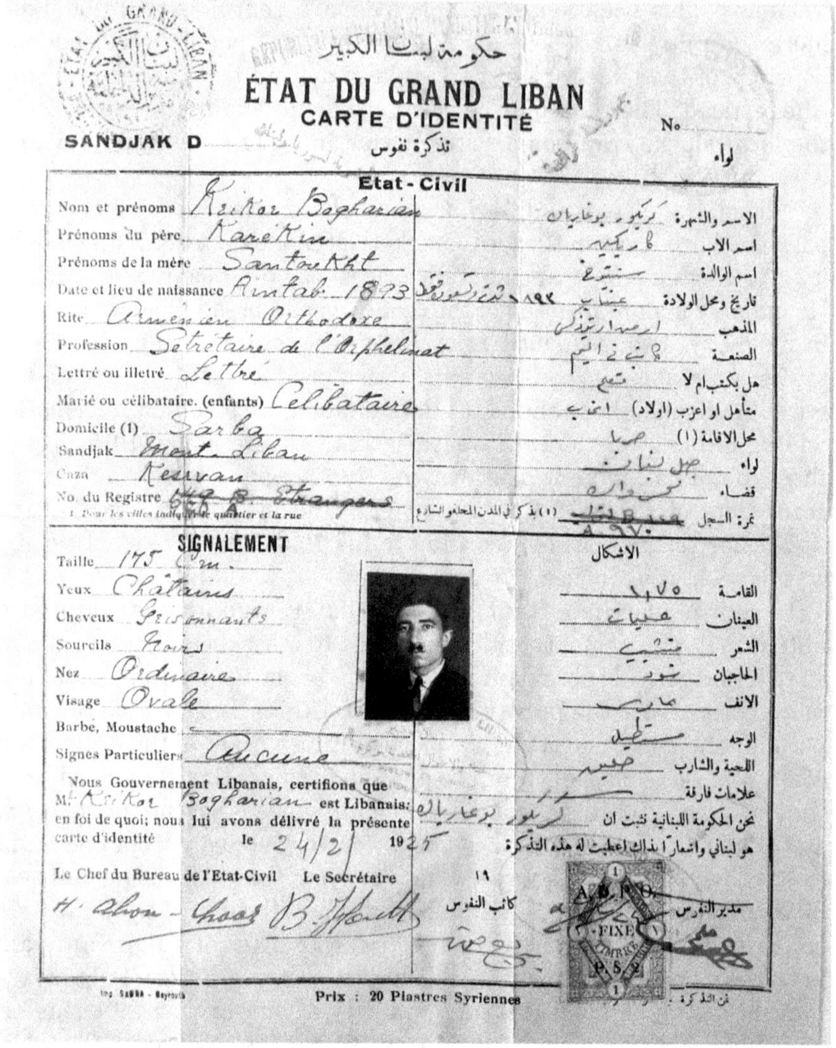

حكومة لبنان الكبير

ÉTAT DU GRAND LIBAN

CARTE D'IDENTITÉ

SANDJAK D ... No.

تذكرة نفوس

Etat - Civil

Nom et prénoms Krikor Bogharian

Prénoms du père Karekin

Prénoms de la mère Santoukht

Date et lieu de naissance Aintab 1893

Rite Arménien Orthodoxe

Profession Secrétaire de l'Orphelinat

Lettré ou illetré Lettré

Marié ou célibataire. (enfants) Célibataire

Domicile (1) Sarba

Sandjak Mont-Liban

Caza Kesrvan

No. du Registre

1. Pour les villes indiquer le quartier et la rue

SIGNALEMENT

Taille 175 Cm.

Yeux Châtains

Cheveux Grisonnants

Sourcils Noirs

Nez Ordinaire

Visage Ovale

Barbe, Moustache

Signes Particuliers Aucune

Nous Gouvernement Libanais, certifions que Mr. Krikor Bogharian est Libanais; en foi de quoi; nous lui avons délivré la présente carte d'identité le 24/2/ 1925

Le Chef du Bureau de l'Etat-Civil Le Secrétaire

Prix : 20 Piastres Syriennes

Figure 3.1. Krikor Bogharian's Lebanese identity card, 1926. (Source: Haigazian University Library, Beirut)

constantly in motion: he went out to make purchases, often took walks in Salamiyya or the environs, and became apprenticed to a carpenter some time after the deportation. Bread and bulgur were the staples that provided both the Bogharians and Der Nerses's family with their essential nutrients. Once conditions forced them to go without these staples, they were hard put to find substitutes and adapt to the new situation.

On the other hand, when these staples were available one could also rather easily find, on the local market and at affordable prices, other kinds of food to supplement the basic caloric and nutritional needs of a young adult like Bogharian, for example, tomatoes and tomato molasses, grape molasses, beets, yogurt, and milk.

Here we should note that the information Bogharian transmits by no means conveys the full picture. It is limited to the period covered by his diary, whose final entries were made in December 1916. Throughout that period, however, Bogharian's entries routinely include information on food prices, which justifies the supposition that anyone with minimal sources of income could survive in the period in question.

To determine what situation prevailed throughout the twenty-two months after December 1916, we have to turn to Der Nerses's diary, which unfortunately does not provide the abundant information Bogharian's does. Compared to the young diarist, the priest from Ayntab does not note daily market prices and refers less often to foodstuffs and their prices, and the few references he does make are limited to staples. Yet even these infrequent references suffice to bring out the profoundly different economic situation that set in around June 1917. As the tables below show, the prices of the most basic foods reached extraordinarily high levels starting in mid 1917. These exorbitant prices doubtless reflected a severe crisis; Der Nerses's diary is replete with references to it and descriptions of its disastrous consequences. Skyrocketing prices also meant that the social and economic equilibrium of survival that had to some extent been maintained among the Ayntab Armenians living in Hama and Salamiyya was likewise upset. Therefore the tables below provide important benchmarks for an examination of the period from mid 1917 to liberation.

A Table of Food Prices Reflecting the Armenian Catastrophe

Table 3.1 shows the prices of wheat, the cereal that was the staple of the typical family of deportees from Ayntab, from December 1915 to October 1918. Wheat served above all to make the flour used to bake bread. Bulgur, another ever-present staple in the Ayntab Armenians' diet, was also made from wheat that was first boiled, then dried and pounded. It is true that *değlip*s (mills that were used to crush the boiled, dried wheat) were not to be had in Salamiyya, but the deportees from Ayntab managed to construct a machine of the same sort.[14] The local *değirmen*, another type of milling machine, was also available.[15]

The market prices shown in this and the following tables are those that obtained in the Hama district, which included the towns of Hama and Salamiyya. All the data they contain are drawn from Bogharian's and Der Nerses's diaries. "Old price" means the price prevailing before the two diarists were deported. The "old prices" of foodstuffs indicated by Bogharian most probably refer to the prices in Ayntab's market.

It is also important to note that in the account books of the day, a unit of measure called the *liter* was in use, known in local parlance as the *lider*. A very old unit of measure, it was not used for liquids alone; nor was it equivalent to the weight of a container with a capacity of one metric liter. Had that been the case, one *lider* of wheat would have weighed about 830 grams. This would, by present standards, be considered an error and possibly lead to mistaken conclusions. The *lider* was in common use in the Ottoman Empire and certain neighboring countries as a measure of weight during the period that interests us. It was used for fruit, vegetables, grains, cotton, and so on. It is hard to give an exact definition of the weight to which one *lider* corresponded. Even within the boundaries of the Ottoman Empire, it proved impossible to establish a general standard for the *lider*. Most probably, it was a variant of a measure of weight still in use in the contemporary Arab world, the *ratl*, the exact value of which varies from one region to another. Like the *lider*, the *ratl* is a common measure of the weight of everyday commodities.

To determine what weight it represented for our diarists, we may look to Der Nerses for help: he transmits crucial information about this in two passages in his diary. First he follows the phrase "one and a half *liders* of wheat," with the explanation "that is, three *okhas*."[16] The *okha* was a well-known measure of weight equal to 1.28 kilograms; thus, one *lider* was the equivalent of 2.56 kilograms. Der Nerses confirms this in another passage, where he writes that one *lider* of bread cost six piasters, or that one *okha* of bread cost three piasters.[17] Thus one *lider* weighed two *okhas* or 2.56 kilograms.

As can be seen in Table 3.1, the price of wheat was relatively stable until late 1916. Indeed, it even fell appreciably in June–July 1916. Unfortunately, after 1916, Der Nerses rarely refers to the price of wheat, so we are unable to observe the radical transformation of the situation. Nevertheless, the price of wheat on 24 March 1918 is unquestionable proof of extraordinary inflation: by that date, the price had increased by 900 percent. The crisis affected all of Bilad al-Sham: for the same period, Dadrian reports on the increase in the price of wheat in the market in Jarash (a big village in the *sanjak* of Hauran) between March 1916 and September 1918, when the market price increased by about 600 percent.[18]

Table 3.1. The price of wheat in the Hama district, December 1915–October 1918.

Date	Cost of 1 *lider* (2.56 kg) of wheat (piasters)
Old price	4
8 December 1915	5
14 December 1915	6.25
17 January 1916	5
10 March 1916	8.125
15 March 1916	6.875
22 April 1916	5.3125
1 May 1916	5
4 May 1916	4.375
15 May 1916	4.375
21 May 1916	7.5
19 June 1916	4.375
13 July 1916	3
5 August 1916	3
17 August 1916	3.4375
23 August 1916	3.75
29 August 1916	3.5
19 Sept 1916	3.5
11 October 1916	5.625
25 October 1916	5
31 October 1916	5.625
26 November 1916	5
7 December 1916	7.5
19 December 1916	7.8125
28 July 1917	11
24 March 1918	40
2 October 1918	10

The evolution of the price of bread presents nearly the same picture, with the same gaps. Thus, by April 1917, the old price had increased 192.6 percent. However, the available sources do not give the impression that the Hama district was suffering from an extraordinary crisis, largely because information on prices is lacking for the following months, when the economic situation had clearly deteriorated. However, the price of bread can be compared with that prevailing in Aleppo in the same period, where the prices of staples were, generally speaking, not very different from those in the Hama district.[19] A *lider* of bread was selling for about 3.5 piasters in Aleppo in May 1915; by February 1917, the price had risen steeply to around 38 piasters,[20] a 985.7 percent increase.

Table 3.2. The price of bread in the Hama district, December 1915–April 1917.

Date	1 *lider* of bread
Old price	4.1 piasters
8 December 1915	5
21 March 1916	6
22 April 1916	5
15 May 1916	4.5*
4 July 1916	6
13 July 1916	6
23 August 1916	5
19 September 1916	5
31 October 1916	5
26 November 1916	6
15 April 1917	12

* For the same date, Der Nerses reports a price of six piasters for a lider of bread (Tavukjian, Diary, p. 112).

Some of the gaps in this picture are filled in in the next table, which shows the price of flour, frequently reported by Der Nerses as well. According to Bogharian, the natives of the Hama district made their bread in *tonir*s (ovens consisting of jars dug into the earth), whereas the Armenians used a *saj*, an acorn-shaped oven about as big as a breadbox, to bake bread in their own homes.[21] Note that all these tables feature a gap for the period extending from early 1917 to April of the same year. By this period Bogharian had stopped keeping a diary and Der Nerses had been deported to Tafile, so there is no information about market prices in Salamiyya or Hama for these months.

Table 3.3. The price of flour in the Hama district, December 1915–April 1918.

Date	1 *lider* of flour
Old price	*3.3 piasters*
8 December 1915	4.5
22 February 1916	4.3
10 March 1916	6.3
21 March 1916	6
22 April 1916	5
15 May 1916	4
19 June 1916	5.5
31 October 1916	5
October 1917	20
23 December 1917	20
25 December 1917	17
9 January 1918	24
1 March 1918	27
24 March 1918	40
10 April 1918	36
15 April 1918	52
26 April 1918	50

Evidently, flour was becoming an unaffordable product for the majority of people from the latter half of 1917 on: by 15 April 1918, the price of flour had risen to 1,475.75 percent of the old price. These price increases and the parallel devaluation of Ottoman currency are proof of hyperinflation. Obviously, this made the deported segment of the population, forced from the day of its arrival to struggle daily to obtain food, vulnerable in every way.

The following table provides a general idea of the prices of dairy products (milk, yogurt, and cheese) in Salamiyya and Hama.

Table 3.4. The price of yogurt in the Hama district, January 1916–April 1918.

Date	1 *lider* of yogurt
9 January 1916	6 piasters
10 March 1916	3
21 March 1916	3
22 April 1916	3
15 May 1916	3.5
21 May 1916	4.3
3 June 1916	5
4 November 1916	10
13 December 1916	7
1 March 1918	8
10 April 1918	5

Both diarists often stress the importance of yogurt and milk. To begin with, both yogurt and milk were regarded as "food for sick people," as Bogharian puts it.[22] People with typhus or fevers were put on a diet of milk, yogurt, and cheese. The prices of these foodstuffs had remained relatively low: in the case of yogurt, a price increase of 233.33 percent can be observed. For this reason, these dairy products were also poor people's staple diet. We learn, for example, that Krikor Sarafian, who had been a well-known teacher in Ayntab, ate nothing but yogurt and bread for months after it became difficult for him to earn a living.[23]

The Deportees and State Aid: Providential Care, or Making a Mockery of a Right

We have already seen, taking the Bogharian family as an example, that a family that had formerly enjoyed an average income was not long able to survive on its savings and the income derived from sale of its possessions. Sooner or later, in the course of these three and a half years of genocide, the overwhelming majority of deported families and individuals had to face the fateful moment of needing to find new sources of income, which in this case will be termed *external sources of income*. Failure in this quest could very rapidly complicate their situation and pit their struggle for survival against insuperable obstacles.

These fundamental problems and our diarists' unbroken will to resolve them open a very unusual world up before our eyes, one that it is important to reconstruct and examine from several different perspectives. The first external source of income mentioned by our diarists is Ottoman state aid. Most deportees who have written eyewitness accounts of the genocide generally use the Ottoman-Turkish word *tayın*, "daily ration" (or the plural *tayinât*) to refer to it. In Ottoman legislation of the same period, this aid is called *iaşe*, which means "maintenance" or "food supplies." The *tayın* or *iaşe* was the sum of money that, by Ottoman government decision, was to be received by every Ottoman Armenian removed from the familial home and "resettled" in his or her new "place of residence"—in other words, place of exile. This is spelled out, notably, in the law (*Talimâtnâme*) of 30 May 1915. Containing fifteen articles, it bears on "on the settlement and livelihood of Armenians transferred elsewhere in view of the state of war and political imperatives."[24] Articles 3, 9, 10, and 11 of this law contain direct references to the state's obligation to guarantee "resettled" Armenians a livelihood.[25] References to such state aid also abound in wartime correspondence between Ottoman state officials. On 9 June 1915, a telegram from the Interior Ministry informed the government of Mosul province of the dispatch of an allocation of 500,000 piasters to be spent on settling and feeding Armenian *muhacirs*.[26] Similar telegrams about providing for the Armenian "settlers" were sent to the government of Aleppo province.[27]

The fact that such state aid existed, and especially the fact that it was in fact distributed, may of course seem incongruous and derisive when we bear in mind that hundreds of thousands of Armenians would, after reaching their places of deportation on the steppes of Jazira and thus qualifying for state aid, eventually be butchered. Similarly, it can seem at first glance that providing state aid in the conditions created by the execution of a genocidal plan is a strange way of squandering state funds. Complicating factors, however, were at work here. They bear examining.

To begin with, it may be supposed that until the moment of the crime, the existence of a law about state aid could serve to save appearances and provide excuses for the executioner. From this point of view, then, we must also examine the fact that a system of *tayın* existed (the extremely erratic distribution of aid notwithstanding) even in the transit camps set up for the deportees east of Aleppo.[28] In other words, this aid was also provided to many Armenians who were then massacred in the vicinity of Der Zor a few months later.

In this connection, we must not neglect another factor: the executioner's or oppressor's dehumanization and brutalization of victims or oppressed groups. This is, in every way, an important stage on the way to their physical annihilation, a stage preparatory to the use of means of mass violence against them. The victim is in a state of complete defenselessness, degradation, and vulnerability and, in equal measure, entirely dependent on the executioner and the latter's dispositions towards him. This state of affairs convinces the oppressing side it is so utterly powerful that it can decide when the victim will eat, as well as what kind of food and how much. Eventually the situation brings the victim to adopt an animal comportment, something that appeared in the clearest possible fashion in the Nazi camps, which, as characterized in Primo Levi's *If This is a Man*, became infernal machines for turning men into beasts.[29] Once the victim has, from the executioner's or more generally the oppressive side's standpoint, been transformed into an animal or taken on still more abominably inhuman forms, it becomes easier to transition into more radical phases and even to exterminate the "animal."

This metamorphosis is most probably not premeditated by the executioner, but no matter what the conditions involve, the fact is that they provide a breeding ground for criminal mass acts and reinforce the will to carry them out. In this respect, Garabed Kapigian's eyewitness account is extremely revelatory. The decimated caravan in which Kapigian was deported from Sivas eventually reached Suruj/Suruç, which, like Ras el-Ain or Der Zor, was the final destination of many Armenians, the place where they would be collectively slaughtered. The future victims were, however, still alive, and even in this place, strangely enough, the guards began distributing state aid to the deportees: a loaf of bread per person. There was bitter irony, as described in Kapigian's account, in the fact that the gendarmes violently beat the beneficiaries even as the aid was being distributed. For that reason, the deportees called such scenes *"tayın-kötek"* (*tayın*-beatings).[30]

In other cases, the authorities' concern to safeguard public health led them to provide aid to the Armenians. Epidemics mowed down more defenseless Armenians than anything else; in fact, so many perished that the large numbers of unburied bodies in the cities or their outskirts jeopardized the entire populace as well as the Ottoman troops passing through these localities on their way to the front. To come to grips with such situations and find practical remedies for them, the Ottoman authorities preferred to work directly with Armenian institutions. From September 1915 to August 1916, Aleppo's Armenian Prelacy received, practically on a monthly basis, a total of 178,518.20 piasters. In the records of the uses to which this money was put, the notations "expenditures for the dead" or "disbursed for the dead" appear constantly. In other words, the Armenian side had to use these funds to bury its dead.[31]

In the case of our diarists, the first reference to *tayın* appears on 26 August 1915—a few weeks, that is, after they settled in Hama:[32]

Bogharian learned of a plan to distribute state aid to the deportees from Ayntab. Ten days or so later, Der Nerses spelled out that the gendarmes' commanding officer and the *müfettiş bey* had ordered the deportees' representatives to draw up lists of names of the Armenians in the place, classified according to town or village of origin, in order to facilitate the distribution of *tayın*,[33] which first took place on 21 October 1915, after the Armenians from Ayntab had been collectively relocated in Salamiyya. There Hovhannes Efendi Levonian, a native of Ayntab who had served as *mal müdiri* (director of the treasury) in his home town, began distributing one *mejid* (20 piasters) to each of the poorest families living in tents.[34] This operation was clearly carried out on the local *kaymakam*'s initiative. Three days later, the deportees living in tents received more substantial state aid: one *mejid* for each adult and half a *mejid* for each child. "Everyone has a happy, smiling face," Der Nerses observed.[35]

The following entries in the priest's diary paint a clear picture of the way state aid was handed out. They afford us a glimpse of another facet of the interesting relationship that had sprung up between the local authorities and the deportees' representatives. The deported Armenians participated directly in the distribution of *tayın*, as Der Nerses did when he took a direct hand by preparing the lists of names. Priority was accorded to the poorest families—those who had initially lived in tents in Salamiyya and then gradually settled in villages in the vicinity. Local officials sometimes distributed the aid themselves. For example, one of them, Jevad Efendi, was a "kindhearted, patient friend of the poor" who "always wanted help to go to the poor."[36] At other times, the deportees' representatives took it upon themselves to distribute these moneys to beneficiary families: in this case, the distribution took place in the *mal müdir*'s office.[37] For this purpose, in fact, an ad hoc committee of Armenians had been formed, most of them from Ayntab; it was presided over by Der Nerses himself.[38]

In Aleppo, the local Armenian Prelacy also cooperated with the *muhacir komisyonu* (settlers' committee) to distribute state aid to the Armenian deportees in the city. The local Committee for Settlers, made up of Aleppo Armenians, itself drew up lists of beneficiaries among the deportees and submitted them to the local authorities.[39] Various accounts confirm that in the first months of the deportation, when Jelal Bey was still the *vali* of Aleppo province, state aid was regularly distributed in the city, in striking contrast to practice in neighboring towns and villages. "In the outskirts, people are begging for bread," Catholicos Sahag II says about places outside Aleppo in a letter dating from this period. "Either Christ's miraculous powers or a royal treasury will be needed to feed half a million natives of Cilicia and perhaps as many people from the eastern provinces, if not more, in the Syrian desert."[40] Indeed, these lines express better than anything else the disproportion between the aid distributed by the state and the deportees' catastrophic condition.

The two diarists often underscore the utter irregularity with which aid was distributed. Evidently, in the first year of the deportation, the promised aid was not distributed at all in November or the first half of December. Only on 16 December 1915 did the 100,000 piasters allocated to the aid program reach the local authorities, and even though distribution then began without delay,[41] the operation dragged out until mid January.[42] Many Armenians from the villages poured into Salamiyya in hopes of receiving their share of the aid, but those living in the districts around Aleppo were manifestly the neediest. These people often had to wait for days in the streets of the little town, without shelter, before receiving their benefits. At such times, Salamiyya presented a heart-rending picture. "Poor women from the villages are roaming the streets and sleeping in them, hungry and naked, and some of them lie dying near the walls."[43]

In the winter months, when aid was most needed, the deportees received almost nothing. Only on 8 March 1916 is the distribution of state aid in Salamiyya mentioned. According to Bogharian, it involved a sum of a few thousand piasters that was distributed to deportees in a few villages.[44] Some two weeks later, on 20 March, state aid amounting to 11,800 piasters was distributed.[45] The impression is that the distribution of *tayın* was regularized in these months. Thus, on 16 April, 592 individuals (widows and orphans) received benefits in Salamiyya: 22.5 piasters for each adult and 15 piasters for each child. The same day, 1,200 more people in villages nearby received aid.[46] On 28 May, 40,000 piasters in aid arrived and was gradually distributed over the next few weeks to some 2,800 widows and orphans who had been settled in Salamiyya and nearby villages. It took the form of banknotes, that is, a devalued form.[47] After an interruption of several months, Bogharian once again mentions, on 16 September 1916, the distribution of new state aid amounting to 50,000 piasters. The task of making a clean copy of the lists of the names of the needy was entrusted to him. Around 1,000 natives of Ayntab benefited from this assistance; every adult received 22.5 piasters and every child received 15 piasters.[48] Nothing is said about the distribution of aid in the first three months of 1917, when Bogharian stopped keeping a diary and Der Nerses was deported elsewhere, not to return until April. Only in October 1917 are there new references to state aid.

By fall 1917, the prices of foodstuffs were soaring to shockingly high levels and the economic crisis had already begun to have devastating effects. This state of affairs would persist until the Allied armies occupied the area. In these circumstances, the local authorities distributed three *okhas* (3.84 kg) of wheat instead of money on one occasion. Der Nerses's family, which had settled in Hama and fallen on hard times, was among those benefiting from this aid. "They gave eighteen okhas of wheat to me, too. We accepted them very gladly as a gift of God." But not everyone was thus satisfied. In this connection, Der Nerses depicts the abuses that accompanied the distribution of aid, which was the responsibility of the Armenians who had drawn up the lists of the needy. It happened, for example, that "widowed women who had perhaps seen no wheat for more than a year" but "had no one to plead their cause" went empty-handed because their names were not on the lists, while people who already had a means of making a living or the preparers of the lists of needy themselves benefited from this assistance.[49]

The examples of Salamiyya and Hama suggest that the distribution of this aid, which had been established by the same state that determined its amount, often depended on the local authorities' goodwill. The law required that the *muhacir* Armenians be provided with food, but the same local authorities could, through unofficial channels, have received diametrically opposed orders reflecting the central authorities' real intentions. Nevertheless, any local official could, at least in theory, insist on the letter of the law and, after long administrative negotiations and delays, obtain this aid in legal fashion.

An interesting variant of this phenomenon occurred in Aleppo, where local Armenians, who were exempted from deportation, had formed a relief committee for deported Armenians with the *vali*'s permission. The committee members were very likely aware of the philanthropic laws protecting the lives of the Armenian *muhacirs* and guaranteeing them food and shelter, the more so as these laws had been officially promulgated and republished in Ottoman newspapers. The relief committee representing Aleppo's Armenians appears to have been appealing to the authorities to apply these laws when it officially requested "the benevolent government's assistance" and, a few days later, asked the local state *muhacir komisyonu* "to immediately seize empty apartments and assign them" to Aleppo's Armenian deportees.[50] The relief committee also appealed to the Aleppo mayor's office to resume distribution of bread to the deportees, which "had not taken place for three days."[51]

These appeals stemmed from nothing more than a wish to see Ottoman law enforced. In the present case it was a group representing the victims that took the initiative, but it seems reasonable to suppose that Ottoman provincial authorities also sent requests of this kind to higher state bodies. The motivation for such requests could vary. For example, in the zone of operations of the Ottoman Fourth Army under Jemal Pasha's command, a region sui generis, the authorities often took steps to distribute state aid. In other cases, the motivation might simply have been the authorities' empathy with and pity for the deportees; these were probably the decisive factors in Aleppo under Jelal Bey (*vali* of the province until 15 June 1915) and his successor, Bekir Sami Kunduh (*vali* until late September of the same year). At other times, presumably, the authorities attempted to access illegal sources of personal enrichment, of which state aid was one of the most lucrative. It seems probable that once an official had, after repeated efforts, succeeded in obtaining state funds, it was easier for him to embezzle money in collaboration with his colleagues. This is the opinion of Krikor Kudulian, an Armenian who had been deported to Amman. In his memoirs, he gives fairly detailed information about the way state aid was distributed there. According to Kudulian, local officials often pocketed funds intended to meet the deportees' needs.[52] Vahram Dadrian, who was deported to Jarash, located in the same general area, depicts the distribution of *tayın* there. His account, too, plainly reveals local officials' mercenary conduct when it came to handing out the state aid entrusted to them.[53] Garabed Kapigian, for his part, provides information about the successive distributions of *tayın* in Rakka, a town outside Bilad al-Sham, and the abuses perpetrated by the state officials involved.[54]

In order to understand Ottoman officials' approach to the funds allocated for state aid programs and the psychology associated with it, it is helpful to know that the source of all the moneys allotted to the *muhacirs* was the Commission for Abandoned Property (Emvâl-i metrûke). This official body, created by government decision, was tasked with managing the Armenian "settlers'" "abandoned" real estate and all their other assets. Moreover, the law of 30 May 1915 stipulated that the Commission for Abandoned Property was responsible for covering the Armenian deportees' living expenses.[55] In other words, this state assistance—which was sometimes a means of salvation and sometimes doled out like charity, generally failed to appear, appeared late, or appeared only to disappear, was at bottom something to which the Armenian deportees had every right: it represented their own assets.

Yet only a small fraction of the wealth that belonged by right to the deportees was distributed to them, and rarely at that, in only a handful of localities.[56] In fact, the law had from its inception served to cover up the crime of the genocide. On other occasions, the distribution of state aid took a curious course: the authorities who undertook to distribute

Figure 3.2. A view from the region of Hama in the 1920s. (Source: AGBU, Nubarian Library, Paris)

it also decided shortly thereafter to massacre the same needy deportees to whom they had dispensed benefits. However, side by side with such cases there is the example of Bilad al-Sham and, of particular relevance to our concerns here, the distribution of aid in Hama and Salamiyya. In these places, the local authorities cooperated straightforwardly with the deportees' representatives to distribute the aid. The deportees relocated to Salamiyya knew that state funds had been transferred by the *mutasarrıf* in Hama even before the money reached their *kaymakam*, and knew as well that they would be receiving it. When payment was delayed, they frequently turned to the authorities in Salamiyya to request that the transfer be speeded up. Moreover, when aid did finally arrive, the local authorities conscientiously distributed it, as eyewitness accounts confirm.

In Bilad al-Sham, accordingly, the existence of state aid was sometimes little short of providential for many Armenians. That is why Der Nerses remarks in 1915 that "if it were not for the rations provided by the government, [the Armenians] would be unable to survive."[57] Undeniably, these benefits were distributed inconsistently and at irregular intervals—shortcomings that could have mortal consequences for the majority of deportees who, having used up their savings, were seeking out new sources of income even as they struggled to secure their daily sustenance. What is more, by the time economic inflation set in in mid 1917 and the Armenian deportees needed outside assistance more than ever before, the distribution of state aid had all but ceased.

Sending Money from Geneva to Salamiyya: The Post Office and the Missionary Network

Another important matter related to that of the deportees' sources of income is the question of postal communications. The post office could mean the difference between life and death for Armenians who faced the threat of starvation in Hama and Salamiyya. In Salamiyya, the post was quite irregular, but mail nevertheless arrived from Hama around twice a week.[58] As already mentioned, some deportees received newspapers in the mail, but what was surely more important for catastrophe victims faced with extreme conditions was being also able to receive letters and money transfers thanks to the post office. These transfers, known as *havale*s, were carried out by mail or by wire.

While our two diarists' entries contain references to correspondence from a very early date, they say nothing about money transfers until August 1916. Krikor Bogharian's father had only recently been deported from Salamiyya, and the family's economic situation had become much worse as a result. It was in this dire situation that the family received a *havale* of four Ottoman gold liras from Zenop Bezjian, an Ayntab native and a leader of the Protestant community. "It arrived in the nick of time," Bogharian notes: "we paid off half of our debts (rent, loans, etc.)."[59] In the same period, the young diarist found himself constantly writing letters on behalf of his own family or that of Der Nerses. The addressees were either relatives or fellow natives of Ayntab living either in Ayntab or Istanbul, or in exile in Damascus, Aleppo, or Ajlun.[60] Later, Bogharian also wrote to people in the United States: Bishop Papken Gyuleserian, who was from Ayntab, and Vahan Kyurkjian, who had been born in Aleppo but had worked in Ayntab for a time. He received answers from both.[61] Obviously, Bogharian invested all this effort in his correspondence in hopes of receiving assistance. The effort bore fruit: *havale*s eventually began arriving one after the other, from Aleppo, Istanbul, Egypt,[62] and even the United States.[63] Bogharian's correspondence with a native of Ayntab living in Istanbul, the lawyer Nazaret Festekjian, is particularly interesting, because the *havale*s sent by Festekjian played a providential role for both Bogharian's and Der Nerses's family, both of which had been left defenseless. "We are truly grateful to Mr. Festekjian, who helped us so that we could buy necessities in these difficult days. To date, nine gold lira have been sent to us," Bogharian writes on 23 November 1916.[64]

At the same time, Bogharian kept up a correspondence with his father, deported to Tafile; he received letters from him and also transferred money to him on various occasions. Der Nerses also corresponded with his family, and his diary show that the *havale*s sent to deported priests arrived at their destination. Vahram Dadrian and Garabed Kapigian likewise attest that money transfers were made by post and wire. Dadrian and his family were deported from Chorum/Corum; upon reaching Aleppo in September 1915, they received money by cable from

Samson and Istanbul. Later, when the authorities relocated them in Jarash, they continued to receive transfers from merchants who had been business partners of Dadrian's father.[65] Kapigian, for his part, confirms that the telegraph and postal services worked relatively well in Rakka and that money was transferred to the deportees by wire and post.[66]

*Havale*s were not only sent in these two ways. The Banque Ottomane had a branch in Hama, and deportees demonstrably took advantage of it to receive money transfers. Der Nerses made the acquaintance of the branch's director, Sheikh Khelil Efendi, who "promised to do such favors as it was in his capacity to do for us from time to time."[67] The memoirs of Yervant Odian provide information about the kind of money transfer that reached Hama: he received sums from Istanbul through the Régie and the *düyunu unumiye* (the Public Debt Administration).[68] Kapigian, in turn, reveals that during the months he spent in deportation in Suruj, Armenians from Erzurum who were living there received cash transfers by way of the Ziraat Bankası (the Agricultural Bank).[69] He himself received cash transfers there from his brother in Sivas.[70]

In addition to all this, there also existed forms of non-state aid. Although our two diarists do not indicate the sources of these funds, they were very likely moneys that Armenians living abroad were endeavoring to get to their suffering countrymen. Der Nerses's first reference to this is dated 5 November 1915, the date on which Bishop Kyud Mkhitarian received an eighty-lira banknote earmarked for widows and orphans from Antioch.[71] The priest from Ayntab went from Salamiyya to Hama and Homs in order to distribute the money, turning it over to the beneficiaries in those two cities.[72] On another occasion, in March 1918, Der Karekin (Krikor Bogharian's father) traveled from Salamiyya to Hama, evidently in order to claim funds intended as aid for deportees, of which he was the nominal beneficiary. He distributed around forty banknotes to poor people in Hama and was expecting to disburse another fifty or so to the needy in Salamiyya as well.[73] Krikor Bogharian, in his turn, writes that 105 Ottoman gold lira donated by a few Protestant Armenians arrived in Salamiyya in July 1916 for distribution to Protestants.[74] Although in all three of the preceding cases the aid in question was obviously not state aid, it is not certain that it was sent from abroad. In this connection, Der Nerses's entry of 26 April 1918 is of greater interest to us, because there the priest from Ayntab clearly identifies the source of 2,500 francs (156.25 Ottoman lira banknotes) that Der Karekin, again the nominal beneficiary, went to a bank in Hama (most likely the Banque Ottomane) to collect. The money had been sent for distribution to Salamiyya's needy. "Last year," Der Nerses goes on, "Der Karekin is supposed to have appealed to Msrian, who lives in Germany, and to have received two thousand marks from him a few months ago; this time, on their recommendation and in response to an appeal from Der Karekin, two thousand five hundred francs have arrived."[75]

This crucially important piece of information, together with other sources, gives some idea of a substantial philanthropic network, and of the paths involved in transferring funds (and in what form) from European capitals all the way to, say, the little town of Salamiyya. More than any other source, Odian's memoirs shed some light on the name that Der Nerses mentions, Msrian. They reveal that the wife of this well-known tobacco trader from Samson was living in Hama with her two daughters. They had been in a caravan of deportees from Samson subjected to massacres and other acts of violence en route; the thirty pillaged, exhausted survivors in this caravan, all women, found rest only when they reached Hama. But the tobacco trader also had children who were engaged in the tobacco business in Germany.[76]

The sequel to this episode unfolded in Europe, where resident Armenian political activists were working to provide material assistance to their suffering compatriots in the Ottoman Empire. We should examine their efforts in a broader framework, bearing in mind that the most important actors in the network responsible for seeing that this kind of aid reached its destination were American and other Western missionaries. In the United States during the war years a popular mobilization emerged, mainly on the initiative of missionary organizations, in favor of the Ottoman Empire's suffering Christians—particularly Armenians,[77] but also famine-stricken Lebanese, Anatolian Rums (Orthodox Greeks), and thousands of Christian settlers who had found refuge in Iran and the Caucasus[78]—and Palestinian Jews.[79] Various organizations created for this purpose came together in November 1915, giving birth to the American Committee for Armenian and Syrian Relief. (From 1919 on, this organization would bear the name Near East Relief.[80]) A large fund amounting to several millions of dollars was collected for the Armenians,[81] and the Committee set about sending these moneys to northern Iran and the Caucasus, where many thousands of Armenians had found refuge. Financial aid also began making its way into the Ottoman Empire by way of the U.S. diplomatic network there. Initially, American funds were usually dispatched to the U.S. Embassy in Istanbul and forwarded from there to U.S. consulates, particularly those in Aleppo and Beirut; then the consulates mobilized their local networks to distribute them to needy catastrophe victims. The American and European (German and Swiss) missionary networks established on

Ottoman territory were also put to work. Thus, in a number of cases, money that had arrived from abroad was turned over to the Istanbul-based Bible House,[82] which sent it on to the interior provinces.

In April 1917, the very existence of this network was threatened when the hitherto neutral United States declared war on the Central Powers and immediately closed its diplomatic missions in the Ottoman Empire. However, it proved possible to create something to replace the diplomatic network in short order. The American missionary William Peet, who until then had acted as the main coordinator of funds distributed by the missionary network from his base in Istanbul, moved to Europe and settled in Geneva; he began to direct the new structure created to receive funds from there. Thereafter, Peet channeled funds collected in the United States and Europe to the Swiss and Dutch Foreign Ministries, which in turn forwarded them to their embassies in Istanbul. All these operations were carried out by three neutral countries, a narrow framework that ensured the success of the enterprise.[83] The missionary network active in the Ottoman Empire, for its part, continued to exist, and even American missionaries pursued their work there. The United States had in fact managed to avoid declaring war on the Ottoman state; the local Ottoman authorities were therefore relatively tolerant of American missionaries.[84]

None of this, of course, bears directly on the subject, the more so as we cannot say how much of this aid went to deportees in Hama and Salamiyya, though we do know that in the last year of the war, an orphanage in Hama received financial support from American and European missionary sources. What is important for our purposes is the fact that the Armenian side, too, started taking advantage of the existence of such networks and sending money to Armenian catastrophe victims, the deportees in Hama among them. There is extensive information on this subject in the correspondence of Boghos Nubar Pasha. This leading Egyptian-Armenian figure lived in Paris at the time and was engaged in political activity in Europe in his capacity as president of the Armenian National Delegation. Moreover, from 1915 on, Boghos Nubar was the main actor in the effort to ensure that relief funds collected by Armenians reached their needy compatriots in the empire. His first success came in March 1916, when he saw to it that a sum of 75,000 francs raised from various Armenian sources reached its intended destination. The money was first sent to the U.S. Embassy in Bern, which forwarded it to the Embassy in Istanbul. In the Ottoman capital, part of it was entrusted to the Armenian Patriarch, Zaven, while the rest was sent on to the American consulate in Aleppo to meet the needs of Armenians living in the city itself.[85]

In the next months, the Armenian side continued to dispatch funds on a regular basis. Boghos Nubar was represented in these matters by an assistant of his stationed in Geneva, Yervant Aghaton. It was Aghaton who maintained contact with the American and missionary networks in Switzerland. In a letter dated 20 April 1917, Aghaton reveals that, of the sum of 18,900 francs that he himself had turned over to the network on that day, 1,500 francs represented a donation from the Msrian brothers.[86] Another letter shows that the Msrian brothers donated another 15,000 francs that October; and, important for our discussion, also that the brothers' family had been deported to Hama, that the Msrians were tobacco merchants with a commercial agency in Dresden, Germany, and that they had been living in The Hague since the outbreak of the war.[87] There can be no doubt that they were part of the Hama-based Msrian family mentioned by Odian and Der Nerses, and that they were making every effort to provide material support for their relatives' struggle for survival.

The Prelacy of the Aleppo Armenians: The Most Important Network for the Distribution of Aid

Examination of the activity of the networks involved in dispatching financial aid to Hama and Salamiyya shows that Aleppo's Armenian Prelacy was one of their main centers. This religious institution in Aleppo was a crucially important station on the road that these Armenian and missionary networks followed to deliver funds to their destinations on Ottoman territory. It is therefore worthwhile to pause over the prelacy's activities in favor of the deportees, the more so as our two diarists and their families benefited from those activities at different times.[88]

One of the clearest indications of the importance of the Aleppo prelacy's role is provided by the account books of the Settlers' Relief Committee, which the Aleppo diocese set up with the government's permission on 24 May 1915,[89] shortly after the deportations began.[90] Among the members of the committee were the Armenian notables Sarkis Jiyerjian (treasurer), Vahan Kavafian, Tavit Jidejian (chairman), Hagop Barsumian, Armen Mazlumian, Rupen Ejzajian, and Dajad Dakesian. The president of the committee was the vice-prelate, Der Harutyun Yesayan, who would be arrested early in 1916 along with Jidejian, Barsumian,[91] and about sixty other Armenians on charges of fomenting rebellion, and imprisoned until the war's end. Albeit deprived of its most important activities, the Settlers' Relief Committee continued its work.

The Aleppo's Armenian Prelacy's archives are excellent sources for the study of many different aspects of the philanthropic activity that sprang up in the conditions of the genocide. It is especially interesting that this work was carried out in a city like Aleppo, which had a native Armenian population of no more than ten thousand that, by a quirk of fate, had been exempted from the deportation order. With little warning, this city's Armenians found themselves playing a pivotal role in the relief effort. From all around the globe, money began to make its way there, and local Armenian community bodies went to work distributing aid in parallel with state institutions and also, in some cases, circumventing those institutions. Close study of the abrupt, hastily scribbled notes that fill the ledgers of the Aleppo Settlers' Relief Committee can bring to light a previously unknown substratum of a whole period.

Evidently, the committee's treasury was constantly replenished with sums arriving from elsewhere. For that very reason, this body was capable of taking on multifaceted tasks of relatively broad scope. At the same time, the mass deportations and massacres were an extraordinary, unprecedented event, and the deportees' needs knew no bounds. The committee's ledgers reflect all these circumstances. After the war, some members of this body faced accusations of having illegally appropriated funds in the days of the genocide. In any case, the main question here concerns the transfer of funds—in other words, the intermediary role the Aleppo diocese assumed to ensure financial aid sent from abroad wound up in the hands of deportees in Aleppo or the villages nearby.

The ledgers repeatedly indicate that substantial sums originated from the Istanbul Armenian Patriarchate.[92] They show that the Patiarchate transferred 768,972 piasters to the prelacy in Aleppo between February and October 1916.[93] This transfer involved funds that the missionary network had sent to Istanbul, addressing them to the U.S. Embassy or Bible House. The Embassy or Bible House put part of this aid at the disposition of the Istanbul Armenian Patriarchate, which in turn went to work transferring the money to places affected by the mass violence, notably Bilad al-Sham. This further highlights the pivotal role of the Armenian Prelacy in Aleppo. Its special function was owed partly to the facts that Aleppo lay close to places that had been affected by the catastrophe and the prelacy was one of the rare Armenian institutions that was still operating. The Istanbul Patriarchate generally made cash transfers to Aleppo through the Banque Ottomane.

For its part, the Aleppo Prelacy also received funds directly from the missionary network. The money was often passed from hand to hand. In this connection, the ledgers often mention the Swiss missionary Beatrice Rohner, who would physically deliver funds to the prelacy. Her name never appears by accident in these ledgers. In the war years, she became this secret international network's main agent and even its source of inspiration. She lived in Aleppo and from there also directed a network of her own made up of believing missionaries, diplomats, and deported Armenians. This network channeled financial assistance from Aleppo as far as Der Zor, where it benefited many thousands of Armenian catastrophe victims. The Americans, aware that Rohner's network was the most reliable and active, entrusted funds directly to her.[94] But hers was not the only network active in these deportation centers. We learn from the memorial ledgers of the Aleppo Prelacy that from March 1916 to February 1917, making transfers approximately once a month, Rohner turned a total of 547,624 piasters (4,313 Ottoman gold lira) over to the Aleppo Diocese.[95] The prelacy of course had its own network, which likewise strove to deliver these sums to Armenian catastrophe victims. Rohner presumably also had faith in the activity of this Armenian network; otherwise, she would not have turned money over to the prelacy month after month.

Initially, these funds were distributed by a simple method: to indicate that cash assistance was available for certain deportees, their names would appear on a list posted on a wall of Aleppo's Church of the Forty Martyrs; once thus informed, the beneficiaries had to apply to the prelacy or to missionaries active in the city to receive the money.[96] But funds were not distributed in Aleppo alone. True, the city was itself a devastated zone filled with Armenian deportees; indeed, tens of thousands of Armenians were living there, whether on a state-issued permit or underground, many of them in dire need. Nevertheless, as the Aleppo Prelacy's ledgers make plain, its Settlers' Relief Committee had its own network for distributing funds, a sort of alternative bank with the purpose of allocating the generous sums entrusted to it to collectively deported Armenians in various towns and villages in the vicinity. Sometimes—as indicated in the previously discussed example of the Msrians in Hama—the sums arriving from abroad were intended for specific individuals. In this case as well, the prelacy had to activate its network to ensure that the money reached its destination. The ledgers show that the Aleppo Diocese sent money to Karlek, a neighborhood on the outskirts of the city, as well as to areas nearby, such as Bab, Katma, Mumbuj, Maara, Jisr Shoghur, Riha, Meskene, Meydan-Ekbez, and Sabka, and others further off, such as Rakka, Homs, Der Zor, Ras el-Ain, Marash, Salt, Kilis, Birejig, Damascus, and Idlib.[97] In the case of Der Zor and Ras el-Ain, the very last of the transfers mentioned were carried out in February 1916, in other words, before the mass murder of Armenians that took place in these localities. By way of the prelacy, money also reached the towns of direct interest to us, Hama and Salamiyya. On 12 January 1916, 5,080 piasters were sent from Aleppo to the Armenians in Hama while a different transfer, made the same day through the same channels, conveyed 762 piasters to six deportees living in Hama.[98] On 15 March of the same year, thirteen Armenians from Hama received 254 piasters sent from Aleppo.[99] As for Salamiyya, 5,080 piasters were distributed to deportees there.[100]

The prelacy sometimes turned to the Ottoman post office to deliver these sums to the deportees, but this was not the preferred channel, particularly because postal officials sometimes embezzled funds. That is why the Aleppo Diocese's Settlers' Relief Committee had trusted men who worked either on their own or with acquaintances at different levels to get the money to its destination. This group of agents was, generally speaking, composed of Diocesan officials and people close to them. Clearly, most of them had long lived in Aleppo and were not subject to the *sevkıyat*'s decisions; consequently they enjoyed relative freedom of action and travel. The ledgers repeatedly name people who belonged to this network and undertook to transfer funds. The name most often mentioned is that of Kavas Sarkis, a diocesan official who, apparently, carried out his task competently. We know that Sarkis had previously been the *kavas* (bodyguard) of the Catholicos of Cilicia, Sahag II.[101] It is not clear, however, whether he had been in the Catholicos's service from the start and had accompanied him from Adana to Aleppo. In any event, when Sahag II was exiled to Jerusalem in October 1915, Sarkis stayed behind in Aleppo and continued to work for the prelacy. In addition to his monthly salary, Sarkis often received other sums from the prelacy; in the ledgers, they are designated "per diem for the *kavas*." This may of course mean that the money covered miscellaneous expenses incurred on official trips. We can also speculate, however, that in the conditions then prevailing, the *kavas* used part of this money to bribe Ottoman gendarmes and other officials, thus overcoming obstacles to the delivery of aid money to deportees. This is only a surmise in this case. In other cases, however, it is clearer that the prelacy resorted to bribery.

Besides delivering food and money to the deportees, the Aleppo Prelacy also endeavored to ensure the security of the caravans of deported Armenians passing through Aleppo and other towns and villages in the vicinity. The success of such an operation depended on whether various people could be persuaded to intervene on the deportees' behalf. One of the best ways to get them to do so, as the memoirs of Armenian survivors often stress, was to bribe lower-ranking officials or the gendarmes who accompanied the caravans or guarded the deportation routes. The account books in Aleppo hold notations such as "A gift for the gendarme going to Bab," "For the gendarme going to Maara," or "Gift for a gendarme."[102] There can be little doubt about the use to which these sums were put.

Beside Kavas Sarkis, the names of Kavas Haji and Kavas Manug are mentioned, albeit less often; they, too, delivered cash aid to deportees. Six other names are repeatedly mentioned in connection with this operation: Vruyr, Onnig (very probably Onnig Mazlumian), Dajad (very probably Dajad Dakesian), Antun, Takvor, and G. Ketmenian (very probably Garabed Ketmenian).[103] All were plainly officials at the prelacy. Priests also played active roles in the aid distribution networks. They either held ecclesiastical posts connected with Aleppo's Prelacy, or were themselves exiles who had succeeded in getting as far as this city and finding refuge in it. The prelacy entrusted these priests with aid money, which they distributed to deportees in nearby towns and villages like Idlib, Bab, Riha, and Maara, but also further off, for example in Der Zor. We often encounter the names of the following priests in this group: Khachadur

Figure 3.3. Aleppo, 1923. Photograph taken in the common courtyard of the Fourty Martyrs and Holy Mother churches, on the occasion of the blessing of the Chrism. First row, left to right - Father Mampre Sirunian, Father Nerses Tavukjian (wearing the miter), Catholicos Sahag II Khabayan (seated), and to his right, Archbishop Papken Gyuleserian (the future coadjutor Catholicos). On the very right of the photograph is Kevork Nalbandian (in civilian clothing). (Source: Grégoire Tafankejian collection, Valence)

Boghigian, Hovhannes Etmekjian, Vahan Manugian, Sahag Momjian,[104] Der Vrtanes, and Der Sarkis.[105] The first two priests had been in Aleppo before 1915. The others most likely were themselves deportees.

All these people were active in distributing money in Aleppo or places nearby. In connection with distributions to more distant places, the names of two Aleppo notables are mentioned: Onnig Mazlumian[106] and Rupen Ejzajian.[107] Mazlumian succeeded in distributing a sum of money to deportees in Hama and Ras el-Ain, for example. It remains uncertain, however, whether these people themselves traveled to these distant localities and, as is said in the ledgers, carried out the distributions "with their own hands." Since there are no eyewitness accounts of the two voyages supposedly undertaken by Mazlumian, the more likely assumption seems to be that he mobilized his many connections in Ottoman circles and in this way managed to get funds to those for whom they were intended.

Basically, the main purpose of these networks was to avoid Ottoman control and deliver money to beneficiaries without going through the classic channels, namely, the post office and the banks operating in the empire. Those who played an active role in these networks were convinced that the Ottoman authorities could at any moment outlaw transfers made for this purpose or appropriate part or all of the moneys for themselves. Their reservations about the Ottoman post office and banks were also based on more concrete grounds: during the war, *havale*s were paid out in paper currency, which sometimes entailed a devaluation of as much as 80 percent.

The Power of Connections: In the Labyrinth of a Corrupt Administrative Apparatus

The corruption of an administrative apparatus and the power of personal connections must not necessarily be regarded as an expression of the law of cause and effect. Without question, in a bankrupt, enfeebled state, bribery and reliance on personal connections are ubiquitous realities that make it possible to carry out certain transactions and take various steps forbidden by law. Yet this does not mean that illegal interventions occur only in an atmosphere of bribe-taking and corruption. Interventions of this sort are not always motivated by the pecuniary interest of some state official. Often the motive is a long-standing friendship or a neighborly bond, a special predilection (for a sport, an art, a dish, etc.), or a strategic necessity. These situations arise in extreme conditions as well, such as when a national or religious group or community is collectively subjected to persecution and its members are deported and unjustly condemned by force of law.

In these circumstances, events in which a bribe constitutes a saving factor for the persecuted side are frequent. There are countless instances of this in writings by survivors. We have a conspicuous example in Bogharian's case: a bribe saved his brother from conscription. In 1917, when Armenian deportees faced the real possibility of being drafted, Krikor Bogharian's brother found himself among those called up by the Ottoman army. With a bribe of five *mejid*s (one Ottoman gold lira), however, the Bogharian family succeeded in having his official date of birth changed, thus saving him from the absolute uncertainty that service in the Ottoman army implied.[108] Der Nerses also discusses the issue of avoiding the draft by paying a bribe.[109]

Even in extreme conditions, however, "connections" do not result from bribes alone. Evidently, the motivations for them vary considerably and are sometimes quite unforeseeable. The illustration provided in Wladyslaw Szpilman's *The Pianist* is famous.[110] Similarly, in the years of the genocide an Armenian might owe his life to, say, his father's reputation as a *kanon*-player. This was the case with Hagop Der Ananian, who was caught by gendarmes as he attempted to flee from a railroad station in Karlek, one of Aleppo's outlying districts. During his interrogation, the gendarmes' commanding officer discovered who the fugitive's father was. The Turkish officer, it turned out, was a townsman of Der Ananian's and an ardent admirer of his father's virtuosity on the *kanon*. Ultimately, for the *kanon*-playing father's sake, he let the son go.[111] In another case, Vahe Gyuleserian, a native of Ayntab, was arrested during World War I on trumped-up charges of giving bribes. Had the prison warden not known he was a talented oud player, he might have been condemned to severe punishment by Ayntab's military court. Before long, Vahe's virtuosity on the oud had made him an indispensable musician at the prison guards' parties and a privileged prisoner. Eventually, he was even pardoned.[112]

There is no lack of similar stories in Der Nerses's and Bogharian's diaries. These writings permit a closer examination of the relations between Armenians and the Ottoman authorities in the places of exile. When the issue is approached "from above"—that is, when the main criterion is the ideology of the ruling Ittihad Party, its decisions to deport and exterminate the Armenians, and the steps it took to implement them—it seems cut-and-dry in every respect. After all, the relationship at issue is between an executioner and its victim. Such a relationship can, of course, have its internal complications, and sometimes the executioner may take contradictory measures when executing a plan that ultimately aims at the victims' collective annihilation. But none of this calls the basic plan into question: its purpose is to destroy the victims or devastate them so thoroughly that they are no longer capable of leading a collective existence on their native soil.

Bogharian's and Der Nerses's diaries afford us the opportunity to study the same relationship at another, lower level: that between Ottoman officialdom and the deportees. By and large, this concerns officials at the secondary level and even those deemed insignificant, every one of whom could nevertheless, thanks to his position and ability to intervene, exercise a direct influence on the fate and the struggle for survival of a deportee or a whole group of deportees. The class of officials at this level would include, for example, the commanding officer of a detachment guarding a train station, a *mukhtar*, the chief of police in a transit station for deportees, a village headsman, and even a *kaymakam* or the military commander of a town. All these officials carried out orders received from above. Meanwhile they were in direct contact with certain deportees—the notables in particular, with whom they often cultivated non-hierarchical relationships. Certain factors operating at this level, such as bribery, solidarity between people from the same town or village, pity, or old or new friendships, could facilitate a deportee's struggle for survival, or even that of a whole group.

Thus, there could arise a direct relationship between executioner and victim from which the oppressed side could reap unexpected benefits and experience "miraculous" moments that might help save it. Of course, the victim had to engage in a certain amount of role-playing in such cases. Nevertheless, in the final analysis everything depended on the comportment and mood of the executioner, who was in an all-powerful position. In this connection, we often encounter two individuals in Bogharian's and Der Nerses's diaries: Hama's military commander, Osman Bey, and Salamiyya's *kaymakam* Nejmeddin Bey. It is worth pausing over both. These two Ottoman officials clearly established close relationships with certain Armenians from Ayntab, wealthy individuals and other notables in particular. The notables, however, sometimes only acted as intermediaries between these officials on the one hand, and Ayntab's Armenian community on the other—a circumstance that once again points to the advantages enjoyed by a group that, in conditions of catastrophe, has to some extent preserved its communal structures. Whereas Nejmeddin Bey saw the Armenians of Ayntab as a strategic means of realizing his plans for improving conditions in Salamiyya, the Ottoman commander Osman Bey had a more complex relationship with this group. He combined qualities of a disciplined military man, a benevolent humanist, and a corrupt official, therefore making it not impossible for deportees—or rather, the notables among them—to meet and cultivate relations with him, propose various deals to him, and come to terms.

Osman Bey was Hama's *merkez kumandanı*, the commander of the garrison there. A peculiarity in this official's character became evident in the very first weeks of the deportation. It is not the intention here to determine the orders Osman Bey may have received from his superiors or how he carried them out. The aim is rather to observe how this Ottoman commander behaved toward the ten thousand plus Armenian deportees under his direct orders.

Der Nerses first mentions Osman Bey's name on 26 August 1915. At the time, Der Nerses's family was one of the approximately four hundred lucky ones to be living in apartments rather than the "transit station" where many thousands of other Armenians had been crowded together. In this place, out in the open on a hill near the town, people lived in tents. But then an order was issued to the effect that all the Armenians living in town had to move to the hill. This threw the deportees into a panic. When Der Nerses himself went to see Osman Bey and asked him to clarify the order, he learned that it applied to all the deportees without distinction.[113] In the next few days, Ayntab's notables held further meetings with Osman Bey and, through his good offices, sent a petition to the *mutasarrıf*; in this way they informed both of their wish—that is, the wish of some hundred families—to reside in houses in the city, rather than in tents on the hill, until they were relocated elsewhere.[114]

Osman Bey did not, of course, receive the notables from Ayntab warmly; rather, he continued to insist that the decision to relocate all of them on the hill brooked no appeal. Interestingly, however, his door remained open to the deportees' representatives, and he did not display a racist attitude or attempt consistently to defame his interlocutors in his relations with them, as a number of other Ottoman officials did in this period, especially in the interior provinces. In connection with the same question about permission to continue living in the city, we may further observe that the Ayntab notables took collective action, seeking always to widen the scope of their relations with the local officials. (This is reminiscent of the steps that natives of Erzurum took in an attempt to be allowed to establish residences in Rakka.)[115] Thus they also met with Hama's mufti, Murshid Efendi, a member of the *meclis-i idare*,[116] as well as other local dignitaries, about whom Der Nerses reveals nothing more than their names.[117]

These efforts ultimately failed: all these families had to move to the hill and live in tents, although only for about two weeks. Most important here, however, is that these notables from Ayntab, in the conditions following deportation, maintained their dynamism and will to work together as a group. Later, after Der Nerses had settled in Salamiyya, he visited Hama on various occasions, maintaining relations with Osman Bey and holding meetings with him. Together, the two examined various issues affecting Salamiyya's Armenian deportees, such as conscription and the distribution of state aid.[118] Still later, after the priest from Ayntab moved back to Hama with his family in 1918, he continued to meet on a regular basis with Osman Bey.

In Der Nerses's estimation, Osman Bey was a "sensitive man" in whom the Armenian tragedy evoked feelings of empathy and sorrow.[119] Bogharian gives a different explanation of this military man's attitude. In the very first days of the deportation, Osman Bey befriended a native of Ayntab, Kevork Nalbandian, who had been a well-known teacher and choirmaster in the Ayntab community and later held a similar post in Kilis shortly before being deported. He was moreover a talented musician who played the violin, *kanon*, and harmonica. His musical talent was to gain him privileged status in Hama. He had five brothers who were themselves all musically gifted and often played together in public. Five of the Nalbandian brothers were deported to Hama (one was in Ethiopia in 1915).[120] In Bogharian's opinion, the bond between Osman Bey and Kevork Nalbandian was a friendship based on "music and the tavern," which, the diarist adds, "proved to be advantageous to the natives of Ayntab and Kilis."[121] Yervant Odian offers a similar description of the Ottoman officer; according to Odian, Osman Bey befriended rich Armenians who "kept him well supplied with food and drink."[122] At any rate, Kevork Nalbandian's position as Osman Bey's protégé did indeed guarantee his safety, and his friendship with the officer profited his brothers and his circle of friends as well. Initially, he, too, moved to Salamiyya with the majority of Ayntab Armenians in Hama. Later, however, he was appointed conductor of Hama's military band and soon clearly became a sought-after musician at Turkish and Arab notables' festivities.[123] Thanks to Kevork, his brother Nazaret (who later became a priest, taking the name Der Garabed) was released from the army and likewise settled in Hama.[124] We also know that Der Nerses's meetings with Osman Bey generally took place at Kevork's request. A few months before the end of the war, Hama, like most other cities in Bilad al-Sham, received an order[125] to create *imalat hane*s (workhouses). Der Nerses notes that four hundred *tezgah*s[126] were to be set up in a workshop in Hama and that Harutyun Efendi Nalbandian was to be its *müdir* (director), while Kevork Efendi Nalbandian was to be appointed *müdir muavin* (assistant director). Osman Bey, whose prerogative it obviously was to arrange these appointments, reserved the position of *nazır* (assistant) for himself.[127] Here Osman Bey's friendship with the Nalbandian brothers is visibly already moving to a higher level. Hama's military commander was obviously about to enter the business world, that is, to launch a career that could bring him material profit. The Nalbandian brothers were probably supposed to be his trusted associates in this partnership. However, no further speculation is warranted here, first because in this period Der Nerses wrote only rarely in his diary, and second because Allied forces occupied Hama a few months later, sounding the hour of liberation for the Armenians.

Osman Bey also tried to reanimate certain elements in the Armenian community structure with an eye to improving the cleanliness and well-being of the town of Hama. Thus he worked together with Der Nerses and other notables from Ayntab to bury the corpses of Armenians dumped in open graves on the town's outskirts, and also to found shelters for the rising numbers of defenseless widows and orphans in the streets.[128]

A more eloquent example of the intertwining of philanthropy and mercenary personal interest is found in Khacher Sarkisian's memoirs. In 1917 Sarkisian was in Aleppo, where he managed to find a job as a clerk in a meat and dried-meat factory (*kavurmahane*) that belonged to the Turkish army. Like many of those in charge of such enterprises, the head of the factory, Tevfik Bey (Beybaba), tended to look among the ranks of deportees for experienced manpower and people able to write well in Ottoman Turkish. Sarkisian, chosen to be his new clerk, was a well-known, highly competent merchant from Everek. Thanks to his ingenuity, Beybaba succeeded in appropriating state funds to personal advantage, among other things. His relationship with Sarkisian went beyond the bounds of ordinary friendship to become a multifaceted business partnership. This allowed Sarkisian not only to obtain food and protection for own family, but also to begin to aid many of his acquaintances among his townsmen.[129]

Salamiyya's *kaymakam* Nejmeddin Bey was a man in the mold of Osman Bey, equally or perhaps even more characteristic of the type. He had much to do with shaping the Ayntab Armenians' destiny. According to our diarists, it was on his initiative as mayor of a city close to Hama that, starting in October 1915, thousands of families from Ayntab were relocated in Salamiyya. This measure proved providential for many families who had been leading an uncertain existence in tents in Hama.

Der Nerses relates that Nejmeddin Bey himself came to Hama in September 1915 and singled out the craftsmen among the deportees there with the firm intention of relocating them in Salamiyya.[130] This

Ottoman official, who hailed from Baalbek,[131] was no stranger to the Armenians and especially not to the Ayntab Armenians, as he had earlier been Ayntab's *kaymakam*.[132] Both of our diarists emphasize that they knew Nejmeddin to be a municipal leader who encouraged building: "he is already familiar to us as someone who promotes construction and improvements, and is good at maintaining law and order," Der Nerses noted the first time he set foot in Salamiyya.[133] Again, Nejmeddin was a man who "promote[d] construction," Bogharian writes as he reflects on the *kaymakam*'s activity in Ayntab.[134]

But Bogharian also remarks that Nejmeddin, during his term of office in Ayntab, was persecuted by the local Ittihadist leaders, and that Armenians from Ayntab took a hand in persecuting him.[135] Apparently, the mayor had been appointed to his post during the reign of Sultan Abdülhamid II. After the Constitution was reestablished, the Ittihadists, now in power, were displeased to see Nejmeddin in the post of mayor, and he was subsequently accused of failing to undertake indispensable reforms in the municipal administration.[136] Yet the impression is rather that, in the new conditions, the Ittihadists were unwilling to accept the idea that the local administrative apparatus should be dominated by someone from outside their ranks or that the *kaymakam* should be running the town together with the class of *agha*s and *bey*s left over from Hamidian times. In the end, the Ittihadists organized a popular demonstration in which Armenians also participated. The demonstrators made their way to the *saray* (the seat of the municipal government), where they were able to break through the police barrier and enter the *kaymakam*'s office. They dragged Nejmeddin out of the building and into the street, where he was beaten and showered with insults while his clothes were torn to shreds. He left Ayntab that night.[137]

We do not know what influence this experience had on Nejmeddin Bey's future relationship with the Ittihad. We likewise cannot say whether there was any connection between this compromising incident and the just attitude Nejmeddin later displayed toward the deportees from Ayntab. It is clearer that one of the main reasons that Nejmeddin Bey brought large numbers of craftsmen from Hama to Salamiyya was his penchant for "promoting construction," that is, his ambition to beautify the town he governed and build new buildings in it. Bogharian writes: "Construction workers have plenty of work, since the *kaymakam*'s house (located outside the town), the State Agricultural School, and an elementary school are all under construction. The *kadı* is also building himself a residence."[138] The *kaymakam* also had plans to construct a club with a cafe (*millet kahvesi*).[139] Meanwhile, it was not just craftsmen who were now relocated in this town, but also the families of hundreds of people who had no trade, most of them Ayntab natives. This radically altered the face of the town. Nejmeddin Bey saw to it that the Armenians found living quarters, and as supervisor of the distribution of the state moneys earmarked for them, he was accordingly in contact with Salamiyya's Armenian notables. The Armenians were therefore deeply upset when, in February 1916, Nejmeddin was named to a new post and replaced by Kemal Bey.[140] On the day of his departure, the Armenians from Ayntab sent a delegation to see Nejmeddin off. "History will judge Nejmeddin Bey to be a righteous man for his actions," Bogharian writes. "He has been the salvation of a few thousand Armenians, most of them from Ayntab."[141]

All this points to a conscientious official who needed qualified manpower to enhance and improve the district under his jurisdiction. He found what he was looking for in the Ayntab Armenians, thousands of whom had settled in the town of Hama. The mayor of Salamiyya had already worked in collaboration with them, and the experience had been a positive one. Thus he knew that there was no lack of competent craftsmen and merchants among them and especially that these Armenians were ready to work at any price, as long as their existence was assured by having the means of earning a subsistence diet and protection against the threat of new deportations. Nejmeddin Bey was obviously prepared to accord these conditions to the deportees from Ayntab. His task was presumably facilitated by the fact that these Armenians had maintained a unified group existence and in so doing maintained their community structure largely intact. In a word, it proved possible to bring, in very short order, a homogenous group of people who knew each other and worked together from one town to another, where they could make a new beginning.

In the Hama-Salamiyya environment, another kind of intervention in favor of the deportees was possible. It took place at the official level but was actually a result of the mutual assistance that relatives and community members offered each other. This holds in particular for the activity of an Armenian Ottoman state official by the name of Artin Efendi Boshgezenian. A native of Ayntab, Boshgezenian was a member of the Ittihad Party. He had been elected to the Ottoman parliament as the representative from Aleppo and continued to serve in that capacity in these fateful years. Bogharian attests that when the deportation of the Armenians from Ayntab began, Artin Efendi had intervened with the Ottoman authorities and succeeded in winning ten or so Armenian families, relatives and friends of his, the right to remain in Aleppo rather than be deported somewhere else.[142] Later, when many Ayntab natives settled in Salamiyya, this Armenian member of parliament intervened again on their behalf; as a result, Sarkis Krajian, Hrant Syulahian (Der Nerses's brother-in-law), the Basmajian, Ghazarian,[143] and Ashjian families, as well as the families of Hajji Rupen Boshgezian (the husband of Krikor Bogharian's maternal aunt)[144] and Hagop Karamanugian received the right to settle in Aleppo.[145]

In other cases, people intervened on behalf of deported Armenians to secure salaried government posts for them. With luck, this could save the individual in question from the threat of being deported again, secure that person a permanent source of income, and become a means of obtaining food. These advantages accrued not just to the deportee who was thus elevated to the ranks of "officialdom," but also to his family. One of the best examples of this is the singling out of craftsmen from among the deportees (by decision of the supreme command of the Fourth Ottoman Army) and their transfer to Damascus, where they went were put to work in army factories. Thus this act was primarily an intervention undertaken by a state authority to meet a military need. Because of it, many helpless Armenians who had been awaiting the meting out of their fate in Euphrates Valley transit stations received permission to settle in Damascus. Some also managed to take those family members who were still alive along with them. In addition, such intervention on behalf of a deportee gave the exile and his family the opportunity to secure a subsistence diet, and thus to pursue their struggle to survive.

The case of Yervant Odian is highly typical in this regard. The Istanbul Armenian writer had been banished for political crimes to Buseyra, a village south of Der Zor near the confluence of the Khabur River and the Euphrates. To Odian's great astonishment, the region's Ottoman military commander appointed him to the post of interpreter, and suddenly he became "the most trustworthy of men," learning state secrets as an interpreter for Turkish military personnel and German officers. His new post conferred an even stranger responsibility on him: when a Turkish soldier in the Germans' employ committed an infraction, it was Odian who had to sling a rifle over his shoulder and take the delinquent under guard to the Turkish barracks nearby. The Turks called Odian "Alman çavuş" (German sergeant). About his unexpected, radical change in status, the writer wryly observes: "These sorts of contradictions could be found only in Turkey."[146] Bogharian, too, would benefit from a providential intervention of this type, when in one of his darkest hours in Salamiyya he became, surprisingly, a government official, as discussed later in this volume.

"To Earn a Living by the Sweat of One's Brow...Will Eventually Become Impossible"

Let us attempt to sum up the general picture that emerges from the various statistics and descriptions presented in this chapter. It is well established that early in 1917 an economic crisis set in in the Hama district, and that it greatly complicated the deportees' struggle to survive; the above-mentioned examples are evidence of this. It is also clear that this severe crisis was not specific to the Hama-Salamiyya area, but rather affected Bilad al-Sham as a whole.

In this general atmosphere, the case of the Aleppo Prelacy's *kavas* may be taken as a measure of the situation. As already noted, the only biographical detail we have about the *kavas* is his name, Sarkis. Yet we also know the monthly salary that this official received in these catastrophic years, as well as the story behind it. This otherwise seemingly insignificant detail in fact provides us with a means of assessing the depth of the crisis. In November 1915, the *kavas* had a monthly salary of 127 piasters (one Ottoman gold lira), almost as much as a worker earned in the prewar period; it allowed him to meet both his own and his family's needs. In the same period, a priest employed in Aleppo likewise received a monthly salary of one Ottoman gold lira, although in his case we must also take into consideration "the priest's right," that is, the additional emoluments that someone serving in this religious office received for spiritual services rendered. In the conditions created by the intensifying crisis, the *kavas*'s monthly salary was far from sufficient, so much so that by late 1916, his salary had been raised to 2.5 Ottoman gold lira (317 piasters). In February 1917, when the crisis had assumed disastrous proportions, the prelacy official's salary was increased to three Ottoman gold lira (381 piasters). Plainly, the prelacy was satisfied with its *kavas*'s performance and also aware that even three Ottoman gold lira did not suffice to cover all the living expenses of this official and his family (assuming he had one). Thus, as of mid 1917, the prelacy supplemented the *kavas*'s monthly salary with another type of remuneration, called "the price of bread"; obviously, its purpose was to help him meet the cost of vital necessities. From time to time the prelacy also agreed to help the *kavas* buy clothes, and once a year it made him a gift of a pair of "boots" and a "suit."[147]

The single example of Kavas Sarkis gives us an idea of the monthly income a family needed to meet its needs during the economic crisis affecting Bilad al-Sham. Only in this respect is the *kavas*'s life comparable with that of the Armenian deportees living in the same region. In the final analysis, Kavas Sarkis is one small part of Aleppo's Armenian community, which had been exempted from the deportation order and remained more or less intact: its institutions continued to function and its members could earn a living by pursuing their usual occupations. The Armenian deportees' daily lives were quite different: many of them had had to begin all over again. Unable to pursue their usual occupations, they had no choice but to try their hands at new kinds of work. The state did not provide them with housing of any sort; therefore they had to find shelter for themselves and their families using their own means. All this left the Armenian settlers in an utterly uncertain situation.

What is more, any failure in their new trades or posts could have grave consequences for deportees and their families, especially in periods when the price of basic necessities reached unprecedented heights. Like food, discussed above, shelter was a fundamental factor in the daily struggle for survival. In this case shelter means a rented room or apartment. Bogharian's diary is full of information about rents in Salamiyya. For example, the monthly rent for a well-ventilated apartment in a good location could be as much as one lira in 1916, whereas an undesirable little room might be had for ten piasters.[148] Unfortunately, in the next two years, during which the economic crisis worsened, Der Nerses's diary contains no direct references to rents. It reveals only that in late 1917, when Der Nerses's family returned to Hama, they often moved from one apartment to another because landlords kept raising the rent and the family could no longer keep pace with rising prices. "Two and a half months have passed, but we haven't yet managed to settle down; may the Lord grant that we live in peace in this house for a while."[149]

In sum, a family with below-average income could eke out an existence on a monthly income of one Ottoman gold lira in the early war years, but during the period when Hama and Salamiyya were wracked by economic crisis, an individual needed a minimum monthly income of two Ottoman lira to rent an apartment and cover the costs of a relatively normal diet. Otherwise, that person's existence was at the mercy of chance. The situation did not differ significantly in Jarash, where Vahram Dadrian spent his years of exile. According to him, his family of five needed 25 piasters a day in September 1917.[150] In other words, monthly expenditures of 150 piasters, almost one and a half Ottoman lira, were required for each family member. All of this was abnormal; it left the majority of deportees in an extremely vulnerable situation. Those who had arrived in their places of deportation with a knowledge of one or another trade tried to find new work. Such knowledge could be vitally important. However, as we saw from Der Nerses's personal example in the previous section, success was not ensured even for these deportees. Ordinary unskilled work was also available: harvesting fields, transport jobs, and so on. Daily wages for unskilled laborers were between three and four piasters,[151] so in the best of cases, working long hours in exhausting conditions could ensure a monthly income of around one hundred ten piasters.

Before long, the savings of our two diarists and their families were no longer sufficient to allow them to cope with their situation and survive. As noted above, in Bogharian's case the family's material assets totaled only 280 piasters in July 1916. Der Nerses reveals in October 1917 that his family's total wealth was between 300 and 400 piasters.[152] From time to time, they sold one of their material assets, such as an object made of gold or a carpet, but these too were insufficient to guarantee their economic security for long.

Beginning in 1917, the prices of staple foods in Hama and Salamiyya increased by 1,000 percent and more, putting the majority of deportees in an unbearable situation. State aid and external aid could of course be vital in their day-to-day struggle. Der Nerses mentions *tayın* only once in 1917 and never again thereafter, which implies that in the conditions of the economic crisis, state aid was essentially non-existent. As for sums arriving from the outside, Der Nerses plainly did not benefit much from them. This may suggest that the sums arriving from abroad, weighed against the deportees' multiple needs, were inadequate to tip the scales. Here, once again, the words of Catholicos Sahag II take on their full significance: in letters he wrote in this period, he often repeated the idea that "a royal treasure would be required to provide even a modicum of relief for this suffering."[153]

It should further be noted that all moneys arriving in Hama by way of the banks reached their beneficiaries in the form of banknotes or paper Ottoman gold lira. For the deportees, both these forms were extremely inconvenient, since the paper Ottoman lira, worth one Ottoman gold lira at the outbreak of the war, was subject to severe depreciation in the following years. By December 1917, it would be worth only 20 piasters.[154] In other words, all aid that arrived in the form of paper currency or banknotes had been devalued by as much as 80 percent by the time it reached the deportees. Funds delivered by hand in the form of solid Ottoman gold were of much greater value. The official value of one Ottoman gold lira was 100 piasters, but its actual value in the provinces was consistently higher.[155] In the war years in Aleppo, for example, one Ottoman gold lira was worth 127 piasters.[156]

In a word, beginning in 1917, the environment in which our diarists were struggling to survive was subject to sharp vicissitudes. The situation had now radically changed. Der Nerses provides a faithful reflection of this dire predicament in his entry for 1 October 1917:

Until today, we lived by selling some of our possessions; with the help of friends; and, occasionally, thanks to the priest's right. But we have nothing left to sell. Our friends' assistance has been exhausted; we have received no priest's rights for more than a year, and they are not forthcoming today, either. We have now begun living by the sweat of our brow. Something else: inflation has reached such heights that it has become very hard to earn a living by the sweat of one's brow and, it seems, will eventually become impossible....From now on, then, we, a six-member family, will have to live by the sweat of our brows in this extremely expensive period. Lord help us.[157]

These lines are dominated by a feeling of helplessness. Living conditions had deprived Der Nerses of the means of supporting his family. He no longer saw anything he could do to come to grips with the situation; he saw only a somber horizon in which everything was now up to chance. These are obvious signs of decline.

Notes

1. Des Pres, *The Survivor*, p. 88.
2. Tavukjian, *Diary*, p. 104.
3. Bogharian, "Diary," p. 188.
4. Ibid., p. 199.
5. James A. Reilly, *Small Town in Syria: Ottoman Hama in the Eighteenth and Nineteenth Centuries* (Bern: Peter Lang, 2002), pp. 93-94.
6. Bogharian, "Diary," pp. 196-97.
7. Ibid., p. 172.
8. Ibid., p. 149.
9. Ibid., pp. 139, 143, 152-153.
10. Tavukjian, *Diary*, p. 140.
11. Bogharian, "Diary," p. 149.
12. Haigazian University Library Archives, "Krikor Bogharian's Archives," Passport for Krikor Bogharian issued by the State of Great Lebanon on 24 February 1925.
13. Father Harutyun Sarkisian ("Alevor"), *Palu, ir sovoruytnere, grtagan u imatsagan vijage yev parpare* [*Palu, its customs, educational and intellectual level, and dialect*] (Cairo: Sahag-Mesrob, 1932), p. 113.
14. Bogharian, "Diary," p. 171.
15. Ibid., p. 181.
16. Tavukjian, *Diary*, p. 140.
17. Ibid., p. 112.
18. Dadrian, *To the Desert*, pp. 136-137, 144-145, 210, 264.
19. The data about Aleppo are taken from the Files on Benefits Programs [*Nbasdits*] in the Archives of Aleppo's Armenian Prelacy (hereafter AAAP).
20. June 1915, 3.5 piasters; November 1915, 6 piasters; April 1916, 7.4 piasters; May 1916, 7.95 piasters; September 1916, 9 piasters; January 1917, 26 piasters.
21. Bogharian, "Diary," p. 144.
22. Ibid., p. 151.
23. Ibid., p. 165.

24. "Ahvâl-i harbiye ve zaruret-i fevkâlede-i siyasiye dolayısiyle mahall-i âhara nakilleri icra edilen Ermenilerin iskân ve iâşeleriyle hususât-ı sâireleri hakkında Talimâtnâmedir," in Doç. Dr. Azmi Süslü, *Ermeniler ve 1915 Tehcir Olayı*, vol. 5 (Ankara: Yüzüncü Yıl Üniversitesi Rektörlüğü Yayını, 1990), p. 114; Taner Akçam, *A Shameful Act: The Armenian Genocide and the Question of Turkish Responsibilty* (New York: Holt Paperback, 2007), pp. 187–188.
25. Süslü, *Ermeniler ve 1915 Tehcir Olayı*, pp. 114–115.
26. BOA. DH. ŞFR, nr. 53/305, Bâb-ı Âlî, Dâhiliye Nezâreti, Iskân-ı Aşâyir ve Muhâcirîn Müdîriyyeti, 19, Musul Vilâyeti'ne, 26 B. 1333, 9 May 1915, in *Armenians in Ottoman Documents*, pp. 45–46.
27. BOA. DH. ŞFR, nr. 55 A/77, Bâb-ı Âlî, Dâhiliye Nezâreti, Iskân-ı Aşâyir ve Muhâcirîn Müdîriyyeti, 73, Haleb Vilâyeti'ne, 25 L. 1333, 5 September 1915, in ibid., p. 98; BOA. DH. ŞFR, No. 57/110, Bâb-ı Âlî, Dâhiliye Nezâreti, Iskân-ı Aşâyir ve Muhâcirîn Müdîriyyeti, 116, Haleb'de Muhâcirîn Müdîri Şükrü Bey'e, 17 Z. 1333, 26 October 1915, in ibid., p. 125; BOA. DH. ŞFR, No. 57/317, Bâb-ı Âlî, Dâhiliye Nezâreti, Iskân-ı Aşâyir ve Muhâcirîn Müdîriyyeti, Adana ve Haleb vilâyetleriyle Urfa Mutasarrıflığı'na, 28 Z. 1333, 6 November 1915, in ibid., p. 130.
28. AAAP, Ledger 38, "Minutes of the Armenian National Council's Settlers' Relief Committee," Twenty-Eighth Session, 7/20 July 1915, Aleppo.
29. Levi, *If This Is a Man*, p. 39.
30. Garabed Kapigian, *Yeghernabadum: Pokun Hayots yev norin medzi mayrakaghakin Sepasdio] [The story of a crime: Poku Hayots and its great capital, Sepasdia]* (Boston: Hairenik, 1924), p. 350.
31. AAAP, File "Benefits," Ledger 23, "Treasury, Settlers, 1915–1916," p. 8 and File "Benefits," Ledger 13/4, p. 10.
32. Bogharian, "Diary," p. 131.
33. Tavukjian, *Diary*, p. 88.
34. Ibid., p. 93.
35. Ibid., p. 94.
36. Ibid., p. 100.
37. Ibid., p. 103.
38. Bogharian, "Diary," pp. 174–175.
39. AAAP, Ledger 38, "Minutes of the Armenian National Council's Settlers' Relief Committee," Twenty-Second Session, 24 June/7 July 1915, Aleppo.
40. Archives of the Cilician Catholicosate (ACC), File Sahag II 100-1, Letter no. 4980/94 of 19 July 1915 from Catholicos Sahag II to Patriarch Zaven of Constantinople, Aleppo, f° 309.
41. Tavukjian, *Diary*, p. 103.
42. Bogharian, "Diary," p. 153.
43. Ibid., p. 103.
44. Ibid., p. 160.
45. Ibid., p. 162.
46. Ibid., p. 166.
47. Ibid., pp. 112, 175, 178–179.
48. Ibid., pp. 193–194, 197.
49. Tavukjian, *Diary*, p. 140.
50. AAAP, Ledger 38, "Minutes of the Armenian National Council's Settlers' Relief Committee," Second Session, 12/25 May 1915, Aleppo. See also ibid., Sixth Session, 18/31 May 1915, Aleppo.
51. See also AAAP, ibid., Ninth Session, 22 May/4 June 1915, Aleppo.
52. Krikor K. Kudulian, *Garmir noter darakri gyankes [Red notes from my life as a deportee]* (Port Said: n.p., 1919), p. 25. Similar accusations are leveled against

local officials in the priest Hovhannes Torosian's eyewitness account, which also contains information about the way state aid was distributed in Sheikh Miskin (in the *sanjak* of Hauran). Hovhannes Torosian, "Pasder sev yegherne" ["Facts about the somber crime"], *Husaper* 3, no. 147 (13 March 1918).
53. Dadrian, *To the Desert*, pp. 94, 195–197.
54. Kapigian, *Story of a Crime*, pp. 117–118.
55. BOA, 16 Receb 331 (18 Mayıs 1915)' de Dahiliye, Harbiye ve Maliye Nezaretleri'nde gönderilen tamim, in Azmi Süslü, *Ermeniler ve 1915 Tehcir Olayı*, pp. 115–116.
56. See Akçam, *The Young Turks' Crime against Humanity*, pp. 367–368.
57. Tavukjian, *Diary*, p. 101.
58. Bogharian, "Diary," p. 160.
59. Ibid., p. 186.
60. Ibid., pp. 187, 190, 202.
61. Ibid, pp. 200, 202.
62. Ibid., p. 192.
63. Funds transferred from the United States passed by way of Aleppo (ibid., p. 204).
64. Ibid.
65. Dadrian, *To the Desert*, pp. 60, 134, 145–146, 154.
66. Kapigian, *Story of a Crime*, pp. 119–121.
67. Bogharian, "Diary," p. 108.
68. Odian, *Accursed Years*, p. 127.
69. Kapigian, *Story of a Crime*, pp. 377, 387.
70. Ibid., p. 398.
71. Tavukjian, *Diary*, p. 96.
72. Ibid., pp. 98, 102.
73. Ibid., p. 154.
74. Bogharian, "Diary," p. 181.
75. Tavukjian, *Diary*, p. 158.
76. Odian, *Accursed Years*, pp. 106–107.
77. Robert L. Daniel, "The Armenian Question and American-Turkish Relations, 1914–1927," *The Mississippi Valley Historical Review* 46, no. 2 (September 1959), pp. 252–255.
78. James L. Barton, *Story of the Near East Relief (1915–1930)* (New York: Macmillan, 1930), pp. 10–14.
79. Merle Curti, *American Philanthropy Abroad* (New Brunswick, NJ: Transaction, 1988), pp. 241–246.
80. Ibid., p. 246. Rich documentation of this philanthropic missionary activity is available in missionary organizations' and other Western (American and European) archives. The most important of these sources are Hans-Lukas Kieser, *Der verpasste Friede. Mission, Ethnie und Staat in den Ostprovinzen der Türkei 1839–1938* (Zurich: Chronos, 2000); Hans-Lukas Kieser, *Nearest East: American Millenialism and Mission to the Middle East* (Philadelphia: Temple University Press, 2012); Keith David Watenpaugh, *Bread from Stones: The Middle East and the Making of Modern Humanitarianism* (Berkeley: University of California Press, 2015).
81. Barton, *Story of the Near East Relief*, pp. 47–48.
82. Bible House was the name given to the American and British Bible Societies taken together. Bible House also served as headquarters for the branch of the American Board of Commissioners of Foreign Missions in the Ottoman Empire.
83. Archives of the AGBU's Nubarian Library. Letter from Boghos Nubar Pasha to W. W. Peet, treasurer of the American Missions in Turkey and the Balkans, 15 June 1917, Paris.
84. Barton, *Story of the Near East Relief*, pp. 63–64.

85. Archives of the AGBU's Nubarian Library. Letter of 8 March 1916 from Aghaton to Boghos Nubar Pasha, Geneva. Letter from Aghaton to the U.S. Ambassador to Switzerland in Bern, 7 March 1916, Geneva.
86. Archives of the AGBU's Nubarian Library, Letter of 20 April 1917 from Aghaton to Boghos Nubar Pasha, Geneva.
87. Archives of the AGBU's Nubarian Library, Letter of 13 December 1917 from Aghaton to Boghos Nubar Pasha, Geneva.
88. One of the rare studies of this question is Vahram L. Shemmassian, "Humanitarian Intervention by the Armenian Prelacy of Aleppo during the First Months of the Genocide," *Journal of the Society for Armenian Studies* 22 (2013): 127–152.
89. AAAP, Ledger 38, "Minutes of the Settlers' Relief Committee," First session, 11–24 May 1915, Aleppo.
90. Ibid., Twelfth Session, 28 May–10 June 1915, Aleppo.
91. Bishop Yeghishe Chilingirian, *Ngarakrutyunk Yerusaghemi-Halebi-Tamaskosi Kaghtaganagan yev Vanagan Zanazan Tibats yev antskeru* [Descriptions of refugee-related and monastical events and developments in Jerusalem, Aleppo, and Damascus] (Jerusalem, n.p., 1927), pp. 32–33.
92. AAAP, File "Benefits," Ledger 13/4, pp. 3, 20, 27, 32, 35, 38, 44, 49, 52; AAAP, File "Benefits," Notebook 5, 1916–1917, pp. 1, 4.
93. AAAP, File "Benefits," Notebook 5, 1916–1917, p. 25.
94. See Hans-Lukas Kieser, "La missionaire Beatrice Rohner face au génocide des Arméniens," in Jacques Sémelin, Claire Andrieu, and Sarah Gensburger, eds., *La résistance aux génocides. De la pluralité des actes de sauvetage* (Paris: Sciences Po, 2008), pp. 383–398.
95. AAAP, File "Benefits," Ledger 13/4, pp. 23, 27–28, 38, 49, 52; AAAP, File "Benefits," Notebook 5, 1916–1917, pp. 23, 53. In this period, an Ottoman gold lira was the equivalent of 127 piasters in the Bilad al-Sham region.
96. H. A., "Bolisen Der Zor" ["From Constantinople to Der Zor"), *Hayrenik Monthly* 45, no. 12 (December 1967): 34.
97. AAAP, File "Benefits," Ledger 13/4, pp. 4, 14, 18, 22, 26, 27, 30–31; AAAP, File "Benefits, Notebook 5, 1916–1917, p. 8.
98. Ibid., Ledger 23, "Treasury, settlers, 1915–1916."
99. Ibid.," Ledger 13/4, p. 26.
100. Ibid., p. 14.
101. Ibid., Ledger 3, "Settlers' accounts," 1 October 1915, p. 3. *Kavas* here means bodyguard. In other contexts, it designates a courier working for a consulate or embassy, or a watchman responsible for the security of an institution.
102. Ibid., Notebook 22, "Treasury, Settlers, 1915," pp. 6, 8; AAAP, File "Benefits," Ledger 13/4, p. 24.
103. Garabed Ketmenian was, from 1906 to 1908, the principal of Aleppo's Armenian Nersesian School and a member of the school board. In 1915, he was the director of the Armenian hospital founded by the Armenian Prelacy in Aleppo's Ayide neighborhood.
104. This priest, a native of Ayntab who had long served in Kilis, was sent to Der Zor to distribute aid in July. AAAP, Ledger 38, "Armenian National Council, Minutes of the Settlers' Meeting," Session 28, 7/20 July 1915, Aleppo; Session 29, 10/23 July 1915, Aleppo; Session 29, 17/30 July 1915, Aleppo.
105. The surnames of the last two priests were not found.
106. Onnig (Baron) Mazlumian (1871–1934) was born in the village of Anchrti (present-day Topkapı) near Arapgir. He settled in Aleppo in 1885. In 1911 he and his brother Armenag built a modern hotel in Aleppo, the Hôtel Baron. During World War I, Mazlumian and his brothers tried to use their friendly relations with high-

ranking Ottoman officials to bring about arrangements favorable to the Armenian deportees.
107. Rupen Ejzajian (1878–1930), born in Nigde/Niğde, attended the American college in Tarsus. In 1901 he graduated the American University of Beirut with a degree in pharmacy. He settled in Aleppo, where he opened his own pharmacy. During World War I, he was conscripted into the Ottoman army and given the rank of a pharmacist-officer. He performed many important services for Armenian deportees.
108. "Khachig Bogharian (1898–1971)," p. 291, in *Ayntabiana*.
109. Tavukjian, *Diary*, p. 154.
110. Wladyslaw Szpilman, *The Pianist: The Extraordinary True Story of One Man's Survival in Warsaw, 1939–1945* (New York: Picador, 2000).
111. Hagop Der Ananian, "Inchbes azadetsa mahvan jiranneren" [How I escaped from death's claws], *Hayrenik Monthly* 43, no. 11 (November 1965): 57–58.
112. V. N. Gyuleserian, "Husher yev pusher, 1915–1918-i sev oreren" [Memories and thorns from the black days of 1915–1918], *Hay Anteb* 5, no. 4 (1964): 3–8; 6, no. 1 (1965): 3–8.
113. Tavukjian, *Diary*, p. 78.
114. Ibid., pp. 78–79.
115. Archives of the AGBU's Nubarian Library, "Aram Andoniani tseghasbanutyan nyuteru havakadzo" [Aram Andonian's collection of materials bearing on the genocide], File Garabed Kapigian, "Rakkayi archev" [Before Rakka], pp. 105–106.
116. The (local) governing council.
117. Tavukjian, *Diary*, pp. 81–82.
118. Ibid., pp. 108–109.
119. Ibid., p. 149.
120. "Hagop Nalbandian (1901–1962)," in *Ayntabiana*, pp. 453–455.
121. Bogharian, "Diary," p. 130.
122. Odian, *Accursed Years*, p. 111.
123. "Father Garabed Nalbandian (1892–1970)," *Ayntabiana*, p. 311; "Hagop Nalbandian," p. 454.
124. "Father Garabed Nalbandian," p. 311.
125. The order was most probably issued by the high command of the Fourth Ottoman Army.
126. A wooden loom for weaving cloth, *tezgah, tezgeah*.
127. Tavukjian, *Diary*, p. 156.
128. Ibid., pp. 149–150.
129. Khacher Sarkisian, *Yotanasun darineru hushers* [My memoirs of seventy years] (Beirut: Donigian, 1970), pp. 734–789.
130. Tavukjian, *Diary*, p. 91.
131. Bogharian, "Diary," p. 141.
132. Tavukjian, *Diary*, p. 93; Bogharian, "Diary," p. 140.
133. Tavukjian, *Diary*, p. 93.
134. Bogharian, "Diary," pp. 140–141.
135. Ibid., p. 140.
136. Nerses (Mahdesean) Hagopian, "Hay Heghapokhagan Tashnagtsutyune Ayntabi mech yev haragits tebker" [The Armenian Revolutionary Federation in Ayntab and related events], in Sarafian, *History of the Armenians of Ayntab*, p. 973.
137. Ibid., pp. 974, 976.
138. Bogharian, "Diary," p. 142.
139. Ibid.
140. Ibid., p. 157.
141. Ibid.

142. Ibid., p. 148; "Levon Krajian (1906-1970)" and "Hagop Karamanugian (1863-1939)", in *Ayntabiana*, pp. 271, 422-423.
143. Archives of the Haigazian University Library, "Krikor Bogharian's Archives," "The Natives of Ayntab in Syria" (unpublished ms.) by Krikor Bogharian, p. 3.
144. Bogharian, "Diary," pp. 148, 188.
145. "Hagop Karamanugian (1863-1939)", in *Ayntabiana*, p. 422.
146. Odian, *Accursed Years*, pp. 188, 194.
147. AAAP, File "Benefits," Ledger 4, "Settlers' accounts," 1 October 1915, pp. 12, 16, 18, 22, 28, 35. Ibid., Ledger 13/4, pp. 24, 33. Ibid., Notebook 5, 1916-1917, pp. 1, 3, 7, 35, 42, 51.
148. Bogharian, "Diary," p. 158.
149. Tavukjian, "Ms. Diary," p. 131.
150. Dadrian, *To the Desert*, p. 210.
151. Tavukjian, *Diary*, p. 137.
152. Ibid., p. 141.
153. ACC, Letter no. 4980/93 of 6 July 1915 from Catholicos Sahag II to Patriarch Zaven of Constantinople, Aleppo, f° 303.
154. Tavukjian, *Diary*, p. 145.
155. Şevket Pamuk, "Money in the Ottoman Empire," in Halil Inalcik and Donald Quataert, eds., *An Economic and Social History of the Ottoman Empire*, vol. 2, *1600-1914* (Cambridge: Cambridge University Press, 1994), pp. 973-974.
156. This is what one Ottoman gold lira was worth according to the account books of Aleppo's Armenian Prelacy. For this reason, we have also taken the market rate of 127 piasters as the value of one Ottoman gold lira in Hama and Salamiyya.
157. Tavukjian, *Diary*, p. 139.

Selected Bibliography

Published Material

Akçam, Taner. *A Shameful Act: The Armenian Genocide and the Question of Turkish Responsibilty.* New York, 2007.

Barton, James L. *Story of the Near East Relief (1915-1930).* New York, 1930.

Bogharian, Krikor, ed. Այնթապականք / *Ayntabiana*, vol. 2. Մահարձան: մահագրութիւններ, դամբանականներ եւ կենսագրական նօթեր [Funeral monument: necrologies, funeral orations and biographical notes]. Beirut, 1974.

———. Ցեղասպան Թուրքը, վկայութիւններ քաղուած՝ հրաշքով փրկուածներու զրոյցներէն [Tseghasban Turke. Vgayutyunner kaghvadz hrashkov prgvadzneru zruytsneren] [The genocidal Turk: Eyewitness accounts from the narratives of people who were miraculously saved]. Beirut, 1973.

Chilingirian, Bishop Yeghishe. Նկարագրութիւնք Երուսաղէմի-Հալէպի-Դամասկոսի Գաղթականական եւ Վանական Զանազան Դիպաց եւ Անցքերու, *1914-1918* [Ngarakrutyunk Yerusaghemi-Halebi-Tamaskosi Kaghtaganagan yev Vanagan Zanazan Tibats yev antskeru] [Descriptions of refugee-related and monastical events and developments in Jerusalem, Aleppo, and Damascus, 1914-1918]. Jerusalem, 1927.

Curti, Merle. *American Philanthropy Abroad.* New Brunswick, NJ, 1988.

Dadrian, Vahram. *To the Desert: Pages from My Diary,* trans. Agop Hacikyan. London, 2006.

Daniel, Robert L. "The Armenian Question and American-Turkish Relations, 1914-1927." *The Mississippi Valley Historical Review* 46, no. 2 (September 1959): 252-275.

Der Ananian, Hagop. "Ինչպէս ազատեցայ մահուան ճիրաններէն" [Inchbes azadetsa mahvan jiranneren] [How I escaped from death's claws]. *Hayrenik Monthly* 43, no. 11 (November 1965): 53–58.

Des Pres, Terrence. *The Survivor: An Anatomy of Life in the Death Camps.* New York, 1976.

Gyuleserian, V. N. "Յուշեր եւ Փուշեր, 1915–1918-ի սեւ օրերէն" [Husher yev pusher, 1915–1918-i sev oreren] [Memories and thorns from the black days of 1915–1918], *Hay Anteb* 5, no. 4 (1964): 3–8, 6, no. 1 (1965): 3–7.

Inalcik, Halil, and Quataert, Donald, eds. *An Economic and Social History of the Ottoman Empire*, vol. 2, *1600–1914*. Cambridge, 1994.

Kapigian, Garabed. Եղեռնապատում, Փոքուն Հայոց եւ նորին մեծի մայրաքաղաքին Սեբաստիոյ [Yeghernabadum: Pokun Hayots yev norin medzi mayrakaghakin Sepasdio] [The story of a crime: Poku Hayots and its great capital, Sepasdia]. Boston, 1924.

Kieser, Hans-Lukas. *Der verpasste Friede. Mission, Ethnie und Staat in den Ostprovinzen der Türkei 1839–1938*. Zurich, 2000.

———. *Nearest East: American Millenialism and Mission to the Middle East.* Philadelphia, 2012.

Kudulian, Krikor K. Կարմիր նօթեր տարագրի կեանքէս [Garmir noter darakri gyankes] [Red notes from my life as a deportee]. Port Said, 1919.

Levi, Primo. *If This Is a Man*, trans. Stuart Woolf. New York, 1959.

Odian, Yervant. *Accursed Years: My Exile and Return from Der Zor, 1914–1919*, trans. Ara Melkonian. London, 2009.

Reilly, James A. *Small Town in Syria: Ottoman Hama in the Eighteenth and Nineteenth Centuries.* Bern, 2002.

Sarkisian, Father Harutyun ("Alevor"). Բալու, իր սովորույթները, կրթական ու իմացական վիճակը եւ բարբառը [Palu, ir sovoruytnere, grtagan u imatsagan vijage yev parpare] [Palu, its customs, educational and intellectual level, and dialect]. Cairo, 1932.

Sarkisian, Khacher. Եօթանասուն տարիներու յուշերս [Yotanasun darineru hushers] [My memoirs of seventy years]. Beirut, 1970.

Sémelin, Jacques, Claire Andrieu, and Sarah Gensburger, eds. *La résistance aux génocides. De la pluralité des actes de sauvetage.* Paris, 2008.

Shemmassian, Vahram L. "Humanitarian Intervention by the Armenian Prelacy of Aleppo during the First Months of the Genocide." *Journal of the Society for Armenian Studies*, 22 (2013): 127–152.

Süslü, Azmi. *Ermeniler ve 1915 Tehcir Olayı.* Ankara, 1990.

Szpilman, Wladyslaw. *The Pianist: The Extraordinary True Story of One Man's Survival in Warsaw, 1939–1945.* New York, 2000.

Tavukjian, Father Nerses, "Օրագրութեան Մեքենագրուած Բնագիր" [Orakrutyan mekenakrvadz pnakir] [Typescript of the diary (Ms. Diary)].

———. Տառապանքի օրագրութիւն [Darabanki orakrutyun] [Diary of days of suffering]. Beirut, 1991.

Watenpaugh, Keith David. *Bread from Stones: The Middle East and the Making of Modern Humanitarianism.* Berkeley, 2015.

Primary Sources

AAAP: Archives of Aleppo's Armenian Prelacy
ACC: Archives of the Cilician Catholicosate
Archives of the AGBU's Nubarian Library
Haigazian University Library Archives, "Krikor Bogharian's Archives"

Chapter 4

Descriptions of the Deportees' Decline
The Deaths of Shoghagat, Hagop, Krikor, Diruhi, and Many Others

On the Way Down: Conscription

Decline was inevitable. It is true that in this environment of survival, money and connections were elements of fundamental importance that could ward it off. Hence at first glance one might have the impression that the deportees were not all equally well-equipped for the struggle, and that there was a clear difference between, on the one hand, the moneyed stratum or the Armenians who had enriched themselves in the conditions of exile, and on the other, the families that had by now lost their possessions and depleted their savings. But even though class differences of this kind were observable in the first years of the deportation, their importance began to diminish as of 1917. The unprecedented economic crisis and the incalculable rise in the prices of foodstuffs made decline a widespread phenomenon in our deportees' world: only a small group of privileged exiles was spared the fatal consequences of the economic crisis.

One type of calamity, however, rode roughshod over class differences: epidemics, which were very widespread among deportees from the very first days of deportations. Material means were needed to care properly for the infected, so the difference between the wealthy and the poor was conspicuous in the struggle against epidemics as well. However, as there obviously were no miracle drugs to be had in this survivors' environment, diseases mowed down deportees of all social strata. The question of epidemics will be examined in detail in this chapter, with a focus on the deaths that occurred in our diarists' families.

Conscription was another calamity. As described earlier, Armenian deportees in Hama and Salamiyya were subject to the draft from 1916 on. This represented a devastating threat to the deportees, because it carried off young men who were capable of working, leaving whole families helpless. The conscription of Armenians was a generalized phenomenon: all Armenian deportees of draft age living in Bilad al-Sham were subject to it. The same chronology of events connected to the draft appears across various eyewitness accounts. Thus, in April 1917, both Der Nerses and Bogharian write about the conscription of Armenians in Salamiyya, while other accounts relate identical events taking place at the same time in Damascus, Homs, Salt, and Jarash. The colors and forms of Vahram Dadrian's account of the conscription of seventy Armenians in Jarash are more appropriate to a scene of mourning.[1] It leaves the impression that for those left behind, the crucial issue of the loss of a capable worker overshadowed the sad fact that a family member was departing. The shaky system established for obtaining a whole family's daily bread suddenly vanished into thin air, leaving the remaining family members confronting still more threatening uncertainties.

Der Nerses was eminently aware of the disastrous consequences conscription had on the deportees' day-to-day struggle. In October 1917, at a time when the question of being recruited into the army had surfaced once again, he writes: "If this military service does indeed materialize, it will deal the final blow to the Armenians still left in Syria."[2] Two weeks later, reflecting on the same subject, he adds: "If inflation were not so severe and if the question of recruiting soldiers from among the Armenians had not come up, the people still remaining would survive, thanks to their industry, initiative, and resilience. But military service is ruining everything, and inflation is attaining incredible proportions."[3]

Yet conscription did not resemble the epidemics. By paying bribes, deportees could avoid military service and remain in their place of deportation along with their families. In reality, it was the poorest who were inducted—those who were incapable of paying bribes and had no connections. Der Nerses's description of a group of 195 Armenian draftees sent from Hama to Damascus in March 1918 is telling in this respect:

> There was not a single man of means among those who were leaving; all were from the poor, beggar class, incapable, for the most part, of doing any kind of work, and already skeletons. Even the families they left behind here, who accompanied them to the station, were heaps of bones who had lost all semblance of humanity....All the [conscripts] had the sad demeanor of people standing around the body of someone who has passed away; those they left

behind kept fainting, as if afraid they were seeing them for the last time. Indeed, for many of them, what they were thinking was true.[4]

In other words, the terrible specter of conscription was once again haunting Der Nerses's world in March 1918. "All the Armenians' faces were ashen, because if all adult men were inducted, all the families left behind would be condemned to death," the priest from Ayntab observes.[5] In one of the severest phases of the economic crisis, it was plain that the decision to draft the Armenians could not but deal a mortal blow to the struggle for survival that the deportees had been waging for three years now. This decision, which was made in May, also clearly left a deep mark on the collective memory of the Armenians of Bilad al-Sham: like Der Nerses's diary, many other eyewitness accounts of the event paint it in somber colors. Many people were even convinced that by taking this step, the authorities had revealed that they were undertaking to annihilate these surviving fragments of the Armenian people. Naturally, every deported Armenian male sought to avoid conscription into the army and the consequent imposition of an utterly uncertain destiny on himself and his family. The authorities, however, pursued draft dodgers with extreme severity. In Damascus, the arrests took on mass dimensions, and more than 1,000 Armenians were drafted.[6] Jarash, too, saw persecution and arrests connected with recruitment.[7]

Utter Helplessness in the Face of Epidemics: Losing Loved Ones in Salamiyya and Hama

Alongside the anxiety caused by conscription, epidemics constituted permanent calamities to which all the deportees were vulnerable. More than anything else in Bilad al-Sham, malaria, typhus, cholera, and various other infectious diseases had become their principle attackers, destroying the nucleus of the family and undermining the struggle to survive. However attentive the Armenian deportees were to their hygiene and diet, the fact was that these diseases targeted them more than any other element of the population. Armenians were settled in places where other caravans of deportees had already arrived or would soon come. These areas of settlement were also transit routes for deportees who were being sent further south. These groups of Armenians from Anatolia and the Armenian homeland were in an exhausted state and made easy targets for epidemics. In a word, rich and poor alike were constantly exposed to zones infested by infectious disgeases of all sorts.

Moreover, the overwhelming majority of deportees, whatever their place of origin, had initially lived at least once in a "settlers' transit station." These were generally open areas, in a town or on its outskirts, that had been marked off for deportees. The exiles lived in tents that were very far from meeting even minimum hygienic standards. Descriptions given by different "settlers" are, in their broad outlines, identical: shaky tents pitched out in the open, defenseless deportees exposed to blazing sun and downpours, unburied corpses, swarms of flies and mosquitoes, open latrines, foul odors, and insufficient water. Obviously, new deportees living in or near such places could very quickly be infected in their turn. These "settlers' transit stations" disappeared after 1916, but the subsequent economic crisis and the poverty and famine it caused did nothing to eradicate the epidemics plaguing the Armenians. The upshot was that throughout the war, the deportees were condemned to remain in these places, permanently exposed to epidemics and waiting helplessly for what fate would bring.

In these conditions, it was by no means unusual that Bogharian had contracted malaria by December 1915, remaining bedridden for nearly one month.[8] A few weeks after he recovered, his brother Khachig came down with typhus.[9] In June 1916, Bogharian writes in his diary: "Malaria has raised its head again; there are houses in which four or five people have taken to their beds at the same time. In my grandfather's house, for example, six people are ill, and my maternal uncle Adur's condition is rather alarming. In my maternal uncle Garabed's house, four people are sick, as are three more in my maternal aunt's house."[10] In these conditions, Bogharian's uncle Adur died at the age of thirty-five;[11] his was the first deportation-related death in Krikor Bogharian's family. This absolute vulnerability to illness may be observed in both the diaries studied here; clearly, the means for battling disease hardly differed from one deportee to the next. In December 1915, Der Nerses notes:

> Disease in Salamiyya isn't getting worse, but neither has it diminished, and no one is safe from infection. There are sick people everywhere and, in many homes, people are living on top of one another; the air is always fetid and very many people lack the material means to care properly for the sick. The result is that eighty percent of those who have fallen ill are left to their fate: if God shows them mercy and their physical strength allows, they are saved; if not, they are committed to the earth ten to fifteen days after being stricken. Lord have mercy on all of us.[12]

Der Nerses's family would likewise not be spared these diseases. The first family member to fall seriously ill was four-year-old Kevork, who was running a fever and suffering from constipation on 19 December

1915. Der Nerses, who generally expresses himself with restraint, writes that the following night, "the boy's condition got so much worse that it began to cause us serious concern."[13] Because medicines were not to be had, the family tried traditional cures: they rubbed the boy's body down with vinegar and mustard, gave him rosewater and senna[14] to drink until he got over his constipation. His fever broke the next morning.[15]

Kevork's recovery was a consolation for Der Nerses, who clearly had gone through some alarming moments due to his son's condition. Yet he enjoyed peace of mind for fewer than six months, for the calamity of ill health was to strike another and this time heavier blow at the Tavukjian family in Salamiyya. On 25 June 1916, in the course of a single day, Kevork and Der Nerses's two daughters, Mariam and Dudu, all fell ill. The infection differed little from the one Kevork had had; the symptoms were high fever, constipation, and headaches. While the three children were still sick in bed, another of Der Nerses's sons, twelve-year-old Nerses, also came down with the same disease.[16]

Der Nerses's diary entries for the next three weeks are among the gloomiest and most woebegone of all. They create the impression of two runners competing in an exhausting race. One is the Tavukjian family, or, more precisely, those of its members who are still healthy, who, in a state of high alarm over the condition of the others, are struggling to nurse them back to health. The other runner is death, who, disguised as illness, has established his lair in the house and is growing steadily more savage, becoming a fierce opponent. This frenzied struggle between these two antagonists spotlights the importance of the assistance the family members received from each other, but at the same time the extremity of the situation cannot but reveal the limits of such assistance, limits beyond which the family's joint efforts can only fail.

Thus, on 2 July, although Mariam's fever had subsided, the same illness befell the youngest member of the household, her sister Shoghagat, who must have been at most a one-year-old nursling during the deportation and would therefore have been two when she got sick. Because her mother was enfeebled by the conditions of their exile, Shoghagat had already been weaned and put on a diet of animal milk and yoghurt. When she began teething, complications arose: she became weaker and contracted an intestinal inflammation. Der Nerses, who had been opposed to weaning her and was even convinced that this had caused her illness, derided those who had persuaded his wife to take this step. Day in and day out, the family lavished care and affection on the little girl, and her condition slowly improved. But then the wave of illnesses of June–July 1916 broke over the family's heads, plunging the Tavukjian household into unaccustomed chaos. One result was that Shoghagat did not always receive the constant attention she otherwise would have.[17]

After Shoghagat fell ill, her mother developed a high fever and was confined to her bed. Der Nerses's diary entry of 3 July, about the condition of the other family members, reads: "Mariam is feeling better today, too, and Kevork is suffering less, but Dudu is still running a fever and Nerses's fever is unabated. Shoghagat's condition is unclear."[18] The following day, the little girl's fever rose.[19] The situation was now out of control, although, like many other deported families living in Salamiyya at the time, the Tavukjians had no trouble obtaining food and seemed to have adapted rather well to conditions in the little town. Yet all this was not enough to bolster the family's capacity to withstand the epidemic. Salamiyya apparently lacked the pharmacists and physicians to whom an urban middle-class Ayntab family like the Tavukjians were accustomed to turn. Now they had to fall back on alternative methods: either traditional medicine or whatever they could recall from their own general knowledge of modern medicine. In these inauspicious June days, they tried a number of remedies. They bathed the sick members of the family in lukewarm water, made them perspire, put coriander on their bellies, rubbed the aching parts of their bodies down with mustard and, when they were running fevers, coated their bodies with vinegar. As for their diet, they fed them yoghurt and had them drink milk. To relieve stomach disorders, they gave them a mixture of sweetened carbonated water and lemon juice (called *gazoz* in Turkish). They had to do without expert advice or suggestions for treatment. In this situation of helplessness, Der Nerses wrote in his diary: "Divine help has taken the place of all medicines and remedies, and it is the best of all."[20]

Thereafter, a four-day gap appears in Der Nerses's diary. The reason for this hiatus becomes clear when he resumes making entries on 9 June: "I, too, came down with the same illness and am still suffering from constant fever, restlessness, sweating, and violent headaches."[21] The epidemic did not spare a single member of this family, but each person's condition improved—except Shoghagat's, which gradually grew worse. By 10 July the little girl was the only person in the house who was still gravely ill. On the afternoon of that day, "a few minutes before two o'clock, when the sun was taking back the last of its rays, God took Shoghagat back to Himself."[22]

They buried Shoghagat after midnight, to the left of the grave of Mariam Syulahian, her grandmother. Der Nerses's mother-in-law had died on 27 April of that year. "May our Lord and Savior Jesus place her among his perfect children,"[23] Der Nerses writes in his diary entry for that day. The mourning father, evidently suffering pangs of conscience over his helplessness in the face of the epidemic, tries to interpret his child's death. In the final analysis, the explanations he finds link directly to the extreme conditions of his family's deportation: "Today, for this reason, two kinds of guilt feelings: we weaned her prematurely and so brought on her illness; and, because we ourselves were ill recently, we weren't able to take the necessary precautions with her."[24]

The omnipotence of the epidemic and the havoc it wrought are frequent themes in survivors' memoirs. A very revelatory scene of this kind is described by Vahram Dadrian, whose family suffered a case of collective illness at their house in Jarash. A devastating disease, most likely typhus, left every member of the family seriously ill (father, mother, two daughters, and two sons). The episode took place late in 1915, when the Dadrians had not yet exhausted their savings; thus they may be described as still rich, and they were prepared to spend a great deal of money to regain health. However, Jarash had neither doctors nor medicine. Moreover, there were frequent downpours that the roofs of even the best houses failed to withstand; water trickled through them, leaving rooms damp. It was during one of these rainy periods that Vahram's father died.[25]

Shoghagat's death is a typical illustration of the deported families' helplessness in the face of epidemics. It occurred in 1916, at a time when inflation had not yet reached its peak in Salamiyya and many deportees could still afford the main staples. In this regard, another account of Der Nerses's, this one about his brother's family, is interesting. The case involved the conditions of the deportees' impoverishment and their vulnerability to infection. This time, the events Der Nerses recounts take place in Hama in 1918—that is to say, in the days when the economic crisis was at its most severe. We know that in 1917, Der Nerses's brother Hagop had left Salamiyya with his family and moved back to Hama in hopes of finding better opportunities for making a living. There were six people in the family: Hagop, his wife, their nine-year-old son, and their three daughters, one of whom was married but lived in Hagop's household because her husband had been drafted.[26] In October 1917 Hagop, too, was conscripted, along with hundreds of other Armenians in Hama, and had to leave his whole family behind without a protector.

Although the first group of conscripts had already been dispatched from the town, transportation had not yet been organized for Hagop's, so the waiting recruits were held in a prison, where they had the status of prisoners.[27] Twenty days after his brother was drafted/imprisoned, Der Nerses traveled from Salamiyya to Hama, where he immediately went to see his brother's family. They had been getting by on a subsistence diet, and in these conditions, Hagop's wife, Diruhi, had fallen ill.[28] "My brother has been in detention for twenty days now; from the first day on, there was no food left in the house. The whole family has come down with jaundice and is deathly pale; their faces showed that they are anemic with hunger."[29] The priest from Ayntab proceeded to buy them what they needed: bread, flour, and raisins. This undoubtedly saved their lives.[30]

Eventually his induction into the army was postponed, and the 44-year-old Hagop was released after spending barely one month in prison. As noted earlier, he then took up weaving in Hama with his brother, but the venture quickly failed, and decline once again loomed on the horizon. In his 3 February 1918 diary entry, Der Nerses himself succinctly retraces the stages of Hagop's family's decline:

> But the rise in prices, which are going up daily, and the increase in the number of *manusa* workers made them weaker daily. In particular, they'd been eating cabbage and leeks[31] for two months, raw. I knew that that wouldn't do my brother's family any good, and I constantly admonished them to eat boiled cabbage and leeks. Diruhi would listen to me, but my brother never did, with the result that he became a little more ravenously hungry every day. A few weeks ago, he began shoveling everything he could get his hands on into his mouth, just to fill his stomach.[32]

One gets the impression that Hagop had abandoned himself to fate, as if his will to survive had evaporated. He was unemployed, and it seems that he now lacked the initiative to take up a new line of work. In these conditions, the family's principal if not sole income was the aid received from Der Nerses. This was insufficient for the long term, especially as the priest's own family was also facing an utterly uncertain future. What is more, throughout these difficult days, Diruhi had been pregnant, and before giving birth she fell ill. The baby was born; they named it Krikor. Shortly afterward, though, the child, too, fell ill. Hagop followed suit.

Throughout this period, Der Nerses provided the family with basic foodstuffs and money, spending two Ottoman gold lira in the course of two months. "I tapped my very tight budget," he writes, "to help them out, but it was never any use."[33] The newborn Krikor died on 1 February 1918.[34] His parents' health had improved somewhat, but Hagop had clearly not altered his behavior of the previous few weeks. Der Nerses's description of the last day of his brother's life is worth quoting at length:

> However, once my brother got back on his feet, he again began shoveling everything he could lay his hands on into his mouth. This morning, Hagop was feeling better; I advised him to find a job, spend what he earned on food

for himself, and eat a great deal of bread, so that I could find him work and [the family] could get by. After that, he went home and ate some unknown plant that was growing in the courtyard; I don't know how much of it he ate. After that, he took a stroll through the market; we don't know where he ate or what he ate, only that he ate some bread and wheat soup at Rupen Syulahian Efendi's house around ten o'clock. When he left Rupen's house, everything suddenly turned black before his eyes and he was unable to go home; they hardly managed to bring him home. After eleven o'clock, he started to thrash about; at half past eleven, he became tongue-tied and could no longer speak, nor could he eat or empty his stomach. They sent me word, and I went to see him around two o'clock. He recognized me, but couldn't say anything; he just pointed to his throat, as if to say that something was stuck in it. He was thrashing about, was in pain, and was growing colder from one moment to the next. I immediately sent for Sarkis Efendi, the pharmacist from Arapgir, so that Sarkis could, if possible, make him vomit. The pharmacist tried to do something or the other, but in vain... Please, doctor, I said, give him some medicine, try some remedy. "It's no use," he said, "because he can't get anything down, and whatever it is in his stomach, his stomach has to be emptied." Sarkis Efendi emptied his stomach and massaged his feet, but that didn't help. A little later, Hagop urinated on himself, saw that he had done so, broke out in a cold sweat and, at half past three [on 3 February] gave up the ghost without a sound.[35]

On July 11, after two straight months of illness, Diruhi also died, leaving behind a ten-year-old son and three daughters, two of them young girls and one a young bride.[36]

The last paragraph of Der Nerses's diary entry for 3 February, the day Hagop died, speaks volumes. The sexton informed the priest from Ayntab that several people who died that night "had eaten grass yesterday and died for that reason."[37] These lines resemble explanations of the Armenian deportees' behavior that Der Nerses proffers more than once as of late 1917. In many of them he had observed a "bestialization," a dangerous metamorphosis that found alarming expression in the fact that people now, "when they said 'live', understood merely eating something and breathing."[38] This meant that the terrible living conditions and the helplessness in the face of the situation that had been forced on the deportees had now begun to paralyze many of them and undermine their will to survive. Once that happened, many deportees found themselves reduced to the state of disarmed creatures with no will to resist: in a purely passive posture, they simply let time go by. Der Nerses was well aware of all this. His 3 February diary entry ends with this pessimistic interpretation: "Seventeen corpses were buried by noon today, all of victims of undernourishment. Lord save us; otherwise, the Armenian people is going to be destroyed by hunger."

Figure 4.1. A view from Hama in the 1920s.
(Source: AGBU, Nubarian Library, Paris)

"For Many, Staying Alive Is Not Living, but Just Breathing"

The relatively secure social and economic situation of Der Nerses and his family, and of the groups of Ayntab Armenian deportees more generally, began to disintegrate in 1917. In fact, though, the human wrecks arriving from the inner Anatolian provinces and the Armenians' historic homeland had constantly been involved in scenes of misery and demoralization in the environment of Hama and Salamiyya ever since 1915. Many members of this group were now drained, defenseless, and thus incapable of continuing their struggle to survive. In his diary entry of 26 August 1915, when Der Nerses and his family had only just arrived in Hama, the priest from Ayntab described the condition of deportees from Kghi/Kiği. The diarist was shocked, and at the same time moved, by these miserable deportees' indifference to what happened to the bodies of their own relatives. Deaths due to famine and disease were already happening at a merciless pace among them, and they had become feeble, powerless creatures, deprived of the ability or will to bury their dead. "The poor people are all living tombs, they have no time even to protect their dead. One of the deceased died at night. During the night, a dog or cat ate his face, and they didn't even notice."[39]

The dates of these entries fall within the period in which eighty plus deportees' bodies were buried every day on the hill in Hama. These were often unidentified corpses that had been brought from the temporary transit station for deportees in Hama: "Only in a very few instances is their name or place of origin clear."[40] In this early phase of exile, however, our two diarists rarely describe or comment on catastrophe. It may be presumed that the catastrophe, with its violence and mortal consequences, had not yet touched their family members, close relatives, or the Ayntab community. In the future, too, after they moved to Salamiyya, it must be said that the population of the village included few such wretches, who, as a rule, had settled in the neighboring villages and died there as well. The depiction of the situation in Der Nerses's diary changes radically in 1917 and 1918, after Bogharian had stopped keeping a diary. From 1917 on, descriptions of demoralization begin to predominate; such cases are daily occurrences among the Armenians from Ayntab, and Der Nerses repeatedly describes, comments on, and analyzes them.

This type of catastrophic situation has been the object of many different kinds of studies in the case of the Jewish Holocaust. It basically concerns a stratum of defenseless people who are not only in a desperate predicament but also demoralized and despondent; their struggle has lost its momentum, their power of resistance has been exhausted, and they have lost their will. Der Nerses's brother Hagop was, in a way, an embodiment of this type in the last months before his death. Alexandra Garbarini's work on this theme is useful. Garbarini shows how Jewish diarists during World War II felt incapable of describing their mode of life in the ghettos or the concentration camps, and tried with various words, sometimes of their own devising, to invest it with significance. The word often repeated in this connection is "vegetating"; it epitomizes, Garbarini writes, both their physical and emotional state.[41] This directly corresponds to what is at issue here. Elsewhere, a Jewish diarist uses the compound word "human plant" (*Menschenpflanze*) with reference to his condition and that of his fellow inmates in a camp. In Garbarini's opinion, the Jewish diarists' compulsion to use neologisms to describe inhuman situations of this kind finds its explanation in the fact that they are convinced that the experiences they are going through are historically unprecedented. The Jewish diarists do indeed—as Garbarini notes, citing a wide range of different examples—repeatedly voice the idea of unprecedented or inexpressible experience.[42]

Here, however, one might ask whether all victims of extreme conditions might have difficulty describing their situations and tend to find the events that befall them absolutely extraordinary. The problem is not to establish which catastrophic situation is "more indescribable" or "more unprecedented." Really, the problem is the victim's powerlessness, during the implementation of a genocidal plan or in an extreme situation resulting from it, truly to understand and explain, in ordinary language, a hellish situation encompassing a whole world. Moreover, the victim is plagued by doubts as to whether people outside the zone of catastrophe will be able to grasp the full scope of the events taking place around him or her. We find a reflection of such a situation in various letters written by Armenians in the Ottoman Empire during the Genocide, particularly in the disaster zone. As early as May 1915, when the mass deportations of Armenians had just begun, Catholicos Sahag II, who was without a doubt aware of the unprecedented nature of these measures, wrote to Patriarch Zaven in Istanbul from Adana. "I imagine that you, too, like us, do not have freedom of movement, that your tongue is tied, that your pen has become rusty, that your heart is overflowing, but that you, too, have no means of expressing yourself and will not have."[43] Two months later, when events were in full swing, one has the impression that the Catholicos of Cilicia believed that people far from the disaster zone might not understand the extreme nature of the situation. Thus he wrote to Patriarch Zaven, who was in Istanbul: "The world has not seen, nor will it again see, so much horror, so much misery and need. The ruin of Jerusalem was a stroke of good fortune in comparison with the destruction visited on the Armenians. Massacre, rapes, countless abductions of children of both sexes, the sale of attractive women, young brides, and virgins for as little as three mejidiyes—there is no giving an account of this, or explaining it."[44] Finally, on 17 March 1916, Patriarch Zaven received a letter from the Aleppo Armenian Prelacy that presented the situation in the darkest possible colors. "The imagination, the tongue and the pen," the letter declares, "are powerless to give a true account of the situation."[45]

As already explained, it is in extreme situations of this kind that the group of despondent and demoralized people appears—in other words, those who "vegetate,"—apparently a human type that is peculiar to catastrophic conditions of this kind. In the rich literary and historical sources on the Nazi camps and ghettos, the most terrifying incarnation of this type is the *Musselman,* as he is called, a word that literally means "Muslim." Here, the assumption is that the appellation was a word coined by the inmates of the camps, one that clearly bears the traces of religious prejudice. That is in all probability contradictory, given that those imprisoned in the camps were themselves the biggest victims of one of the most ruthless forms of racist discrimination. In any event, like the frequency among Armenian deportees of clichés about Arabs and Bedouins, the surprising incidence of this negative stereotype of Muslims and their faith in the world of the camps is very likely a reflection of the heavily prevalent Orientalism of the period.

On the other hand, Frederic Homer establishes a sharp contrast between the *Musselman* and what he calls the Hobbesian hero or Hobbesian man, who was likewise a type peculiar to the environment of the Nazi camps. What rules Hobbesian man is the idea of surviving, surviving at any cost, often to the point of exhibiting an egoism toward others that rules out any sort of self-sacrifice whatsoever. The camp inmate who did not adopt this attitude could very soon be condemned to undergo the

Musselman's fate.⁴⁶ It also could happen that a Hobbesian hero would, in moments of profound despair, behave like a *Musselman* and begin to resemble one—though these could be merely transient moments. The chief difference between the Hobbesian man and the *Musselman* was that the former, if his decline was not irreversible, could very soon shake off the behavior characteristic of the latter, assume the features of Hobbesian man again, and pursue the struggle to maintain his existence. In the case of the *Musselman*, in contrast, the way back had as a rule disappeared for good, so that he inevitably went to his perdition.⁴⁷

The names given to this type may differ from one environment to the other. In the Soviet Gulag, for example, the *Musselman* was given the Russian name *dokhodiga*, which, literally, means "totally exhausted"; it designates a state like no other, in which a person suffers in the zone between life and death.⁴⁸ The *dokhodiga* was an individual of the same type as the *Musselman*, one in whom the state of physical and moral disintegration has become permanent; as Terrence des Pres puts it, for such people "the collapse was too much, too many psychic and physical blows too fast, until the momentum of decline increased beyond reversal."⁴⁹ Plainly, they could not make friends with others with whom they could maintain relations based on mutual interest, for they no longer had the will to organize and systematize their lives at all. In the camps, they would receive the minimum daily ration prescribed by the regulations, although it was clear to all that it was impossible to survive on so little; an inmate who wanted to live had to struggle to find ways of supplementing his diet. However, in the case of these "non-men," as Levi writes, "the divine spark [was] dead within them, [they were] already too empty to really suffer."⁵⁰ "One hesitates to call them living," Levi goes on; "one hesitates to call their death death, in the face of which they have no fear, as they are too tired to understand."⁵¹

Der Nerses, too, wrote long descriptions of, and commentaries on, people in this state. Of course, the diarist was not familiar with theoretical discussions of the concepts of *Musselman* or Hobbesian man, which come from the post-Holocaust period. But the exceptional diaries of the priest from Ayntab afford us an opportunity to conduct in-depth comparative observations and analyses in this field. These passages in Der Nerses's diaries are a rarity in Armenian survivors' writings and undoubtedly represent the most valuable aspect of the priest's diary. The other known Armenian eyewitness accounts of the genocide generally confine themselves to a chronological narrations of events or general descriptions of scenes. Very seldom do they hold penetrating views of the inner recesses of the deportees' lives, sociological or philosophical commentary, or profound analyses.

When Der Nerses reflects on the deportees' demoralization or, generally, on their decline, his motivations are often religious. Put another way, he ascribes deportees' decline to their having distanced themselves from the Christian faith and neglected its ceremonies and rituals, so his analyses often have a theological coloration. But these passages represent only one part of his descriptions. This paragon of a conscientious priest also had close contact with all strata of the community of deportees. As an eyewitness to what was happening on the ground, he exhorted and encouraged his flock and did what he could to halt their accelerating demoralization. Thus his daily jottings reflect the thoughts of a despondent priest who was directly experiencing that decline and trying to understand and analyze the deportees' unusual mode of life, while simultaneously condemning their indifference, utter passivity, and renunciation of social and Christian values. From this point on, Der Nerses became the author of an eyewitness account of moral decline.

One of the recurrent images in the priest's diary is that of the deportees' "bestialization"—in other words, the collapse of a whole social structure, under whose ruins ordinary human relations have disappeared. "For many people, staying alive is not living, but, rather, just a matter of breathing; already, a number of poor, helpless people are living the lives of animals, and unfeeling animals at that. They have forgotten everything. I would never have imagined how low misery can make a human being sink."[52] This remark comes in an entry made in December 1917, after Der Nerses's move with his family to Hama, where he was trying to earn a living making *manusa* in the face of very serious problems. He was already detecting the exhaustion and indifference that were in the process of gaining the upper hand among many of the people around him. "Now all that people mean by 'living' is eating and breathing," he adds. "Life's moral demands and spiritual needs have been left completely to one side. The mind no longer functions or rules, noble sentiments have been benumbed, and people act only on instinct, their one thought being to keep breathing a little longer."[53]

Conspicuous scenes of decline were visible on the ground: as the number of deaths gradually increased, unburied Armenian bodies could be seen in Hama's streets. "Very early every morning, the corpses of deported Armenian orphans of both sexes who had been left without anyone to care for them and had been sleeping out in the open are gathered up in *silejeks* [big bath towels] or *arabas* [carts] and transported from the city, to give yet another portion to the soil that is so hungry for Armenian bodies; there they are dumped in ditches, like heaps of refuse."[54] Alongside people's physical decline, the sight of dead Armenians who had been left without protectors was also, for Der

Nerses, one of the most shocking signs of demoralization. In his capacity as priest, he knew a great deal about the domestic lives of the families around him, and of the tragedies that were taking place in them. "The father of a family all of whose members are sick just died," he writes, "and they only just barely managed to bury him four days later. In the course of the week, the members of a family of four or five starved to death; it was two days before people noticed the corpses. They were loaded onto *belediyeyi tambur*s [small carts belonging to the municipality] and deposited outside the city limits."[55]

For Der Nerses, such things were unbearable; giving the dead a decent Christian burial was a priority in his eyes. In January 1918, with this in mind, he succeeded in convening a meeting of Ayntab notables at which he convinced them to raise the small sums required to finance burials for the dead. Later he would discuss the same problem with Hama's *merkez kumandanı* (garrison commander), Osman Bey, who promised to see to it that funds from the state budget were allocated for burials. It was around this time that the priest from Ayntab visited the caves near Hama, located on the heights near the banks of the Orontes (al-Asi) River. Although they faced the sun, dirt and humidity made them insalubrious and uninhabitable. Yet these caves had become shelters for impoverished Armenian deportees. In every one of them, dozens of families lived piled up on one another. Der Nerses clearly was strongly affected by the sight. "I was confronted with a dreadful, wrenching condition," he writes.[56] "Families of eight to ten members lie there, squeezed together, withered, dejected; large numbers of once strapping young men are so faint with hunger that they lie stretched out on the ground, ignoring even those who call out to them. Whenever they catch sight of someone," he continues, "those who stall have breath left in them cry out, 'Bread, give us bread.'"[57] The priest, however, could not satisfy those demands; he had come here to see about burying the dead, which was the only way he could help these poor people. Thus the caves' inhabitants were disappointed, for all they wanted was food. There was even one man among them who said that after they died, he preferred that he and others like him should serve as food for dogs. Der Nerses found the incident terrifying. He wrote that very day in his diary: "Ah, what a terrible condition: it has become natural for that most sensitive of all creatures, man, to picture the body of his loved ones as food for the ravenous beasts that feed on corpses. He can bear that."[58]

In these lines, it is as if Der Nerses's religious and human feelings have become one. He sees this indifference to the dead as a supreme embodiment of moral degradation, and the utter defeat of the struggle for survival. It is on this occasion that he pens one of the most impressive passages in his diary. "Are there still deeper levels of misery? How deep can one descend? We go one step further down every day; we think that we have taken the last step, but then we see that there must be still deeper depths. Will we ever find the bottom of these endless abysses, and start to climb back up out of them?"[59] The reality of the situation was unbearable for Der Nerses; everything around him was on the point of being destroyed. He could not stand to see more of these scenes of extreme misery and managed to visit only a scant handful of families in these caves. "I went back, because my heart could not bear visiting all of them."[60]

Here, Der Nerses is actually describing the stratum of morally degraded deportees for whom the race against time is already over. These are the defeated, whose circle of "money-food-connections" has ceased to function. They are physically spent or, as the priest often puts it, "withered": they cannot take on tasks that require strength, and nor "can they shed the tears that often serve as a means of venting deep anguish."[61] Had someone given them bread, they would certainly not have refused it, but beyond that, they lacked all spirit of enterprise or even common sense. Like Der Nerses's brother, they ate whatever came their way. The priest from Ayntab detected this state of utter exhaustion in these demoralized people's eyes above all: "their eyes are dry; they are no longer eyes, but black holes that you can see only if you look hard."[62] In a word, these people had adopted a waiting attitude. Though in a state of extreme despair, they were not suicidal: as Bruno Bettelehim notes, such people are incapable of doing anything calling for personal effort, and effort to commit suicide.[63] Sooner or later, death would come on its own to take their lives.

Figure 4.2. Father Nerses Tavukjian (Source: Kevork Sarafian, ed., Պատմութիւն Անթէպի Հայոց [History of the Armenians of Ayntab], vol. 1. Los Angeles, 1953)

The Diarist as Witness to Catastrophe: Depictions of the Deportees' Moral Decline

If the stratum of utterly wretched people described in the previous section represent the morally degraded—that is, inevitable candidates for death, given the prevailing conditions—then how does Der Nerses qualify the remaining deportees, who were, relatively speaking, better able to pursue the struggle for survival? Primo Levi, reflecting on the world inside the Nazi camps, writes: "Here the struggle to survive is without respite, because everyone is desperately and ferociously alone."[64] Plainly, those who had not yet succumbed to the *Musselman*'s fate had to scramble every day to obtain a little more food, to stay healthy, to avoid making a false move. "One has to fight against the current; to battle every day and every hour against exhaustion, hunger, cold and the resulting inertia; to resist enemies and have no pity for rivals; to sharpen one's wits, build up one's patience, strengthen one's willpower."[65] Levi goes still further: "Or else, [one has] to throttle all dignity and kill all conscience, to climb down into the arena as a beast against other beasts."[66] Such descriptions have led Frederic Homer to the conclusion that the inmates of the camps had entered into a "Hobbesian social contract." In other words, the prisoners who failed to adopt the harsh principles of "Hobbes's laws" or to practice the very often unscrupulous art of survival were ineluctably condemned to decline.[67]

Der Nerses's interrogations are not cast in this mold. For him, it was the general demoralization and immorality in the deportees' ranks that constituted the catastrophe. The demoralization he saw was not confined to the fact that people left their relatives' corpses unburied, a phenomenon that was peculiar to those in decline. Der Nerses describes a moral decline that was more comprehensive, involving others along with the wretched or the exhausted. "Unfortunately, immorality of every kind is spreading day by day; and, in the state in which this deportation has left us, what has done our nation the greatest harm is the intensifying immorality on all sides. Woe to the Armenian nation! It was unimaginable that it would fall so low; but this has been a natural process, and it has now reached its term."[68] And just as Der Nerses bewails the Armenians' deepening immorality, he also denounces their "bestialization"—this noun occurs repeatedly in his diary, where it sometimes designates a generalized state that extended to the majority of deportees of all social strata. He writes:

> The rich and the poor alike are becoming more like animals every day. The bestialization of the poor is due to their exhaustion, which is caused by the

suffering due to hunger. That of the rich stems from their fear of an uncertain future: with the ignominious deaths caused by starvation before their eyes, their minds, hearts, and souls are diminished; they start to behave like animals, and lose all feeling. Brother even turns ruthlessly against brother.[69]

Here, then, the subject is a generalized moral decline. The priest from Ayntab judges these deportees with extreme severity. They have conspicuously estranged themselves from the Christian faith, and the spirit of intra-community assistance has died in them. The lives of such people are distinguished by their selfishness. These are, basically, the traits of the Hobbesian man. The individuals Der Nerses depicts were people in whom the social contract had been fundamentally ruptured, as Todorov would put it: they reacted to events as animals would.[70] We might say that Der Nerses's criticisms basically constitute his expression of disapproval of the deportees' adoption of a Hobbesian social contract and their retreat from principle—which in fact were ways of ensuring their survival. Ultimately, his real targets, generally speaking, were the individuals making up the segment of the community who, despite the conditions of their exile, had discovered new methods of making a living. They had set out on new lives as merchants and more or less become successful, while also violating social, moral, or national and community norms in order to adapt to the surrounding extreme situation. Their life was not yet on the final, mortal, dead-end road; they continued to pursue their race against time. Simultaneously, however, they exhibited the great indifference that Hobbesian men typically show to compatriots who are in unenviable situations. When all is said and done, these people were, as the priest from Ayntab himself writes, haunted by "the fear of an uncertain future," or else were exposed daily, in their immediate surroundings, to their starving compatriots' "ignominious deaths."

By no means does Der Nerses spare this group of deportees in his diary. "Such people are just out to stay alive; their immoral concupiscence and their lusts have made them forget everything else, and there is not an iota of man's lofty ideals left in them. But, when there are none to think or reflect among the living, who will attend to the dead?"[71] At this point, the diarist is suspected of changing the meaning of the "immorality" he condemns, so that what he has in mind is licentiousness and prostitution—even though the priest from Ayntab makes no direct allusion to either. A rare allusion to the subject appears in July 1917, when he writes that Salamiyya's municipal physician is subjecting people to medical examinations "on the pretext" that there are prostitutes in the city, as well as men whom they have infected with syphilis.[72] In the same entry, he writes: "Physical immorality can now be seen in those in whom one would never have expected it."⁷³ Here he is very likely alluding to prostitution. Bogharian, for his part, writes more openly about this subject and notes the existence of female Armenian prostitutes in the Hama-Homs-Salamiyya region.⁷⁴

Of course, the phenomenon was not limited to this zone but it had become widespread among Armenian deportees in Bilad al-Sham.⁷⁵ Consequently, there is a convincing case that Der Nerses was well aware of the situation but confined himself to making reserved allusions to it in his diary or engaging in general analyses of immorality. In addition, the priest from Ayntab was a helpless witness to the decline of family mores in the extreme conditions of the deportation: relatives had sex with each other; parents sold their own children or encouraged them to prostitute themselves. Although our two diarists never allude to any of this, such phenomena are mentioned repeatedly in various eyewitness accounts of life in Bilad al-Sham. It seems unlikely that the Salamiyya-Hama area constituted an exception in this regard.⁷⁶

For Der Nerses, meanwhile, the "immoral" also included the sycophants, swindlers, thieves, and egotists among the Armenian deportees. In these people the ethos of mutual assistance had completely died; their mean-spirited actions made the harsh conditions in which impoverished, helpless deportees were forced to live even harsher. Bitterly, the priest observes that "lying, swindling, purse-snatching and robbery, pretending that goods weigh more or less than they in fact do—all this is common and is considered to be simple alertness."⁷⁷ He then lists living examples: "Among the Armenians who sell flour, some mix salt in with the flour, as well as cheap cereals of all kinds; some wet goods to make them heavier, and, on top of all this, some add dirt to them. A brother gives his brother dirt to eat and gets 5 or 6 piasters per *okha* for it."⁷⁸ The bitterness evinced here intensified when Der Nerses took up the *manusa*-maker's trade in Hama and had to make purchases from Armenian merchants from Marash and Ayntab who caused him to feel ill-treated and exploited. Aggrieved by a merchant from Marash, for example, he writes: "He was unwilling to perform even [a] small service for a priest who has taken it upon himself to earn his daily crust of bread by weaving cloth on a loom with his own two hands."⁷⁹

According to Der Nerses, these examples proved that the spirit of mutual assistance had disappeared from the community in the Hama-Salamiyya area. This was, at bottom, a consequence of the increasingly miserable conditions there, as was very clear to the priest from Ayntab. "The greatest misfortune is the fact that, the more people suffer, the less hope, faith, and charity they have."⁸⁰ Was it possible, in such an environment, for the deportees to reject the "Hobbesian social contract" and strive to remain true to themselves, to honor the social and moral rules that they professed, to avoid the compromises of principle that extreme conditions imposed on them? Der Nerses has a characteristic answer to these questions: "For a people that numbers in the tens of thousands and is living, like this one, in an Evil Empire, there is a handful of individuals among the Armenians—perhaps ten—who shine like stars of the first magnitude,—stars that, with all their moral strength, earn and give and help others as they should."[81] These lines recall Levi, who writes that only a very few people managed to survive without sacrificing part of their moral code. He calls people of this sort superior individuals, embodiments of the martyr and the saint.[82] Todorov, for his part, observes that in the world of the camps, according to the witness of the survivors themselves, acts of heroism or saintliness were few and far between.[83] Let us once again give the floor to Der Nerses, who, in the environment in which he lived, which had "become bestial" and "immoral," points to the existence of heroes and describes his own vision of them: "Heroes, perfect believers, too, are always to be found among those who are dying of starvation, people who courageously battle all sorts of difficulties and, in the end, commend their souls to God, triumphing spiritually, even if they are physically defeated."[84]

What conclusions can we draw? For the priest from Ayntab, the hero—the antithesis of the Hobbesian hero—was an individual who worked honestly to earn a living, lived in a spirit of devotion and self-sacrifice, was ready to help others, was free of sexual aberrations, displayed exemplary conduct, did not fornicate, and remained true to his Christian faith.

Was Der Nerses himself not one of the people who corresponded to this type? Was he himself not one of the little group of "perhaps ten" superior people? All these traits were in fact united in his person in the first years of exile, even when conditions were at their most extreme. Yet the inclination is to classify the priest from Ayntab instead as a Hobbesian man, that is, one of the great many who were prepared to make various concessions in the interests of surviving, and to commit acts of the kind they would have shunned under normal conditions. To be sure, no such "aberrations" appear in clear-cut form in Der Nerses's diaries, and it is not possible to liken him to the negative types painted in such somber colors. At the same time, however, it seems there are no clear definitions of the "Hobbesian social contract" and no fixed rules underlying it: it is, rather, a behavioral style, or a modification of a former behavioral style, that is widely adopted in extreme conditions. Some can, of course, take illicit advantage of it by radicalizing the behavioral modification and, in this new environment, acquiring the profile of the profoundly cynical. In his diary, Der Nerses devotes a great deal of space to describing and condemning such people. Alongside such depictions, the priest's everyday jottings feature moments in which his conduct as a deportee veers noticeably toward that of the Hobbesian hero. More specifically, he commits acts he never would have undertaken in normal life, and they are sufficient to justify the conclusion that in extreme conditions, Der Nerses, too, was inevitably confronted with the necessity of adapting to the situation.

Questions of this sort arise upon re-examination of, for example, the conditions surrounding the death of Der Nerses's brother Hagop. Der Nerses makes clear that in this period, Hagop had no work, and his family, with no source of income, was surviving on the aid provided by Der Nerses. In the two months preceding Hagop's death, the priest from Ayntab gave them a total of two Ottoman pounds. This can certainly be regarded as an act of fraternal devotion, yet it could not do much to alter the family's ongoing decline. It was a family of six, and in the general conditions of this period, an eight-member family needed a minimum of upwards of seven Ottoman pounds a month for its basic diet alone (as is pointed out in chapter 3) to say nothing of rent, medical costs, and so on. Could Der Nerses have come up with this sum or provided the family with food? It is of course difficult to answer this question. However, months after Hagop's death, his brother discussed this question in a letter to his fellow clergyman Karekin Bogharian, who was then living in Salamiyya. "Since coming to Hama," Der Nerses declares, "what has tormented me the most has been wanting to help and not being able to. I even involuntarily slackened in my duty toward my brother."[85] Here the confession or heartache is not just about the insufficiency of the help the priest offered his brother, but also about the fact that he was powerless to do the "more" required. Providing his brother with additional help would presumably have meant endangering his own family's already extremely vulnerable financial equilibrium and food supply, and thus hastening their own decline. It appears that Der Nerses made the difficult choice of trying to save at least his own family.

The problem of making principled choices recurs when the figure of Sahag Efendi Aramian crops up in Der Nerses's diary. This name first appears on 18 October 1917, at a time when Der Nerses had traveled from Salamiyya to Hama to buy things needed to pursue the weaver's trade in Salamiyya. He had suffered one setback after another as a weaver and was deeply discouraged. On the date mentioned, the priest met with his townsman Kevork Efendi Nalbandian, who, as described earlier, enjoyed a good relationship with the local authorities and a relatively enviable situation. Kevork Efendi suggested that Der Nerses settle with his family in Hama and work there. Der Nerses replied that he lacked the money to pay for a move of that kind. Kevork Efendi thereupon invited him to dine with his family that evening. A number of well-off deportees were also present at the dinner, including Sahag Efendi Aramian,[86] a deportee from Antioch. When Aramian learned of Der Nerses's predicament, he immediately made him a present of five Ottoman pounds to cover the costs of the priest's move to Hama.[87] Less than one month later, Sahag Efendi displayed the same generosity and devotion, giving the priest, who was on the verge of dire poverty, another three Ottoman pounds and twenty *lider*s (around 50 kg) of wheat and flour,[88] worth more than three Ottoman pounds at the going rate.

In Hama, Der Nerses and his family endured an extremely somber period. All their arduous efforts to earn income by working ended in failure: "we had had no food in the house for four or five days, and I was in very low spirits."[89] "Divine grace," however, intervened once again. Late in December 1917, Der Nerses encountered Sahag Efendi in the street. This time, Sahag Efendi gave him two French gold pounds and had twenty *lider*s of flour sent to the priest's house that very day. "We couldn't have hoped for a greater blessing," the grateful priest writes. "It seems that God has specially inspired this man to help me in the last few months, and, when I am in narrow straits, he turns up and takes me by the hand. In all my years as a priest and in exile, I had not seen a single rich man as benevolent as he is."[90] "They say that this man," he goes on, "has extended a helping hand to many others on the way down by giving them large sums of this kind."[91] And his diary entry for 1 January 1918 clearly shows the crucial importance of the assistance that Der Nerses and his family received from their benefactor and fellow Armenian from Antioch at this critical moment in their lives. Der Nerses writes that without Sahag Efendi's help, he and his family "would have been terribly weakened, materially speaking, and utter poverty would have been [their] lot."[92]

It might naturally be supposed that, at last, one of the rare stars shining in the firmament of the "Evil Empire" or one of the "heroes" swimming against the current of "immorality" had appeared in the pages of Der Nerses's diary. But this, too, would be mistaken. Sahag Efendi Aramian was an Armenian who, to ease the extreme conditions of his exile, renounced his faith and converted to Islam, changing his name to Muchhad.[93] Kevork Efendi Nalbandian, who had shown the priest from Ayntab such great sympathy and friendship, had likewise gone over to Islam and had taken the name Jemil.[94] In his diary, Der Nerses is unsparing of Armenians in this category. He severely berates deportees who neglect their "moral and spiritual needs," singling out apostate Armenians for special reprobation.[95] For him, "of all human feelings, the best and most noble" are moral and spiritual values, and he considers "extinguishing and doing away with this component" of existence "the greatest of all ruins."[96] And the person who had presented himself to Der Nerses and extended him a helping hand was, however noble his intentions, the Islamicized Muchhad—someone who symbolized human "ruin" of this kind.

At the same time, however, Der Nerses had sunk into economic misery and was powerless to provide for his family with his earnings. Starvation and decline seemed inevitable for them all. In this situation, it is not likely that the priest from Ayntab hesitated for long. In those agonizing times, he accepted the convert's gift and, in the following weeks, continued to repeat—to adopt his perspective—that "sinful" act. By taking this step, Der Nerses manifestly compromised one of his principles, himself becoming a Hobbesian figure. He appears to have been aware of this contradictory reality when he wrote about his honest friend: "Now I believe more than ever that, if God wants, he can bring forth children for Abraham from stones."[97]

Notes

1. Dadrian, *To the Desert*, pp. 139–140.
2. Tavukjian, *Diary*, p. 139.
3. Ibid., p. 139.
4. Ibid., pp. 154–155. Two other groups following this one were made up of 95 and 75 Armenians, respectively; ibid., pp. 156, 158.
5. Ibid., p. 153.
6. Archbishop Malachia Ormanian, *Khohk yev khosk* [Reflections and remarks] (Jerusalem: St. James, 1929), pp. 353–354; Manase Sevagian, "Tamasgos yev Hayere kaghakin angumen arach" [Damascus and the Armenians before the fall of the city], in *Arev* 4, no. 79 (13 November 1918); A. N. Genjian, "Hayere Tamasgosi mech (Azadakrumen arach yev yedke)" [The Armenians in Damascus before and after liberation], in *Yeridasart Hayasdan*, n.d. [1919]; Chlingirian, "Descriptions of Jerusalem-Aleppo-Damascus," pp. 41–42; Aram Sahagian, "Tamasgosen-Akaba (Husher Medz Yegherni oreren)" [From Damascus to Akaba (Memoirs from the days of the Great Crime)], *Hayrenik Monthly* 28, no. 2 (289) (February 1950): 73–74.
7. Dadrian, *To the Desert*, pp. 237–240.
8. Bogharian, "Diary," p. 151.
9. Ibid., p. 154.
10. Ibid., p. 181.
11. Ibid., p. 184.
12. Tavukjian, *Diary*, p. 100.
13. Tavukjian, "Ms. Diary," p. 89.

14. Der Nerses uses the word սէլէմէքի [selemeki], no doubt a corruption of *sinameki*, the Turkish name of the cassia plant whose leaves senna is produced. Senna was used as a laxative.
15. Tavukjian, "Ms. Diary," p. 89.
16. Ibid., p. 98.
17. Ibid., pp. 99–100.
18. Ibid., p. 99.
19. Ibid.
20. Ibid.
21. Ibid.
22. Ibid. "Two o'clock" here is two o'clock on the Turkish system of keeping time, six hours ahead of the European system, by which the time of Shoghagat's death would have been around eight in the evening.
23. Ibid.
24. Ibid., p. 100.
25. Dadrian, *To the Desert*, pp. 116–220.
26. Ibid., p. 134; Tavukjian, *Diary*, p. 161.
27. Tavukjian, *Diary*, pp. 139–140.
28. Tavukjian, "Ms. Diary," p. 133.
29. Tavukjian, *Diary*, p. 140.
30. Ibid.
31. Der Nerses uses both the Armenian and Turkish (*lahana*) words for cabbage and the Turkish word for leek (*prasa*).
32. Tavukjian, "Ms. Diary," p. 133.
33. Ibid.
34. Ibid., p. 134.
35. Ibid., pp. 133–134.
36. Tavukjian, *Diary*, pp. 159, 161.
37. Tavukjian, "Ms. Diary," p. 134.
38. Tavukjian, *Diary*, p. 103.
39. Tavukjian, *Diary*, p. 75.
40. Ibid., p. 83.
41. Garbarini, *Numbered Days*, p. 155.
42. Ibid., pp. 154–155.
43. ACC, Letter no. 4980/86 from Sahag II to Patriarch Zaven.
44. ACC, Letter no. 4980/86 from Sahag II to Patriarch Zaven, 19 July 1915, Aleppo, ff 309–310.
45. Archbishop Zaven, *Badrarkagan hushers, vaverakirner yev vgayutyunner* [Memoirs of a patriarch, documents and testimonials] (Cairo: Nor Asdegh, 1947), p. 179.
46. Frederic D. Homer, *Primo Levi and the Politics of Survival* (Columbia: University of Missouri Press, 2001), p. 103.
47. Ibid., p. 105.
48. Chalamov, *Récits de la Kolyma*, pp. 11–12.
49. Des Pres, *The Survivor*, p. 88.
50. Levi, *If This Is a Man*, p. 103.
51. Ibid.
52. Tavukjian, *Diary*, p. 143.
53. Ibid.
54. Tavukjian, "Ms. Diary," p. 128.

55. Ibid., p. 130.
56. Tavukjian, *Diary*, p. 148.
57. Ibid., p, 149.
58. Ibid.
59. Ibid.
60. Ibid.
61. Tavukjian, "Ms. Diary," p. 137.
62. Ibid.
63. Bruno Bettelheim, *Surviving the Holocaust* (London: Fontana, 1986), p. 98.
64. Levi, *If This Is a Man*, p. 101.
65. Ibid., pp. 105–106.
66. Ibid., p. 106.
67. Homer, *Primo Levi*, pp. 103–104.
68. Tavukjian, *Diary*, p. 137.
69. Ibid., pp. 151–152.
70. Todorov, *Facing the Extreme*, p. 39.
71. Tavukjian, "Ms. Diary," p. 135.
72. Tavukjian, *Diary*, p. 137.
73. Ibid.
74. Bogharian, "Diary," pp. 173, 175, 195.
75. See Vahé Tachjian, "Gender, Nationalism, Exclusion: The Reintegration Process of Female Survivors of the Armenian Genocide," *Nations and Nationalism* 15, no. 1 (2009): 60–80; idem, "Mixed Marriage, Prostitution, Survival: Reintegrating Armenian Women into Post-Ottoman Cities," in Nazan Maksudyan, ed., *Women and the City, Women in the City: A Gendered Perspective to Ottoman Urban History* (New York and Oxford: Berghahn Books, 2014), pp. 86–106.
76. ACC, Correspondence no. 50, Letter from Father Vahan Gyuldalian to Catholicos Sahag II (Jerusalem), 15 June 1919, Ayntab; ACC, Correspondence no. 50, Letter no. 10, from Father Nerses Tavukjian (on behalf of Ayntab's religious assembly) to Catholicos Sahag II (Jerusalem), 1919, Ayntab.
77. Tavukjian, *Diary*, p. 137.
78. Ibid.
79. Ibid. p. 147.
80. Ibid., p. 139.
81. Ibid., p. 152.
82. Levi, *If This Is a Man*, p. 106.
83. Todorov, *Facing the Extreme*, p. 54.
84. Tavukjian, *Diary*, p. 152.
85. Haigazian University Library Archives, "Krikor Bogharian's Archives," Letter from Father Der Nerses Tavukjian to Father Der Karekin Bogharian, 15 September 1915, Hama.
86. Der Nerses calls Aramian "Sahag Efendi Sahagian" in his 18 October diary entry.
87. Tavukjian, *Diary*, p 141.
88. Ibid.
89. Ibid., p. 147.
90. Ibid.
91. Ibid.

92. Tavukjian, "Ms. Diary," p. 130.
93. Tavukjian, *Diary*, p. 141.
94. Ibid., p. 148.
95. Tavukjian, "Ms. Diary," p. 125.
96. Ibid.
97. Tavukjian, *Diary*, p. 148.

Selected Bibliography

Published Material

Bettelheim, Bruno. *Surviving the Holocaust*. London, 1986.
Bogharian, Krikor. Ցեղասպան Թուրքը, վկայութիւններ բաղուած՝ հրաշքով փրկուածներու զրոյցներէն [Tseghasban Turke. Vgayutyunner kaghvadz hrashkov prgvadzneru zruytsneren] [The genocidal Turk: Eyewitness accounts from the narratives of people who were miraculously saved]. Beirut, 1973.
Bogharian, Krikor, ed. Այնթապականք / *Ayntabiana*, vol. 2. Մահարձան: մահազրութիւններ, դամբանականներ եւ կենսագրական նօթեր [Funeral monument: Necrologies, funeral orations and biographical notes]. Beirut, 1974.
Chalamov, Varlam. *Récits de la Kolyma*, trans. Sophie Benech, Catherine Fournier, and Luba Jurgenson. Lagrasse, 2006.
Chilingirian, Bishop Yeghishe. Նկարագրութիւնք Երուսաղէմի-Հալէպի-Դամասկոսի Գաղթականական եւ Վանական Զանազան Դիպաց եւ Անցքերու, 1914–1918 [Ngarakrutyunk Yerusaghemi-Halebi-Tamaskosi Kaghtaganagan yev Vanagan Zanazan Tibats yev antskeru] [Descriptions of refugee-related and monastical events and developments in Jerusalem, Aleppo, and Damascus]. Jerusalem, 1927.
Dadrian, Vahram. *To the Desert: Pages from my Diary*, trans. Agop Hacikyan. London, 2006.
Des Pres, Terrence. *The Survivor: An Anatomy of Life in the Death Camps*. New York, 1976.
Garbarini, Alexandra. *Numbered Days: Diaries and the Holocaust*. Ann Arbor, 2006.
Genjian, A. N. "Հայերը Դամասկոսի մէջ (Ազատագրումէն առաջ եւ ետքը)" [Hayere Tamasgosi mech (Azadakrumen arach yev yedke)] [The Armenians in Damascus before and after liberation], *Yeridasart Hayasdan* (1919).
Homer, Frederic D. *Primo Levi and the Politics of Survival*. Columbia, MO, 2001.
Levi, Primo. *If This Is a Man*, trans. Stuart Woolf. New York, 1959.
Ormanian, Archbishop Malachia. Խոհք եւ խօսք [Khohk yev khosk] [Reflections and remarks]. Jerusalem, 1929.
Sahagian, Aram. "Դամասկոսէն-Ագապա (Յուշեր Մեծ Եղեռնի օրերէն)" [Tamasgosen-Akaba (Husher Medz Yegherni oreren)] [From Damascus to Akaba (Memoirs from the days of the Great Crime)], *Hayrenik Monthly*, 28, no. 2 (289) (February 1950): 73–84.
Sevagian, Manase. "Դամասկոս եւ Հայերը քաղաքին անկումէն ետք" [Tamasgos yev Hayere kaghakin angumen yedk] [Damascus and the Armenians after the fall of the city], *Arev* 4, no. 79 (13 November 1918).

Tachjian, Vahé. "Gender, Nationalism, Exclusion: The Reintegration Process of Female Survivors of the Armenian Genocide," *Nations and Nationalism* 15, no. 1 (2009): 60–80.

Tavukjian, Father Nerses. Տառապանքի օրագրութիւն [Darabanki orakrutyun] [Diary of days of suffering]. Beirut, 1991.

Tavukjian, Father Nerses. "Օրագրութեան Մեքենագրուած Բնագիր" [Orakrutyan mekenakrvadz pnakir] [Typescript of the diary] (Ms. Diary).

Todorov, Tzvetan. *Facing the Extreme: Moral Life in the Concentration Camps*, trans. Arthur Denner and Abigail Pollack. London, 1999.

Zaven, Archbishop. Պատրիարքական յուշերս. վաւերագիրներ եւ վկայութիւններ [Badriarkagan hushers, vaverakirner yev vgayutyunner] [Memoirs of a patriarch, documents and testimonials]. Cairo, 1947.

Primary Sources

ACC: Archives of the Cilician Catholicosate
Haigazian University Library archives

Chapter 5

From Forced Islamization to Emancipation

Two Historical Episodes and Their Contradictions

Islamization of the Armenians Deported to Bilad al-Sham

In the extreme conditions that prevailed in Bilad al-Sham, one of the most shocking dimensions of the "Hobbesian social contract" was, without a doubt, the deportees' collective Islamization. More than any other, this event shows how abnormal the deportees' environment had become. The endangered, impoverished, and in many respects now unrecognizable Armenians were summoned to make a concession fraught with consequences. There are essentially no individual studies of this subject, and Islamization is rarely mentioned in Armenian eyewitness accounts, whose authors, generally speaking, only briefly allude to collective conversions. Nonetheless, a handful of exceptional authors have deemed this theme deserving of more detailed and more comprehensive description and analysis. Der Nerses and Bogharian are two examples, as both men's diaries contain a great deal of information on the subject.

In fact, in the modern Ottoman context, the Armenians' forced conversion was not seen as an unusual event. Such conversions were a widespread phenomenon during the anti-Armenian massacres that took place in 1895–1896 under Sultan Abdülhamid II.[1] Accordingly, Islamization of the sort imposed on the Armenian deportees in Bilad al-Sham was for many people a part of their local histories; they had heard about, seen, or in some cases themselves experienced it. In the past, however, Islamization had tended to involve isolated village communities. During

World War I, it embraced nearly the whole community concentrated in Bilad al-Sham. In that sense, it was unprecedented.

The following discussion of this subject will be based primarily on survivors' eyewitness accounts. The aim is to reconstitute this episode and arrive at an understanding of its multiple facets. Armenian deportees' narratives on the subject roughly concur in their chronologies, which justifies the assumption that Islamization had an organized character, that it concerned all the deported Armenians grouped together in Bilad al-Sham, and that this disposition or decision was put into practice in coordinated fashion. Meanwhile, various survivors' memoirs confirm that many Armenians were Islamicized in regions beyond the zone under the Fourth Army's command as well. Generally speaking, these were individual acts; however, episodes of collective Islamization in such areas have also been documented. They were carried out in a manner distinct from that of the Islamization typical of Bilad al-Sham.[2] Whether Islamization took place in Hama, Salamiyya, Jarash, Damascus, Salt, or Amman, it involved a broadly uniform ritual, which prompts the supposition that Islamization was pre-programmed in Bilad al-Sham and accomplished in the same period in all towns in the area in. What might this act of collective Islamization have meant for the authorities? Fuad Dündar, whose work is largely based on Ottoman state archives, very clearly points out that the central authorities had such great reservations about Armenian conversions that Talaat Pasha issued a circular warning Ottoman governors about Armenians' "sham" apostasy.[3] Presumably, then, the events in Bilad al-Sham were once again due to the initiative of the leaders of the Fourth Army and its supreme commander, Jemal Pasha. If so, the question again becomes what motivated Jemal Pasha to take the steps that he did. Was it a desire to reinforce his defense of the Armenians under his protection in the face of the central authorities' genocidal intentions?

According to Yervant Odian, the suggestion that the Armenians in Hama convert came from the local *mutasarrıf*, Khairi Feruzan, a "very good, noble and enlightened man, who had the affection of both Arabs and Armenians."[4] The *mutasarrıf* summoned Artin Nersesian, a leading member of the Adana Armenian community, and through him requested that all Adana Armenians living in Hama go over to Islam so that he could continue to protect them: "The *mutesarif* said that, if we didn't accept Islam, he wouldn't be able to protect us and that we'd probably all suffer very badly."[5] Odian considers the *mutasarrıf*'s concern justified, the more so as it was later learned that he took this step in the days when mass killings of Armenians were taking place in Der Zor.[6] We find exactly the same explanation in Vahram Dadrian, who noted the way the Armenian notables in Jarash interpreted the conversion issue: in their view, "this is a great favor that Jemal Pasha is doing the Armenians." That is, even as the Armenians in Der Zor were being wiped out, the Armenian notables were convinced that the deportees' Islamization would enable the commander of the Fourth Army to prevent a repetition of the mass slaughter in, this time, the Bilad al-Sham region.[7] After all, it was Jemal Pasha who, reacting to Catholicos Sahag II's protests over the wave of conversions to Islam, received his emissary, Bishop Kyud, in October 1917 and told him: "I look at the problem from a humanitarian standpoint. Stop hounding this poor people. So that it can survive to the end of the war, let it be Islamic if it wants, or Jewish, or giavur, or a monkey. Let it even be an ass, if it wants. It's enough that it survive. Go tell your Catholicos what I said."[8]

One may, however, also speculate that the conversions reflected a long-range intention to transform the deported Armenians in Bilad al-Sham into an element loyal to the Ottoman authorities. In the minds of people such as Jemal Pasha, Armenians' Islamization, deportation from their natural habitat, and resettlement in a strange environment were probably basic conditions for further reinforcing the bond between these Armenians and the local imperial authorities, while simultaneously increasing their dependency on their Ottoman "protectors."

The Diarist Becomes a Clerk in the Conversion Office

Of all the known sources, Der Nerses's and Bogharian's diaries provide the fullest picture, relatively speaking, of this important Islamization episode. They show the evolution of the attitude of the deported Armenian community in Hama and Salamiyya in this regard. In the very first weeks in which the Ayntab Armenians were transported to Salamiyya, Der Nerses reflected on the deportees' gradual estrangement from spiritual life. In the first days of their exile, Sunday services were held in the Aposhian family's house;[9] a few weeks later, however, the Aposhians refused to receive the faithful.[10] Weeks went by without any church services at all: "Holidays and feast days have become just like ordinary days of the week," Bogharian writes, unhappy about what he sees.[11] Der Nerses was more pessimistic, for he took this neglect of religion as evidence of a general decline: "Wretched nation: it has been exposed to the severest of catastrophes, the absence of the Word of Life; but the greatest misfortune is the fact that the people feels no pain over this. Indifference is the order of the day; no one feels that something is missing."[12] It later proved possible to rent a room and begin holding services again. Nevertheless, as Bogharian remarks on 3 April 1916, "the number of those who go to church and take part in the service has diminished appreciably."[13]

Was this a consequence of extreme conditions? Caution on the part of the endangered deportees? A retreat of faith, a retreat from God? In any case, the available information is insufficient to explain the Salamiyya Armenians' gradually increasing indifference to religion or estrangement from it. What is known is that Der Nerses, a priest, was dissatisfied with his flock and especially the Ayntab Armenian notables, and that he was also disappointed when they took the first steps toward conversion. The first reports of this to reach Salamiyya indicated that around mid June, the *mutasarrıf* of Hama had suggested to the deported Adana Armenians that they convert.[14] Only a few days later, the Armenians in Salamiyya learned the names of the Islamicized Armenians living in the neighboring town.[15]

Odian, who was in Hama at the time, provides an excellent account of these events. After the *mutasarrıf* had made his suggestion, the Adana Armenian notables deliberated and decided to reject it.[16] Feruzan Bey thereupon summoned the Armenian notables a second time and exhorted them to agree to convert. The deportees in Hama continued to deliberate. At the same time, reports arriving from Homs and Damascus indicated that mass Islamization of the Armenians was already underway in those cities. Apparently the main concern in Hama was the prospect of mixed marriages: many Armenian families were convinced that if they converted, they would have to give their daughters in marriage to Muslims. While the arguments pro and con were raging, one of the Ittihad's leaders in Damascus, Ali Kemal Bey, arrived in Hama, obviously intending to speed up the Islamization process.[17] He began by arresting the chief personalities opposed to Islamization. Then, rumors that every Armenian opposed to conversion would be driven into the Syrian desert started making the rounds. The threat had an immediate effect, and it was in this atmosphere that the mass Islamization of Hama's Armenians began.[18] In December 1916 Ali Kemal Bey traveled to Salamiyya with the mission of preparing a report on the number of Armenians living there and their occupations.[19]

Salamiyya's Armenians were of course aware of what was going on in Hama. Thus they were not surprised when, on 27 June, Hama's *kaymakam* received a telegram from the *mutasarrıf* demanding that the priests in Salamiyya be sent without delay to Hama; from there, they were sent on to exile in Jerusalem. In a word, the groundwork for mass Islamization was being laid here as well. It was under these circumstances that Der Nerses and Krikor Bogharian's father, Der Karekin, left for Hama.[20] All the Armenian priests from the neighboring villages also arrived in the city at this time, having also received deportation orders.[21] All these clergymen were sent to the village of Buseyra, located in the *nahiye* of Tafile in the Kerek *sanjak* (today in Jordan). In all, some twenty clergymen were deported, mostly Apostolic priests with a few Protestant ministers. They were all put in a barn.[22]

In the next weeks, officials charged with monitoring and supervising the Islamization process were sent to Salamiyya, as they had been to Hama. Thereafter, deportees from the surrounding villages began to stream into Salamiyya with the intention of accepting Islam. There seem to have been two motivations in this race to convert. First, the deportees were terrified by threats the authorities circulated to convey that those who did not comply with the Islamization decision would be sent elsewhere. Second, throughout that period, the local authorities continued to distribute state assistance to Armenians in Salamiyya and the surrounding villages, and the deportees were persuaded that those who refused to convert would no longer receive state aid.[23] Similar developments were observed in Jarash and the area around it. After a number of people were arrested there in October 1916, a five-man ad hoc committee made up of the mufti of Erbid, one Armenian, two state officials, and a policeman arrived in Jarash. Their first act there was to summon the Armenian notables who had settled in Jarash to a meeting at which they informed them of the decision about Islamization.[24] Krikor Kudulian indicates that a committee of the same sort, headed by the *kadı* of Kerek, arrived in Salt in September 1916. Kudulian notes that the deported Armenians in the Hauran and Kerek-Ma'an were Islamicized in the same weeks.[25] The deportees in Damascus were likewise converted to Islam under duress. According to Antranig Genjian's eyewitness account, they faced a clear-cut choice: go over to Islam or be driven into the desert.[26]

Together, these events show that the organized Islamization of Armenian deportees in Bilad al-Sham took place smoothly and encountered no noteworthy obstacles. Militating in favor of this, probably, was the local authorities' effort to publicize the operation as little as possible in their area and to provide no occasion for acts that might humiliate the apostates. In such an atmosphere, the dominant idea among the Armenians was that the process was a mere formality and that they could return to their original faith after conditions had gone back to normal. In an extreme situation, however, it seems likely that the prevailing feeling about conversion, among the majority of those living lives of agony, was indifference. This pressure to convert might have elicited a completely different reaction under ordinary circumstances. The daily life of the deportees in Bilad al-Sham, however, was completely extraordinary. It was a race against time to solve vital problems such as, to begin with, obtaining food or battling disease. Moreover, it was necessary to prevent the authorities from making certain decisions that could break the momentum of their struggle for survival, confront them with new problems, or accelerate their decline. In this sense, the deportee, or in this case the community of deportees, was prepared to negotiate with the ruling side and make reciprocal concessions on fundamental questions in hope of finding some middle ground. In a word, the deportees' main strategy was to play for time, so they were prepared to accept suggestions heavy with consequences that could, with the passing years, alter their identity. Staying alive for months and years in extreme conditions calls for knowledge of the art of survival, which frequently entails compliance with merciless laws dictating compromise with one's principles. After all, for people who find themselves in this abnormal environment, past and future are concepts devoid of meaning or even completely absent from day-to-day existence. In his eyewitness account of the Soviet Gulag, Varlam Shalamov writes that for an inmate of the camps, "real were the minute, the hour, the day—from reveille to the end of work. He never guessed further, nor did he have the strength to guess. Nor did anyone else."[27]

Of course, there was an alternative to this situation: resistance, which in such conditions often led to death. One Armenian survivor successfully explains his abnormal mode of life—his Hobbesian behavior, throughout the years of the genocide, when he often stifled his elementary need to resist, bowed to necessity, and survived—in simple language: "It is by surviving that you will triumph," he writes. "Either life or death," he goes on; "choose life."[28] Evidently, the deported Armenian community's position on conversion was no different. Of course, acts of resistance have been documented as well, in the present case. One of those who resisted was Krikor Sarafian, an intellectual from Ayntab who had received his higher education at Yale University in the United States and was teaching at Ayntab's Cilician High School when the deportations began. Rather than convert, he fled Salamiyya. He had no family and was thus exempt from worries about obtaining daily bread for relatives, a circumstance that surely did much to shape his decision. Nevertheless, Sarafian remained a fugitive and, in the eyes of the law, a criminal who had not complied with a decision of the authorities. Initially, he remained in the Hama region, but he later turned up in Damascus, where he was arrested in 1918. He managed to flee once again, taking refuge in Zahle. The end of the war saved him from this irregular mode of life, whereupon he found his way back to Hama.²⁹ Likewise resistant to the conversion plan were Der Nerses and Der Karekin, who, despite the trying conditions they faced after being exiled again, remained true to their Christian faith, whereas other priests who had been banished with them ultimately accepted Islam. However heroic this act of resistance on the two priests' part, one must also take into consideration the basic fact that the authorities did not directly demand that exiled clergyman go over to Islam. The priests were simply separated from their flocks to make it possible to carry out the deported Armenians' conversion smoothly. Moreover, once this process was complete, the priests and Protestant ministers were allowed to join their families again. Kudulian mentions the case of a less fortunate priest, Der Vartan from Kars Bazar (present-day Kadirli). Exiled to Salt, this clergyman refused outright to convert to Islam and was consequently subjected to a public beating by the commander of the gendarmerie, Bedri Bey, as a result of which he died. Another priest, Der Bedros Aprahamian from Karaduran, who was also living in Salt, was given more than three hundred blows with a cane and imprisoned for weeks.³⁰

Another interesting example in this connection is that of some Armenian women who had been deported from their native Samson to Hama. Yervant Odian tells their story in his memoirs. They were the only remaining survivors in their families, as their husbands and adult children had been killed during their deportation. These women considered conversion unacceptable and said often that their husbands had made the supreme sacrifice so that those who survived would not abandon their faith. The resistance these women put up was apparently the only obstacle standing in the way of the authorities' efforts to convert the Hama Armenians. Odian writes that the Ittihad's Damascus delegate, Ali Kemal Bey, sent representatives to the deportees three times a day to inquire whether the women from Samson had changed their minds, and to threaten to send them to the desert when the answer was negative. By the time these events took place, the absolute majority of the deportees in Hama had already accepted the idea of conversion, so the women were under pressure, not just from the authorities' threats but from the other deportees as well, who tried daily to convince them to accept the authorities' proposal. In this situation, the women from Samson ultimately gave in and converted to Islam.³¹

These examples once again show how in various villages and towns in Bilad al-Sham, the local authorities successfully implemented this crucial decision by utilizing the compatriotic and community structures that had been maintained among the deported Armenians. The authorities basically dealt with the Armenian community leaders: it was with these notables that they negotiated, it was from their ranks that they singled out and ejected those they thought likely to resist, and it was these men, again, whom they exhorted to convert to Islam. In sum, once the authorities won the notables over to the idea of Islamization, they had succeeded in their mission. Thereafter, these community representatives would simply play the role of intermediaries. In a sense, they were delegated by the authorities to represent them to the mass of deportees.

The rest, that is, the act of accepting Islam, was nothing more than a series of formalities that, again, unfolded in almost exactly the same way throughout Bilad al-Sham. Moreover, local Muslim populations generally reacted to it in the same way. Yervant Odian's case was typical. Odian and two friends presented themselves to Hama's *mutasarrıf* and announced that they were prepared to convert. An official was summoned immediately and led them to the department that was to draw up their new *nufus teskeresi* (identity papers). Here they were asked what Islamic forenames they wished to be given. Odian took the name Aziz Nuri, and his two friends became Ali Feruzan and Khiusrev. All three were given the surname Abdullah and the second surname Udullah, like all other Armenian converts. "The whole task took less than an hour. The change of name was just that and nothing else," Odian writes.[32] The Armenian writer from Istanbul was one of the first to be Islamicized in Hama. Later, after Islamization became a mass phenomenon among the Armenians in that city, Ittihad's party headquarters became the stage for the conversion process. There, officials prepared the application/request forms that were given to every deported Armenian who appeared. The deportees wrote their names on these forms with their new Muslim names alongside them, and signed. In return, each was assigned a number that would later be presented in order to receive the new identity papers.[33]

Bogharian, for his part, gives fairly detailed descriptions of the conversion process in Salamiyya, which is hardly surprising, given that he worked as a clerk in the conversion office. According to the young diarist, there were two ways of accepting Islam. In the first, the male head of a family appeared personally before the local *kadı* and, on behalf of his family, recited the *šahāda*, the Islamic credo. Then he would submit the new Islamic names he and the other members of his family had chosen for themselves. The second way of converting was much simpler and involved less public display. The head of a household would go to the conversion office with a list of the old names and, beside them, the new Islamic names of all the family members, and then the clerks in the conversion office would copy these names into a single general register, thus making the family's Islamization official. The Bogharians opted for the second method. Since the head of the family had already been banished, Krikor Bogharian, as the oldest male child in the house, presented himself in person at the conversion office, where he was given the name Shehab and his mother was renamed Meriem.[34] Almost exactly the same scene was staged in Jarash: in the district mayor's office, the deportees resident in Jarash prepared a list of Armenians' names, each with a new Islamic name beside it. The register of names was then ratified by an ad hoc state committee that had come to the town to supervise the conversion process. After that, the local Armenians were considered to be Muslims.[35]

The local Muslim societies were the first to turn a skeptical eye on Armenians Islamicized in this fashion. On that subject, too, Odian's witty, often satirical sketches are noteworthy. Thus he remarks on how the local Arabs refused to greet Islamicized Armenians with the formula betokening Muslim identity, *al-salamu alaykum*; rather, they used the word *marhaba*,[36] a more neutral Arabic greeting that tends to be used between Muslims and Christians or Christians and other Christians. Odian also recounts how, when a number of Armenians tried to perfect their conversion by frequenting a mosque; the local Muslims refused to let them set foot in their places of worship. With the same motivation, other Armenians went to the *kadı* to request advice on circumcision. The answer was firm: "This isn't the right *mevsim* [season]." Other sheikhs dissuaded Armenian converts from circumcision by saying the ritual was not one of the main Islamic duties. After listing examples of this kind, Odian adds: "In the final analysis nobody seriously considered us to be Muslims."[37]

Figure 5.1. Krikor Bogharian (Source: AGBU, Nubarian Library, Paris)

Christianity: Second Skin or Mere "Costume"?

However true Odian's conclusion may be, it is safe to assume that in the long term, the apostate Armenians and their descendants would eventually have become accustomed to the new state of things and been gradually assimilated into local Muslim society. Der Nerses, who was an embittered and, at the same time, perspicacious eyewitness to the conversion phenomenon, remarks in one diary entry: "If, God forbid, this state of affairs should persist for even a few years, the [Christian] religious feeling that has already grown faint will simply die."[38] Basically, the apostate Armenians' real goals were to survive to the end of the war, be allowed to live under normal conditions, and return to their former social and religious situation. But at the same time they were also well aware that the decisive factor in the case of conversion, as in other questions too, was time and that sooner or later the harsh consequences of their change of religion would make themselves felt.

Conversion in the environment of Bilad al-Sham must be seen as a maneuver in the art of survival. But the longer the deportees were weighed down by severe hardship, the worse their condition could become, whereupon Islamization could have undesirable results. Islamicized Armenian families with young daughters were especially worried. On the one hand, conversion was a victory they had gained against time; on the other, it was a step fraught with risks that could deal a heavy blow to their conceptions of what was socially proper. "The first fruits of our conversion to Islam have begun to appear," Bogharian writes in this connection on 1 September 1916. "In the villages, some (Muslim) young men have sought to marry Armenian girls, now that they are of the same faith."[39] *Nikah* (Muslim marriage) between Armenian women and local Muslims was clearly many Armenian families' nightmare. In his memoirs about Damascus, Genjian even calls Islamization a "catastrophe" because of the boost it gave to forced marriages and abductions of Armenian girls.[40] In other words, the conditions defined by the Armenians' Islamization in Bilad al-Sham threatened to ride roughshod over Armenian's traditional opposition to mixed marriages between Muslims and Christians, a stance rooted in a context of centuries of Armenian co-existence with Muslims. (As a rule, the fundamental problem here was marriage between Muslim men and Armenian women.)

These realities notwithstanding, the authors of eyewitness accounts are inclined, overall, to downplay the importance of their Islamization and present it as a mere alteration, a formality, a matter that passed unperceived: such is the image they convey when depicting the act of conversion, generally speaking. There is doubtless a certain truth to these descriptions. Thus, after their Islamization in different places in Bilad al-Sham, deportees were observed leading the same collective existence as before, facing the same vital problems and health concerns and fighting the same battle against starvation and death without having undergone any particular shock. However, changes besides mixed marriages soon began to make themselves felt. For example, the deportees used their Christian names in communicating with each other, but in the outside world they were more cautious and used their Islamic names. Bogharian, for example, signed all his letters "Shehab" after converting, even stamping them with a newly designed stamp bearing that name.[41]

Motivated by the same prudence, there emerged a general desire to wipe out and banish every trace of the Christian faith. This is well attested by Der Nerses, who returned from exile to find his Armenian flock in Ayntab solidly converted to Islam. Like many other authors of survivors' accounts, Der Nerses had no need to justify himself because he had never renounced his faith. Meanwhile, his diary contains criticisms—usually merciless—of the Islamicized mass. His arrival in Salamiyya roughly coincided with the Easter holidays, but "there is neither church nor a church service," he comments bitterly on what he found there. "The people have opened their stores the way they do every other day." Months later in 1918, during the first week in January, when the Armenian Church celebrates Christmas, the priest similarly describes the people's indifference to the most important of the Armenian high holidays. While still in Ayntab, that city's Armenian community had been characterized by its fervent faith, but now it sought ostentatiously to exhibit, if not its Islamization, then at least its estrangement from Christianity.

> I didn't bless homes in the prescribed manner but, as I had announced, visited only those who wished me to. No more than eight or ten people invited me to their homes, and I went to see as many again among those with whom we have very close relations. Not one person came to see me, not even to extend holiday greetings. From the very first day, a few stores you could count on the fingers of one hand were, exceptionally, closed; all the others remained open for business as usual. People who think "it's Christmas," "it's Easter," are very rare exceptions indeed.[42]

Der Nerses deems people's explanations of their Islamization altogether incomprehensible:

> It's supposedly natural to be deprived of our religious needs. Either they regard this deprivation that way, as if someone had stripped a costume off them that those who survive will put back on some day—for the moment, that costume is regarded as harmful and has been taken off. In the final analysis, just as, in the fifth century [an allusion to the war the Armenian

general Vartan Mamigonian led against the Zoroastrians, supposedly in defense of Christianity], religion was a second skin for the people, was flesh, was something they could not change, now it is a costume."[43]

All this was unacceptable to Der Nerses. "This is regrettable."[44] "The feeling of veneration for God or of maintaining national and ecclesiastical tradition is over," he continues in another diary entry; "faith, hope, and charity have withered away."[45]

Der Nerses would perhaps have displayed a more tolerant attitude toward his Islamicized compatriots if he had known that in his absence, his family, too, had converted. Bogharian, establishes this, noting in his diary that he himself took the list of the names of the members of the exiled priest's family to the conversion office, where their Islamization was ratified along with their new names.[46] He leaves the impression, however, that after Der Nerses's return, his family and close friends concealed the facts from him. "Our wife held out a bit longer and didn't go hand in an application, and no one came looking for her afterward; this way, our family remained in the Christian faith."[47]

Even though most Islamicized Armenians kept a distance from their new religion, very few approached Der Nerses to request that he celebrate a baptism or Christian marriage for them. Upon receiving such requests, the priest from Ayntab at first refused them, objecting that because they came from people who "had renounced their faith" he "could not administer a mystery of the Christian religion" to them.[48] He was equally severe with fellow clergymen who undertook to perform such rituals for converts. This state of affairs of course made Der Nerses's and his family's economic situation worse: in the new, Islamicized environment, there was little demand for his services as a priest, which was precisely the situation that, as described earlier, led him to turn to other kinds of work. The priest's dire economic straits may partly explain why, some three months after returning from banishment, he tempered his attitude and began celebrating christenings and weddings for Islamicized Armenians himself.[49] There were no alternatives: the general situation closely corresponded to the conditions that Lawrence Langer has described as "choiceless choice."[50]

The Life-Saving Initiative of Krikor's Mother, Santukhd

The Armenians' collective Islamization was only a means of adapting to extreme conditions and prolonging survival. By no means can it be regarded as a way of guaranteeing access to sources of income. The

Bilad al-Sham Armenian deportees' overriding concern was to obtain their daily bread and save their families. Krikor Bogharian's mother Santukhd emerges as a distinctive figure at this critical stage of events.

She is one of the rare females whose actions are described in this book. This inevitably throws up the question of gender, given that the overwhelming majority of self-narration sources at our disposal were written by men. Santukhd's presence in this homogeneous environment—even though all the accounts of her are likewise the work of a man, her son—is a unique phenomenon, yet sufficient to warrant gender-based interpretations of the opposition or cooperation between men and women in this catastrophic situation. As this section will show, Santukhd, thanks to her flexibility in a period when her husband was absent, scored a number of decisive successes that helped ensure her family's survival. Can we, generalizing from her case, conclude that initiatives undertaken by women in extreme conditions were more effective, more productive, and less inhibited by various constraints? I know of no studies of this question of gender. One thing, however, is clear: Santukhd's intervention represented a turning point in the Bogharian family's struggle for survival in the Hama-Salamiyya region. Let us take a closer look at this micro-history.

It might supposed that there is no information about Bogharian in the last months of the war, since he ceased to keep a diary in 1917. Abstractly considered, this may be true, but it is also possible to examine the question from a different angle in search of certain answers about the period of interest to us. In reality, "liberation"—in the sense of simply meeting nutritional needs and thereby attaining general security—for Bogharian and his family came in the last months of 1916. This period seems to have been a turning point in the Bogharian family's life in exile, and one of the principal roles in this major shift was reserved for Santukhd Bogharian. It is important to attempt to reconstruct these months, for they are vital to understanding this family's success in the struggle to survive.

Father Karekin Bogharian was banished to Tafile in July 1916. His family of six remained behind in Salamiyya in an exceedingly difficult predicament: in the absence of the head of the family, they had no source of income. In this period, Krikor Bogharian began writing to compatriots of his from Ayntab living in other cities, asking them for assistance. But although such assistance was forthcoming, it was not enough to guarantee the family's long-term security. In these conditions Santukhd emerges as a figure in her own right. Up to this point, Krikor Bogharian's mother has basically been absent from his diary; now, suddenly, she emerges from the shadows to try to take leadership of the family into her own hands. The steps she took in the following weeks and months are worth pausing over.

To begin with, as we have already seen, Santukhd had made no special effort to resist Islamization: like her compatriots, she and her family had converted to Islam. She had taken the name Meriem. Later, Krikor Bogharian simply takes note of his mother's wish that her oldest child will find work and begin "earning money." Krikor, however, was convinced that he was unable to engage in such work, especially because in the conditions obtaining in Salamiyya, "work" for him meant a trade. Krikor had no knowledge whatsoever of any trade.[51]

It would seem that Krikor's mother was better acquainted with the situation in Salamiyya. The steps she now proceeded to take played a crucial role in determining the family's fate. Santukhd was an accomplished seamstress and had brought with her from Ayntab various samples of her embroidery that were plainly chefs d'œuvre. In these extreme conditions, she had no choice but to put these cherished creations of hers up for sale. Tellingly, she did not turn to just anybody in hopes of selling them, but offered them to the wife of Jevad Efendi, the director of the *arazi mülkiye* (the Sultan's properties) and assistant mayor of Salamiyya. She succeeded in selling one of them and made a gift of another. But she used this encounter to seize the opportunity to tell Jevad's wife about her family's desperate plight and ask her to intercede with her husband, a state official, to find a clerk's post for her son.[52]

Krikor Bogharian was in fact a qualified candidate for a post of this kind. He had an excellent command of Ottoman Turkish, had mastered Ottoman calligraphy, and had already demonstrated his skills in these domains in his post as clerk in the conversion office. In the wartime conditions of the day, young clerks with these qualifications were hard to find outside the deportees' ranks, especially in the Empire's Arab-speaking provinces. Further, Krikor Bogharian's legal name, the one he used in signing documents, was already Shehab, something that was doubtless an advantage for an Armenian seeking a state post in such times. And Santukhd, who (like all the Armenians of Ayntab of her generation) had a native command of Turkish, would have had no trouble communicating all this information about her son to Jevad's wife. On the other hand, it is unlikely that she simply happened to appeal to Jevad at this point. He may have held a high-ranking post in Salamiyya and therefore been considered a man of influence, but he was already known to the Armenian deportees for his benevolent attitude, as Der Nerses attests.[53] Krikor Bogharian, for his part, notes that Jevad's father was a Turk from Baghdad and his mother an Arab, and that he was of the Ismaili faith.[54]

Santukhd's appeal to Jevad's wife produced immediate results. On the very next day, 26 October, Jevad Efendi accompanied Krikor to the office of Salamiyya's *tahrirat katibi* (the *kaymakam*'s general secretary), Tevfik Efendi, and there the young man from Ayntab was appointed to the post of assistant secretary.[55] Thus he now had a post that was directly associated with the *kaymakam*'s, and he worked in Salamiyya's government building. It was in this period that Krikor Bogharian had the stamp with the name "Shehab" made, in all probability for use in his new position.[56] The diarist from Ayntab clearly had a heavy workload, for the secretary who was his superior traveled often, leaving all the work to be done to Bogharian. This is probably why he writes that there "was no time left for reading or writing" at home,[57] which had earlier been one of his main occupations.

The first tangible consequence of the young diarist's new employment appeared one month after he took the job. On 26 November, Jevad Efendi, justifying his reputation as a just man, sold one-quarter of some wheat he had just received to the Bogharians for the trifling sum of 45 piasters. Although there is no indication as to exactly how much wheat was involved, it was clearly a sizable quantity, since Bogharian notes that they were now assured a supply of wheat for the next four months.[58] The *kaymakam*, too, soon perceived Krikor-Shehab's conscientiousness and competence and instructed that he be paid his first salary of 250 piasters. Thereafter, Bogharian occupied two posts: he worked in the *tahrirat*'s office in the morning and worked as the *mutemed katibi* (clerk in charge of running accounts) in the afternoon.[59] In addition, he began helping the director of the *ziraat bankasi* (agricultural bank), Jemil Efendi, with secretarial tasks in his free time.[60] Then, on 5 December, a few days after receiving his first monthly salary, he reaped the most important benefit of his new post: like all state officials, Bogharian, too, was accorded the right to claim a certain share of wheat, for which he paid 570 piasters in paper currency, the equivalent of 260 metal piasters. It is unclear exactly how much wheat he received, but it was presumably a great deal because Krikor now began helping out his family's close relatives and friends. The Tavukjians were among those he assisted: they received 16.5 *liders* of wheat at one point during Der Nerses's banishment.[61]

Krikor Bogharian was now solidly positioned within the stratum of state officials in Salamiyya. As he writes in the afterword to his diary, he had gained the *kaymakam*'s "absolute confidence" and was consequently entrusted with the task of censoring letters exchanged between Armenians. In other words, Bogharian's command of Ottoman Turkish, which he had acquired in Ayntab's Armenian school, and surely also his trustworthy character and scrupulousness on the job, had rather suddenly opened for him the kind of doors that deportees living in extreme conditions could usually only dream about. In summer 1917, another promotion brought Bogharian's career to new heights: he was named to a post as clerk and secretary in Salamiyya's provisions warehouse. He held this post until the Ottoman army withdrew from the city.⁶² The young diarist was not the only Armenian working at this state warehouse: he mentions someone from Marash, Nshan Saatjian, who been given a post as *terazu* (an official responsible for weighing provisions) there.⁶³

For the Bogharian family, which not long ago had struggled to obtain its daily bread, this new post was simply the best possible guarantee of receiving enough to eat. Bogharian was now not only able to support his family, but could presumably derive additional benefits from his position. By paying small bribes, he could doubtless gain access in the warehouse to items whose prices began soaring to new heights from 1917 on. In the Ottoman environment, and especially in wartime, bribing state officials was a common practice to which Bogharian is unlikely to have remained a complete stranger. To be sure, there is not a single reference to this in his diary. Yet various other information at our disposal makes it highly probable that the income Bogharian derived from his government job was more than his monthly salary.

Thus Krikor's brother Khachig, who must have been around eighteen years old in 1917 and had previously worked as a common laborer for an Armenian tinsmith in Salamiyya,⁶⁴ suddenly became a flour merchant.⁶⁵ In the severe economic conditions prevailing in Bilad al-Sham, flour had become an extremely expensive commodity that was sometimes unavailable and, for many, unaffordable when it was. So the mere fact that someone was a flour merchant meant that he had either the high income required to trade in flour or a way of illegally obtaining flour, such as smuggling or theft from a state warehouse. Later, when Der Karekin returned from exile, he joined Khachig in the flour trade.⁶⁶ Father and son gradually expanded their business, opening a grocery store in Salamiyya they sold products other than flour as well. Der Karekin often went to Hama to obtain such other products for their store. And in May 1918, Der Nerses, who by then had settled in Hama, became an agent for the Bogharians' store in Salamiyya, where he purchased basic commodities on their behalf.⁶⁷

The Bogharian family's new economic position made it possible for them to aid other deportees. Testimony to this appears, again, in Der Nerses's diary: on 15 September, he received a gift of four *mejid*s (80 piasters) from the Bogharian family and, directly from Krikor Bogharian, twenty-five *lider*s of wheat. In his letter of thanks to Der Karekin, Der Nerses writes that the wheat he had received "was as pure and unsullied as [Der Karekin's] heart and Krikor's character."⁶⁸ Despite the copious praise found in his letter, however, it is improbable that Krikor Bogharian could basically be considered, in Der Nerses's estimation, one of those rare individuals who, although living "under the Empire of Evil," had managed to preserve his moral integrity and was that "star of the first magnitude" that could serve as an example to others. For the fact is that Bogharian, too, had gone over to Islam and changed his name to Shehab, and that this had most likely been a major factor in getting him the new job that later allowed him to help close friends such as Der Nerses's family.

In the priest's case, this was another contradiction of the position he had adopted toward the "immorality," repeatedly excoriated in his diary, that held sway in the environment of Hama and Salamiyya. We have already seen one instance of such a situation in the relations between Der Nerses and his benefactor, Sahag/Muchhad Efendi. The following lines by Der Nerses may even hold a direct reference to Bogharian, for after adducing various deplorable examples of the decline of the spirit of mutual assistance among Armenian compatriots in his entourage, he adds: "On the other hand, an Islamicized Armenian who makes his living working as an official among the Turks is giving me very generous help, although he does not have the courage to make his way up my stairs, visit me, and leave, or to receive me in his home."[69]

Let us, however, return to Santukhd, to whose initiative Krikor Bogharian owed his new career as an Ottoman clerk. Krikor himself credits her with this success. In his biography of Santukhd Bogharian, written many years later, he observes that he was beholden to his mother's "wisdom" and "courage" for his position as a clerk.[70] Elsewhere, in a passage of his diary produced shortly after he had begun to keep one, Bogharian, referring to his mother's difficult situation, writes that she succeeded, despite all, in being "both mother and father to five children."[71]

The whole meaning of Santukhd's role resides herein. In a traditional society—in the present case, that of the Ayntab Armenians—the mother and the father have very distinct familial duties. Plainly, it was up to the father to choose the family's friends as well as to define its relations with the outside world and its political and ideological positions. He did all this autocratically, without interference from his wife. As seen here, however, extreme conditions could upset these conventions. Der Karekin Bogharian had been exiled, and although Santukhd had shouldered the heavy burden of caring for a large family, she was relatively free to act as she saw fit: she was the one who had to make the "paternal" decisions. Thus the mother played the "father's" part in her own fashion, unconstrained, perhaps, by masculine prejudices.

The meeting between Santukhd and Jevad's wife, it might be said, distilled the essence of this state of affairs. That simple act of selling embroidery became a historical event in the Bogharians' family life, one that changed their destiny. Had Der Karekin been present, Santukhd would probably not have been capable of a step calling for such audacity and enterprise. As for Krikor's father the priest, he would very likely have proved incapable of describing Krikor Bogharian's abilities before the just Jevad with the same suppleness and tact with which Santukhd approached Jevad's wife. Indeed, he would perhaps never have taken such initiative in the first place.

In any case, Santukhd's act marked the beginning of Krikor Bogharian's success. Despite the reign of extreme privation, the Bogharians no longer had to worry much about getting

Figure 5.2, Father Karekin Bogharian (Source: Krikoris Bogharian family collection)

by. In the following months, they would continue to live in Salamiyya in relatively comfortable circumstances. Bogharian's activity as a clerk plainly kept him exceedingly busy and may have been the main reason he stopped keeping a diary. When the Ottoman armies retreated from the area late in 1918, the Bogharians found themselves among the rare exiled families who, despite the drastic conditions of their exile, survived intact: the family had had seven members when it was deported, and all seven of them left Salamiyya behind in April 1919 to go first to Hama, and then to Ayntab.

The Agony of Der Nerses's Family in the Last Months of the War

In the world of the Armenian deportees of Bilad al-Sham, those as fortunate as the Bogharians were rare, as the previous section has demonstrated. Armenians who, like Krikor Bogharian, "found an easy way of making a living at the government's door" were a small minority, according to Der Nerses. As for the majority, he divided it into two groups. The first comprised those who "pursued, panting and moaning and enduring a thousand and one difficulties, the means of prolonging their lives"; the second was made up of people who linked their fate to "the angel of death."[72] He himself undoubtedly belonged to the first group. In spite of all the failures and disappointments he encountered in his work, he continued struggling to secure his family's and his own survival. The aid he received from friends, though extremely important, was clearly insufficient; more was needed. To a certain extent, the letter he wrote to Catholicos Sahag II reflects this state of affairs; albeit undated, it was most likely written in May–June 1918, during the Cilician Catholicosate pontiff's exile in Damascus, to acknowledge that Sahag II had sent the priest from Ayntab a gift consisting of three banknotes. In the letter, after the appropriate expressions of gratitude, Der Nerses adds: "But would that the means at your disposal made it possible for you to give more help to the humble son that you love so well, for, although three or four banknotes in the course of several months is much, much better than nothing, it is very little for a husband and father a family of eight to ten people who lacks the means and capacity for physical work; it hardly suffices to buy a few days' worth of bread."[73] Here Der Nerses is presumably counting the surviving members of his late brother Hagop's family as part of his own. In any case, these few lines addressed to the Catholicos contain a condensed expression of the prevailing situation and state of mind. In the same period, Der Nerses notes in his diary: "If peace is not established in the world by an act of Divine grace, there will be still greater and more terrible destruction on this earth, and remnants of the Armenians will be found only abroad [outside the Ottoman Empire]."[74] Truly, the conditions of existence of Der Nerses and many others like him were still unbearable. Now, having given up the weaver's trade, Der Nerses was to give a new fillip to his career as a priest, which had very nearly ceased altogether in the Islamicized environment.

We may consider this, too, to be a retreat from principle, a Hobbesian figure's deviation from the straight and narrow—especially taking into consideration the fact that Der Nerses had earlier refused to bless the homes of Islamicized families after births or at Easter, reserving this ritual only for those who asked him to do it, or for very close relatives and acquaintances. Yet it is clear that extreme conditions eventually compelled Der Nerses to adapt to the situation, in the interests of his family's and his own survival. As discussed above, he had, with the approval of Ayntab notables and the local military commander Osman Bey, assumed the obligation of burying helpless, demoralized families' dead. In exchange, he was allotted one or two *mejid*s per day, of which, undoubtedly, only a small amount accrued to him. In addition, in January 1918 he began to celebrate mass in Hama's Syriac Orthodox church once every two weeks. Very few of the faithful attended mass, which was perhaps the reason the local authorities tolerated this activity. In his autobiography, Der Nerses writes that the authorities of the day had demanded that Armenian notables compile a list of the names of the Armenian Christians in the Hama area. Der Nerses observed that no one, apart from himself and Der Karekin (in Salamiyya), had authorized the inclusion of his or her name in the list.[75] This time, Der Nerses himself reached out to this Islamicized community, visiting approximately eighty homes in the space of three days and collecting the sum of 80 piasters in the process.[76] This clearly was a source of satisfaction for the priest from Ayntab.

Meanwhile, the best way to reconstruct an authentic picture of Der Nerses's daily life on the eve of liberation is to consider the scene of his wife Anitsa's illness. This act in the drama of his life in exile sums up his onerous day-to-day existence and also that of the majority of Hama's and Salamiyya's deportees—their agonizing life-and-death struggle, and the pervasive fear of, and utter uncertainty about, the future.

By early 1918, disease and poverty had already taken the lives of Der Nerses's brother Hagop and the priest's infant daughter. Hagop's widow, Diruhi, later fell seriously ill in her turn. Anitsa often took care of Diruhi, and in these dark days, on 21 May, the priest's wife herself fell ill with stomach pains, fever, and headaches. This condition persisted for several days with no sign of improvement. On the contrary, Anitsa took a turn for the worse and her fever shoot up to over forty degrees Celsius. "The sad thing," Der Nerses writes, "is that no doctor is to be had." In fact, there were doctors in Hama, but the priest from Ayntab did not have the money to pay them. On 26 May he turned to the municipal physician, Dr. Shukri, begging him to come see Anitsa, but in the end the doctor did not come. Another physician was nowhere to be found. "We can appeal only to God for help. May the Lord come to our aid," Der Nerses writes.[77] Fortunately, his wife's condition improved somewhat in early June, but she was far from recovering completely. Describing his family's dire economic straits in the same period, the priest from Ayntab writes that in May, his "earnings and the money that happened [his] way are not sufficient to cover costs."[78]

About one month later, on 11 July, Hagop's widow Diruhi died. Notwithstanding her weak condition, Anitsa had to lift and dress the body of the deceased, since no one else was available to do so. In a word, she had to render her the final services, a task that called for physical strength. The day immediately following the burial, she took to her bed again, gravely ill.[79] On 18 July her condition deteriorated sharply; death seemed near. The day before, Dr. Shukri had come to see the priest's suffering wife and diagnosed her with *hummaai rajia* (remittent fever), which meant her fever had been caused by a virus. The doctor therefore came to see her again the following day, and this time vaccinated Anitsa. Immediately after the inoculation, however, her condition deteriorated further. Her fever again rose to over forty degrees, and, according to her husband's diary "she went into the first stage of a death agony."[80]

Evening had fallen in Hama. Still hoping to find a doctor, the breathless, desperate Der Nerses hurried through the streets. He went to Dr. Shukri's house three or four times, but every time Shukri was absent; it turned out he was at a soirée. Der Nerses found the pharmacist Sograd Efendi and went with him to Dr. Abdulrahman's house to try to convince him to come see Anitsa. But the doctor refused on the grounds that Der Nerses lived too far away. By now it was midnight. Exhausted, not knowing what else to do, with no one to help him, Der Nerses went back home without a doctor, once again putting his hope, in his own words, in "the chief physician, Jesus." Anitsa was still in her dying agony; then "she nodded off for a little while and we, too, went to bed."[81] Early in the morning of 19 July, Der Nerses again tried to find Dr. Shukri, who finally came to see his patient at two o'clock in the afternoon. He found Anitsa's fever had gone down, which he took as confirmation that the vaccination had had a positive effect. Over the next few days, her condition actually did improve. Although her fever rose again, she gradually got better until early August.

Der Nerses's main preoccupation was now his economic doldrums. On 1 August, he writes that "Anitsa's illness caused me great expense," adding:

> We are already incapable of covering our expenses; in these days of illness, we have doubled our debts. Until today, we had somehow muddled through, but now my debts have gotten the better of me. More than anything else, this has been a grueling, oppressive situation [for me], so much so that I am having trouble sleeping at night—because, for example, my earnings do not cover my expenditures, my debts are increasing daily, and I do not know where the money to pay them off is supposed to come from.[82]

In Der Nerses's case, it is obvious that the uncertainty was absolute: vulnerability to disease, poverty, and, on top of everything else, debt. Plainly, the passage of time made the effort to survive impossible for those in this situation. Death hovered over them and sooner or later mowed many of them down. Indeed, since the beginning of the deportation, the Tavukjians had suffered many losses: Mariam Syulahian (Anitsa's mother), Shoghagat, Krikor (Hagop's son), Hagop, Diruhi.

Here the basic problem of Bilad al-Sham's Armenians is glaringly obvious: the plan to resettle them in the Arab provinces had left them largely without state aid and abandoned them to their fate; therefore the majority of deportees experienced it as a catastrophe. The mass relocation of an entire people and its resettlement in a new environment is a difficult enterprise to carry out, one that rarely meets with success. Furthermore, carrying out an operation of that sort is plainly much more complicated in the conditions of a world war. The unprecedented inflation and severe economic crisis create unbearable situations for even the autochthonous population, while most of the relocated people find their new environment to be a zone of extremes that reduces life to a daily struggle to survive. The more time goes by, the more their ability to struggle diminishes and the more deaths occur in their ranks. In Bilad al-Sham, the deported Armenians' numbers plummeted, with the result that in a few years' time, an entire people found itself facing the threat of extinction. Regarding the resettlement of deported Armenians in the Bilad al-Sham region—a policy pursued by a number of Ottoman rulers—one can only express amazement at certain historians' attempts to invest it with the character of a philanthropic act.[83]

Figure 5.3. Aleppo, ca 1923, Armenian religious leaders. Seated (from left): the first person is Father Nerses Tavukjian; the forth person is Sahag II Khabayan (Catholicos of Cilicia); the seventh person is Father Karekin Bogharian. (Source: Mihran Minassian collection)

The First Months after Liberation: The Bitter Taste of Freedom

Liberation. For a helpless people such as the Armenians in exile, the Ottoman army's retreat from the Hama district and the concomitant flight of Ottoman officialdom could mean only one thing: salvation, an authentic liberation. Yet this enthusiasm is not immediately perceivable in Der Nerses's diary. Clearly, the priest needed time to assess the new situation, familiarize himself with it, come to the realization that the Ottomans had gone down to defeat, and become acquainted with the new rulers. Thus, in the role of a simple but also cautious eyewitness, and in phrases that evince no great enthusiasm, he describes the entry of the Arab Sharifian Army into Hama on 19 October.

Under the prevailing conditions, it was not easy for ordinary deportees to understand what "liberation" meant. They were of course aware that the Ottoman authorities were the real authors of the catastrophe they had suffered, and that the Ittihadist rulers had left the Bilad al-Sham region. This was by itself providential. Nevertheless, the entry of the Allied armies had not immediately solved the deportees' basic problem of securing their daily bread, although that, one might reasonably suppose, was what the impoverished, weakened, suffering Armenians of Bilad al-Sham were waiting for more than anything else. Moreover, the Ottoman army had been the mainstay of survival for many Armenians, especially in the last phase of the war, when thousands of deported Armenian men and women had found work in its workshops. In these structures they found themselves in semi-servitude; nevertheless, they received the daily nutrition that prolonged their survival. This whole system, centered on the Ottoman army, had vanished into thin air with the general retreat of the Ottoman forces. However contradictory it may appear, the fact is that with the collapse of these military structures, many Armenians living in Bilad al-Sham were left defenseless, bereft of any means of support.

The Allied forces marched northward, from Palestine toward Syria and Lebanon and from Basra toward Mosul. Along these strategic routes, the advancing armies encountered emaciated, exhausted Armenian deportees. The Allied commanders directing these military operations had established their headquarters in Egypt, where the Armenian community closest to Bilad al-Sham, geographically speaking, was also to be found. It must be said that the Allies were entirely unprepared to cope with the existence of tens of thousands of hungry, homeless Armenian deportees in the regions they were occupying. It also seems safe to say that they did not make a priority of providing this mass of starving people with humanitarian relief. The supplies and basic structures of the Allied—primarily British—armies served first and foremost to provision their own troops. As for the Armenian deportees, everything had to begin from the beginning. In these circumstances, any aid dispatched to them came mainly from Egypt and tended to arrive late.

This delay was unbearable for the deportees, whose dying agonies thus were only being prolonged. In November and December, we find expressions of uncertainty and fear in the letters Der Nerses now wrote to Catholicos Sahag II. "The numbers of the needy and hungry are rising daily. Material assistance is not arriving from anywhere and we have been plunged into a confused, difficult situation."[84] The priest from Ayntab admits that the local Armenians "are happy and pleased" to have been freed "from dangers and threats and the anguish occasioned by them,"[85] but adds that a wretched multitude is waiting for the massive aid that, albeit indispensable, is not forthcoming: "No Armenian heart can bear the thought that the handful of Armenians who have survived to the present day, after enduring fire and the sword and tearing themselves free of death's cruel claws, should again be ravaged by hunger."[86]

In a letter to a correspondent in Egypt in this period, Sahag II likewise alludes to the desperate condition of the Armenian deportees in Bilad al-Sham. Obliquely, the Catholicos of Cilicia observes that the deportees' miserable state has gotten still worse due to the collapse of the Ottoman system. He begins by listing all the channels of communication that are blocked and all the routes that are impracticable, and then points out that the new conditions mean that many deportees are no longer receiving material assistance from their relatives and friends. Finally, he alludes to Armenian officials who are now unemployed and unable to adapt to the new situation because they lack a command of Arabic; they, too, he writes, must gradually be counted among the ranks of the needy.[87] It is clear that the allusion to unemployed officials concerns, generally, Armenians formerly employed in the Ottoman army's workshops.

Hmayag Ughurlian, a deportee from Caeserea living in Damascus, offers a clearer, more detailed analysis of the same question in this period. In a letter also written to someone in Egypt, he writes:

> With the withdrawal of the Turkish army, the Armenian settlers have been left without work, and their poverty has become still more acute. Armenian settlers furnished the Turkish army with its uniforms. Armenian women spun wool, and knit and sewed, and the workshops were all full of Armenian settlers. Armenian farmers, carpenters, and tailors, and craftsmen of all nations, were employed to fill the Turkish army's needs and received just enough to afford themselves food and shelter.[88]

More than two and a half months would pass before the humanitarian relief network became fully operative and started providing real assistance to Bilad al-Sham's Armenian deportees. Interestingly, only at this stage—after witnessing the Ottoman army's defeat and the Armenian deportees' liberation—does Der Nerses voice authentic enthusiasm. For example, on 31 December 1918 the priest from Ayntab, recalling the dark, somber reality of the deportation, writes in his diary:

> None, neither those who have found a means of making a living, nor those who, lacking other means, are living on refuse dumps, nor, again, those who have fallen into the clutches of the monster known as hunger and are now suffering from disease—none ever hoped to see this day. But, today, everyone is filled with hope and rejoicing in the rays of the dawning sun.[89]

Figure 5.4. Homs, 15 November 1933. Seated (from left): Archbishop Ardavast Surmeyan (Armenian prelate in Aleppo), Sahag II Khabayan (Catholicos of Cilicia), Papken I Gyuleserian (coadjutor Catholicos of Cilicia), Archbishop Yeprem Dohmuni (prelate of Damascus). Standing (third from left): Father Nerses Tavukjian. Standing behind Papken I: Mikayel Nathanian. Next to him, on his right: Father Mashdots Vosgerichian (from Homs)
(Source: AGBU, Nubarian Library, Paris)

Notes

1. On the Islamization of Armenians in the Ottoman Empire in the decades preceding 1915, see Vahakn Dadrian, *The History of the Armenian Genocide: Ethnic Conflict from the Balkans to Anatolia to the Caucasus* (Providence and Oxford: Berghahn Books, 1995); Hovan H. Simonian, "Hemshin from Islamization to the End of the Nineteenth Century," in Hovan H. Simonian (ed.), *The Hemshin: History, Society and Identity in the Highlands of North-East Turkey* (London and New York: Routledge, 2006); Selim Deringil, "'The Armenian Question Is Finally Closed': Mass Conversions of Armenians during the Hamidian Massacres of 1895–1897," *Comparative Studies in Society and History* 51 (April 2009): 344–371; Selim Deringil, *Conversion and Apostasy in the Late Ottoman Empire* (New York: Cambridge University Press, 2012); Nazan Maksudyan, *Orphans and Destitute Children in Late Ottoman Empire* (Syracuse, NY: Syracuse University Press, 2014).
2. E.g., see Khacher Sarkisian, *Yotanasun darineru hushers* [*My memoirs of seventy years*] (Beirut: Donigian, 1970), pp. 654–660; Khoren Tavitian, *Gyankis kirke* [*The book of my life*] (Fresno: 1967), pp. 193–204.
3. Dündar, *L'ingénierie ethnique*, p. 270.
4. Odian, *Accursed Years*, p. 113.
5. Ibid.
6. Ibid.
7. Dadrian, *To the Desert*, p. 241.
8. Kyud Mkhitarian, *Husher yev verhishumner (1918–1935)* [*Memories and recollections (1918–1935)*] (Antilias, Lebanon: Cilician Catholicossate, 1937), pp. 77–78. These lines appear in Turkish written in the Armenian alphabet. Two years later, they appeared in Armenian translation in a book by Catholicos Papken I, *Badmutiun Gatoghigosats Giligio (1441en minchev mer orere)* [*History of the Catholicoses of Cilicia (from 1441 to the present)*] (Antilias, Lebanon: Cilician Catholicossate, 1939; 2nd ed. 1990), p. 951.
9. Tavukjian, *Diary*, p. 95.
10. Tavukjian, "Ms. Diary," p. 84.
11. Bogharian, "Diary," p. 151.
12. Tavukjian, *Diary*, p. 98.
13. Bogharian, "Diary," p. 164.
14. Ibid., p. 178.
15. Ibid.
16. Karekin Bogharian, "Kahanayits tasin aksore" [The priests' exile], *Hay Anteb* 6, no. 2 (1965): 21.
17. Hasan Amja (*Les dessous des déportations: Souvenirs de Tcherkess Hassan bey*) also mentions Ali Kemal's activity in connection with questions relating to the Armenian deportees in the Hama-Homs region.
18. Odian, *Accursed Years*, pp. 114–115.
19. Bogharian, "Diary," p. 205.
20. Ibid., p. 185.
21. Tavukjian, *Diary*, p. 114.
22. Ibid., pp. 116–117. Karekin Bogharian, "The Priests' Exile," pp. 19–24.
23. Bogharian, "Diary," p. 192.
24. Dadrian, *To the Desert*, p. 239.
25. Kudulian, *Red Notes*, p. 29.
26. Genjian, "The Armenians in Damascus."
27. Shalamov, *Kolyma Tales*, p. 12.

28. Aramian, *The Armenians' Purgatorio*, p. 138.
29. "Krikor A. Sarafian (1880–1966)," in *Ayntabiana*, pp. 207–208.
30. Krikor Kudulian, "Anabadi gyanken, darakiri me husheren" [Life in the desert: Memoirs of a deportee], *Arev* 3, no. 35 (2 August 1918).
31. Odian, *Accursed Years*, p. 115.
32. Ibid,. p. 114.
33. Ibid,. p. 115.
34. Bogharian, "Diary," pp. 188–189.
35. Dadrian, *To the Desert*, pp. 164–165.
36. Odian, *Accursed Years*, pp. 115–116.
37. Ibid., p. 116.
38. Tavukjian, *Diary*, p. 150.
39. Bogharian, "Diary," p. 192.
40. Genjian, "The Armenians in Damascus," p. 2.
41. Bogharian, "Diary," pp. 191 and 200.
42. Tavukjian, *Diary*, p. 150.
43 Ibid., pp. 134–135.
44. Ibid., p. 135.
45. Ibid., p. 138.
46. Bogharian, "Diary," p. 189.
47. Ibid., pp. 135–136.
48. Ibid., p. 136.
49. Ibid., p. 138.
50. Lawrence L. Langer, *Versions of Survival: The Holocaust and the Human Spirit* (Albany: State University of New York Press, 1982).
51. Bogharian, "Diary," p. 193.
52. Ibid., p. 199.
53. Tavukjian, *Diary*, p. 100.
54. "Santukhd Bogharian (1877–1949)," *Ayntabiana*, p. 25.
55. Bogharian, "Diary," p. 200.
56. Ibid., p. 200.
57. Ibid., p. 203.
58. Ibid., p. 204.
59. Ibid., p. 205.
60. Ibid. p. 206.
61. Ibid., p. 205.
62. Ibid., p. 207.
63. Ibid., p. 246.
64. Ibid., p. 201.
65. Ibid., p. 207.
66. "Father Nerses Tavukjian (Autobiographical notes)," p. 58.
67. Tavukjian, *Diary*, p. 159.
68. Der Nerses, Letter of 15 September 1915 to Der Karekin, Hama.
69. Tavukjian, *Diary*, p. 148.
70. "Santukhd Bogharian (1877–1949)," p. 25.
71. Bogharian, "Diary," p. 203.
72. Tavukjian, "Ms. Diary," p. 157.
73. ACC, File "Correspondence," no. 50, Undated letter from Der Nerses Tavukjian to Catholicos Sahag II (in Damascus), Hama.
74. Tavukjian, "Ms. Diary," p. 139.
75. "Father Nerses Tavukjian (Autobiographical notes)," p. 58.
76. Tavukjian, *Diary*, p. 159.

77. Tavukjian, "Ms. Diary," pp. 141-142.
78. Ibid., p. 142.
79. Ibid.
80. Ibid., p. 143.
81. Ibid.
82. Ibid.
83. To a certain extent this attitude makes itself felt in an essay of Hilmar Kaiser's (Kaiser, "Regional resistance").
84. ACC, File "Antilias II," no. 26/1, Hama-Homs (1916-1940), Letter of 13 December 1918 from Der Nerses Tavukjian to Catholicos Sahag II, Hama, p. 3.
85. ACC, File "Antilias II," no. 26/1, Hama-Homs (1916-1940), Letter from Der Nerses Tavukjian to Catholicos Sahag II, Hama, p. 1.
86. Ibid., p. 3.
87. Archives of the AGBU's Nubarian Library, Correspondence—Armenia, 1918, XIV, Letter of 2 November 1918 from Catholicos Sahag II to Bishop Torkom Kushagian (Prelate of Egypt), Damascus.
88. AGBU Central Archives, Cairo, File no. 12, DAMASCUS (21 June 1910—26 March 1931), Letter of 13 November 1918 from Hmayeag Ughurlian (Chairman of the Armenian National Union in Damascus) to the Chairman of the AGBU in Egypt, Damascus, p. 2.
89. Tavukjian, "Ms. Diary," p. 158.

Selected Bibliography

Published Material

Amja, Hasan, "Faits et documents: Les dessous des déportations, Souvenirs de Tcherkess Hassan bey," *Renaissance*, no. 1 (22 July 1919).

Aramian, Hayg A. Հայոց Տանթէական. Մեծ եղեռնի պատգամ. Քավարան եւ հրաշալի Յարութիւն [Hayots Danteagan: Medz yegherni badkam. Kavaran yev hrashali Harutyun] [The Armenian Purgatorio: The message of the Great Tragedy; Purgatory and miraculous resurrection]. Beirut, 1970.

Bogharian, Krikor. Ցեղասպան Թուրքը, վկայութիւններ քաղուած՝ հրաշքով փրկուածներու զրոյցներէն [Tseghasban Turke. Vgayutyunner kaghvadz hrashkov prgvadzneru zruytsneren] [The genocidal Turk: Eyewitness accounts from the narratives of people who were miraculously saved]. Beirut, 1973.

Bogharian, Krikor, ed. Այնթապականք / *Ayntabiana*, vol. 2. Մահարձան: մահագրութիւններ, դամբանականներ եւ կենսագրական նօթեր [Funeral monument: Necrologies, funeral orations and biographical notes]. Beirut, 1974.

Dadrian, Vahakn. *The History of the Armenian Genocide: Ethnic Conflict from the Balkans to Anatolia to the Caucasus*. Providence and Oxford, 1995.

Dadrian, Vahram. *To the Desert: Pages from my Diary*, trans. Agop Hacikyan. London, 2006.

Deringil, Selim. "'The Armenian Question Is Finally Closed': Mass Conversions of Armenians during the Hamidian Massacres of 1895-1897," *Comparative Studies in Society and History* 51 (April 2009): 344-371.

———. *Conversion and Apostasy in the Late Ottoman Empire*. New York, 2012.

Dündar, Fuat. *L'ingénierie ethnique du Comité Union et Progrès et la Turcisation de l'Anatolie*, doctoral thesis. Paris, 2006.

Genjian, A. N. "Հայերը Դամասկոսի մէջ (Ազատագրումէն առաջ եւ ետքը)" [Hayere Tamasgosi mech (Azadakrumen arach yev yedke)] [The Armenians in Damascus before and after liberation], *Yeridasart Hayasdan* (1919).

Kaiser, Hilmar. "Regional Resistance to Central Government Policies: Ahmed Djemal Pasha, the Governors of Aleppo, and Armenian Deportees in the Spring and Summer of 1915." *Journal of Genocide Research* 12, nos. 3–4 (September–December 2010): 173–218.

Kudulian, Krikor. "Անապատի կեանքէն, տարագրի մը յուշերէն" [Anabadi gyanken, darakiri me husheren] [Life in the desert: Memoirs of a deportee], *Arev* 3, no. 35 (2 August 1918).

———.Կարմիր նոթեր տարագրի կեանքէս [Garmir noter darakri gyankis] [Red notes from my life as a deportee]. Port Said, 1919.

Langer, Lawrence L. *Versions of Survival: The Holocaust and the Human Spirit*. Albany, 1982.

Maksudyan, Nazan. *Orphans and Destitute Children in the Late Ottoman Empire*. Syracuse, NY, 2014.

Mkhitarian, Kyud. Յուշեր եւ վերյիշումներ (1918–1935) [Husher yev verhishumner] [Memories and recollections]. Antilias, 1937.

Odian, Yervant. *Accursed Years: My Exile and Return from Der Zor, 1914–1919*, trans. Ara Melkonian. London, 2009.

Papken I, Catholicos. Պատմութիւն Կաթողիկոսաց Կիլիկիոյ [Badmutiun Gatoghigosats Giligio] [History of the Catholicoses of Cilicia], 2nd ed. Antilias, [1939] 1990.

Simonian, Hovan H., ed. *The Hemshin: History, Society and Identity in the Highlands of North-East Turkey*. London and New York, 2006.

Tavukjian, Father Nerses, "Օրագրութեան Մեքենագրուած Բնագիր" [Orakrutyan mekenakrvadz pnakir] [Typescript of the diary] (Ms. Diary).

———. Տառապանքի օրագրութիւն [Darabanki orakrutyun] [Diary of days of suffering]. Beirut, 1991.

———. "Ներսէս Քհնյ. Թաւուգճեան (Ինքնակենսագրական նօթեր)" [Nerses Kahana Tavukjian (Inknagensakragan noter)] ["Father Nerses Tavukjian (Autobiographical Notes)"], *Shirag* 51, no. 8 (August 1987): 55.

Primary Sources

Archives of the AGBU's Nubarian Library
ACC: Archives of the Cilician Catholicosate
AGBU Central Archives, Cairo

Afterword

Cease-fire and liberation of the deportees. A new chapter was opening in the history of the Armenians of the Ottoman Empire. This afterword recounts an episode that will help us understand the significance of that moment. There were very many like it in the period immediately following the genocide. It has to do with a debate raging in the Armenian press in Istanbul, Izmir, Aleppo, Adana, and elsewhere that had been touched off by a speech of Artin Efendi Boshgezenian, a former member of the Committee for Union and Progress (i.e., the Ittihad Party) and an Ottoman parliamentary representative from Aleppo. Boshgezenian happened to be a native of Ayntab. His name is mentioned in the third chapter of the present book, and both Bogharian and Der Nerses knew him. His example was chosen from among many similar episodes because Boshgezenian was a friend of our two diarists.

What did Artin Efendi declare in his speech? Taking the floor of the parliament on 18 November 1918, he said: "The Turkish nation today stands accused before the civilized world.... Today there is an enormous crime which stands as the most sorrowful and bloody page of Ottoman history. The immense crime, which has shaken both heaven and earth, is known as the massacre of the Armenians, the Armenian calamity."[1] The deputy from Aleppo went on to describe the perpetrators of this mass crime:

> For this reason, the Turkish nation stands accused. The real perpetrator, however, is not the Turkish nation, but the former Turkish government and administration.... The nation is one thing, the government is another.... I say that this great crime, of which an entire nation stands accused, was carried out by the former regime or, more correctly, by the hooligan regime....[2] That government was the most appalling link in the chain of the crime that has been hung around the Turks' necks, namely, responsibility for the Armenian tragedy. That crime was the work of a special organization made up of a handful of evildoers in the capital and the state officials at their orders in the provinces, namely, valis, mutaserifs, kaymakams, and commanders in the gendarmerie.[3]

Boshgezenian next evoked Turks who had opposed the government decision to massacre the Armenians, insisting, in this perspective, on the same idea: "It is not right...to accuse an entire nation for the crimes of a handful of murderers and madmen."[4] Yet Artin Efendi also pointed out that in a number of places, the common people, too, had taken part in the crime.

> Those responsible for this evil are the kind of people who are incapable of weighing up the consequences of their acts. If sheep fall into a swamp, who is to blame: the sheep, the bellwether[5] who led them into it, or the shepherd who took them from the fold? I say that, while some among the multitude may have had a hand in the crime, the real culprits were their leaders, the state officials. Gentlemen, fanatical feelings are to be found in the depths of the multitude's heart even in the most civilized of countries. They slumber there, and are only rarely awakened. If some factor or the other does not intervene to rouse those fanatical feelings, they continue to slumber. Sometimes, however, vile, dishonorable men appear and arouse those savage emotions. When they come to life, turmoil and confusion break out everywhere. People then butcher each other, and civil chaos, banditry, and rebellion raise their heads.[6]

As the native of Ayntab spoke, a representative from Trabizon/Trabzon, Hafez Bey, interrupted him to declare that a relatively small number of Ottoman state officials had participated in the crime. Artin Efendi demurred: "There were not just a few of them; there were many more than you think. If I were to list their names one by one, night would fall before I was through."[7] The representative from Aleppo then turned to the question of arresting and punishing all those responsible for the massacres without delay, remarking that this obligation was incumbent on the state.[8] He added that it was also the state's task to free abducted Armenian women and orphans and to see to it that the Armenians received reparations for the material losses they had suffered.[9]

At first sight, it may seem that nothing untoward was said in this speech, from the victims' point of view. On the contrary, it may even seem audacious, given that it was delivered in an assembly still dominated by the idea that the Armenians had been deported for acts of treason toward the Ottoman Empire.[10] Yet a storm of protest against Artin Efendi broke out in the Armenian press in the weeks following his speech. His remarks came in for ferocious attacks and he was the object of personal attacks as well, in the form of articles impugning his honor.

The central target of the criticisms was Artin Efendi's contention that the empire's former government was mainly to blame for the crime, not the Turkish people collectively speaking. A. Gebenlian, writing in the Aleppo newspaper *Hay Tsayn*, expressed a diametrically opposed view: "We cannot call a single Turk good or attribute a single Turk's friendly behavior to pro-Armenian feelings. Those who truly tried to help Armenians cannot be called Turks. Those who imagine that any Turk at all harbors humane feelings can't be called Armenians."[11] It is obvious here that the genocide had seriously perturbed Armenian-Turkish relations, and that in the minds of many Armenians, the words "Turkishness" and "Turk" had taken on a new coloring and definition. Artin Efendi's words so scandalized many Armenians that A. Jyunbyushian, writing in the Istanbul Armenian newspaper *Verchin lur*, objected to the Armenian parliamentarian's speech on the one hand, while on the other observing that the Armenian nation bore no blame for his words: "The bodies [of people of Boshgezenian's ilk] are Armenian, but their souls are not."[12] Rage and insults also came from writers whom the deportation had led as far as Der Zor and who had only recently returned, such as Yervant Odian or Kevork-Mesrob. Thus Mesrob writes: "You do not speak on behalf of the Armenians, gentlemen. Speak on the Ittihad's behalf and in its spirit.... The Ottoman parliament is not the tribunal to give a fair hearing to the Armenians' case, you may be sure of that. Have the decency to blush, gentlemen; do not toy with the misery of your race."[13]

One is left with the impression that Artin Efendi's simple words sparked a debate among Armenians about the Turks' collective responsibility for the genocide or the question of their collective guilt. To forgive or to punish, to remember or to forget: it seems that the debate could have developed further, taking on fundamental significance in the formation of the modern postwar Ottoman society that Artin Efendi himself so ardently championed. Germany later went through such a stage after the Nazis' defeat, when a similar debate sprang up around the central issues of collective guilt (*Kollektivschuld*), collective liability (*Kollektivhaft*), and collective responsibility (*kollektive Verantwortung*) for Nazi crimes.

The comparison, however, stops there. True, in the conditions brought on by defeat and occupation, self-criticism and self-reproach had begun to manifest themselves in Istanbul's Turkish newspapers. The Armenian press and politicians such as Artin Efendi had, with this question, assumed a historical role and often stimulated or propelled this progressive phenomenon. It is even possible to speculate that Turkish intellectuals' attitude could have evolved to the point of entertaining the idea of collective responsibility, a development that would probably have positively influenced the Armenian side, dispelling their extreme suspiciousness and terror and instilling in them a degree of confidence about the prospect of continued coexistence with the Turks. Yet all this turned out to be no more than a short phase in Turkey's history, lasting barely one year. It is well known that thereafter, modern Turkey steered an altogether different course, nipping this nascent debate in the bud.

The main idea informing rebuttals of Artin Efendi's speech was that the Armenians had ruptured their ties with the Ottoman-Turkish World. Ottoman Armenian intellectuals would gradually sanctify this idea in light of the geopolitical transformations then rapidly taking place. The genocide and the military defeat of the Ottoman Empire had ensured the ascendancy of the view that Armenians no longer had a place in the Ottoman system. New borders were being drawn, and new states were coming into existence. The Armenian press, community, and national organizations were also steeped in the spirit of these historical transformations, and the idea that Armenians should seek their future outside the Ottoman state was steadily gaining ground. In this regard, the views of "The Native of Mush" (probably Kegham Der Garabedian), one of those who took sharp issue with Artin Efendi's speech, were very clear:

> Gentlemen, the time for your drivel and the day when it carried weight have now passed. You are mercenary advocates working for the Turks' cause. Argue as much as you like: our fate has been settled, because the twentieth century's great legislator of genius, unrivaled champion of liberty, and peerless apostle of peace, Mr. Wilson, is crying from the depths of his heart, the olive branch of Reconciliation and Liberty in his hand: "The Scriptures declare, 'My Temple will be a house of prayer, but you have made it into a den of thieves'; I have come from the civilized world in order to scatter this band of thieves and give every people the absolute right to live freely and independently."[14]

Artin Efendi had come to resemble an obsolete legacy of the past as he struggled against this new, resolute, commanding current, his frail bark rocking perilously on the wild waves of a sea unfamiliar to him. At the same time, however, the victorious Allies lacked the strength and will to impose a new and different future on the Ottoman Empire. Meanwhile, Turkish society was giving birth to the Kemalist movement that would lead to victory after victory, but also to denial of the crime of genocide. The Armenian elite, for its part, had put its trust in the Allies and their promises of free development independent of Turks and separate from Turkey. In these conditions, Artin Efendi was repeating ideas that now seemed untimely, even treacherous. In the same period, in giving an interview to the Turkish newspaper *Menber*, the parliamentary deputy and Ayntab native was asked by a reporter for his opinion of the U.S. President Woodrow Wilson's Fourteen Points and the ways and means of implementing them. The rapidly shifting developments then occurring on the political stage had plainly thrown this Ottoman Armenian, a representative of the old school, into a state of severe shock. Having already witnessed the annihilation of his people by his own state, he was now witnessing the slow disintegration of that same state and the dismemberment of the empire. The whole world of the past was crumbling before his eyes. The man was clearly groping in the dark, yet he endeavored to keep faith with his principles. Thus he declared that his top priority was to see the realization of justice and equality. "Let justice be done, whether by the hand of a Wilson, or a Lloyd George, or even that of a Turk."[15] As for Wilson's principles and the right of the peoples to self-determination:

> There's the sticking point, and it's beyond my understanding. That there must be equality surely can't mean that separate governments ought to be established in one and the same country.... Muslims and Christians have never been equals in this country. What I seek is equality. My honor, my possessions, my soul must be safe. Let whoever wants to ensure that. As long as the vintage is brought in, the vineyard can belong to anyone it likes.[16]

* * * * *

Far from Istanbul, in Hama, Der Nerses and Krikor Bogharian were likewise moving in step with the times.

Survivors of the Armenians' ordeal included listless human wrecks, a huge multitude of Armenian orphans, and Armenian women in Turkish, Arab, and Kurdish families, or working as prostitutes. Obviously, this somber picture could not be transformed overnight. The Allied forces had reached this part of the Empire and the Armenians had been liberated, but for many Armenians the tragedy continued unabated.

Regardless, the Armenians strove to recover and to organize themselves with characteristic and impressive rapidity and single-mindedness, mobilizing to this end in every town and village in Bilad al-Sham to which they had been deported in unified groups. Der Nerses and Krikor Bogharian were part of this current. In Hama on 18 October, on Der Nerses's initiative, twenty-one Armenian notables convened for the purpose of to discussing the urgent questions of the day. The diarist observes: "This is the first time since we Armenians were exiled to these regions that we have convened a meeting freely and without danger."[17] The meeting was followed by another, bigger one, in the course of which a seven-member National Assembly was elected to handle matters concerning the church, orphans, relief for the poor, and relations with the new authorities. Subsequently, from 30 December on, this newly created body was called the Armenian National Union. Der Nerses was elected its president.[18] In the course of these weeks the orphanage in Hama was reopened, and measures were taken to ensure that the orphans would be fed and clothed.[19] The orphanage also began providing Armenian language instruction, something that would have been impossible only a few months earlier. It was also in this period that our two diarists' paths crossed once again: Krikor Bogharian came with his family to Hama, where he was named secretary of both the newly organized Armenian National Union and the orphanage.[20] Although the details are not known, it is likely that Der Nerses played an important part in securing this double appointment.

Der Nerses's and Bogharian's subsequent lives did not differ much from those led by the rest of this survivor generation. In 1919 Krikor Bogharian, like many of the survivors among his townsmen, returned to Ayntab, where the occupying Allied forces had already established an authority. In Ayntab, Bogharian worked as a teacher in an Armenian orphanage. In 1920, the Allied armies' weakness and the Kemalist movement's successive military triumphs caused the town's Armenians to feel that their lives were once again in danger. Thus, in May 1920 the children and staff of this Armenian orphanage left Ayntab and moved to the Lebanese coastal city of Jounieh. Bogharian was in this group of people who had abandoned their hometown. He continued to teach in the orphanage for a while and then moved to Aleppo, where he was named principal of Aleppo's Ayntabi Grtasirats school. He died in Beirut in 1975.

In June 1919 Der Nerses also returned to Ayntab, where he was named an official representative of the Catholicos and president of the board of overseers of the local Armenian orphanage. "Others have destroyed our house; that is easy to do. It remains for us to build it: that, of course, is the hardest," he wrote in his diary on 15 September.[21] In

1920 he became president of the local Armenian National Union, a post he held during the Ayntab Armenians' movement of armed resistance against the Turkish armies. In 1921 he was forced to leave his hometown and settle in Aleppo. There he founded the Compatriotic Union of Natives of Ayntab with the main objective of providing relief to settlers from Ayntab. Der Nerses was murdered in Aleppo on 3 July 1934. The crime was motivated by the priest's decision in a familial dispute that he had adjudicated: he had ruled that the child of a divorced Armenian couple should remain in its mother's care. Enraged by the decision, the child's father reacted violently, putting an end to the priest's life.[22]

Let us turn back to the period of central interest here, the first months after the genocide. It appears that Der Nerses and Bogharian had no choice but to follow the new current, which itself was heavily dependent on the course charted by the victorious Allied states and the decisions they made. The British and French military authorities laid plans to evacuate all the Armenian deportees from Bilad al-Sham and resettle them in their native towns and villages, especially in Cilicia. These plans were indeed carried out, and Bogharian and Der Nerses found themselves in Ayntab again. The multitudes of repatriated survivors were supposed to serve as the occupying Allied armies' and occupation authorities' main means of exercising leverage in Cilicia and the region just east of it. They did, in fact, play this role: despite the weakness of the local French forces, Ayntab's Armenians organized resistance in the city and succeeded in stopping the Turkish troops' advance. Ultimately, France signed an agreement with the authorities under Mustafa Kemal Pasha's direction and withdrew from Cilicia. The Armenians joined the retreating French forces; thus did Der Nerses and Bogharian find their way to Syria and Lebanon.

At bottom, the two currents, Artin Efendi's and the one opposed to it, closely resembled each other in their weakness and helplessness. Both represented surviving remnants of the fragmented, utterly exhausted Armenian community. Both relied on a powerful external force to ensure their future development. In Artin Efendi's case, this force was the contemporary Ottoman state: he wanted to believe that this time, the new regime would adopt a course based on the equality of all citizens without discrimination and on the principle of respect for human rights. The mass deportation and massacre had also constituted a powerful shock for Artin Efendi and those like him. After all, as a native of Ayntab who had lost close family members during the deportation and tried to help many of his relatives and townsmen, he certainly was profoundly aware of the horror of the crime. Nevertheless, he had placed his bets on Turkish intellectuals and the Turkish elite, hoping they would be won to progressive ideas and universal human values and that these would guarantee that he and his fellow Armenians could continue to live side by side with Turks.

The opposite current was radical and nationalistic. The Ottoman Armenians who supported it were convinced that the rupture with the Ottoman-Turkish world was irremediable. For them, the party responsible for conceiving and executing the plan for genocide was Turkish society as a whole, toward which they had now adopted an intolerant attitude. "'A united Ottoman fatherland': all that must now be regarded as history," *Nor Gyank* wrote.[23] "You are all Ittihadists," Kevork-Mesrob exclaims, addressing Turkish intellectuals generally.[24] "If you are afraid to say so," he went on, "we state the matter plainly and demonstrate that the Ittihad is the one national Turkish party to which you have given birth, which you have fed and raised, which you have supported and will support in future."[25] Such Armenians considered all talk of solidarity and coexistence to be inappropriate: "That 'fraternal solidarity' was ruptured on the day when the Armenians, dripping with sweat, were slaughtered in their fields by their 'brother's' knives, when their wives and daughters were ravished before their eyes, when the desire to shatter the foundations of their existence made itself felt with a barbaric savagery never before recorded in history," Onnig wrote.[26]

The watchword of the day was *national reconstruction*. It was imperative to find and regroup the fragments of a people that had been massacred and deported. Gathering its thousands of orphans and ensuring that they would enjoy an Armenian education was a crucially important part of this task. "Wipe clean" or "purify" are frequently recurring verbs in the Armenian rhetoric of this period, whenever the subject of discussion is the orphans' education and "Armenization." The Armenian orphanages were supposed to form Armenians of this kind, "tomorrow's Armenians," and Bogharian and Der Nerses hastened to take on the task. The nationalist current sought to make the memory and pain of the genocide, mixed with hatred for the Turks, the principal cement of the nascent process of national reconstruction. In the Armenian schools established in Syria and Cilicia in particular and, thereafter, in Lebanon and Greece, these two elements were transformed into the central means of ideological homogenization.

To *remember* the genocide and which side had planned it and carried it out, to keep the memory of the martyrs alive, to *forget* and outlaw the Turkish language and various other phenomena, as well as ways of life that bound the Armenians to the Ottoman world. Like every nationalist process, this one was marked by inner contradiction. An effort was underway to create a new Armenian society whose largest segments were composed of Armenians who had been deported to Bilad al-Sham. Der Nerses was eminently familiar with these people, having witnessed their suffering and, as he himself puts it, their degradation, demoralization, and bestialization. Now he was needed to work with this same segment of his people, to provide it guidance, to forget the bitterness and anger that he had felt toward it. Obviously, this would not be an easy experience. Der Nerses was anguished, as the entries in his diary also attest. On 24 November 1918 he celebrated mass before a big crowd in the church in Hama:

> But I continued to feel the prick of conscience in my heart, as did, no doubt, everyone else as well. All the people had changed their names and all still bear that stain today. I looked around me during the church service: the priest officiating, the deacon, the members of the choir, and the congregation had all become Muslims, for a time, in their dread of suffering. Unfortunately, feelings of repentance have not yet sprung up in their hearts, and they are not aware that they erred; most of them think that they had to act as they did and that the Lord does not consider "what little they did" wrong.[27]

The newly created situation required Der Nerses and all other surviving Armenians to demonstrate a spirit of unity and solidarity. However, the priest from Ayntab found it difficult to forget the recent past and the bitterness associated with it: "'The people are eternal sheep'; some find fault with others for converting to Islam and no one recalls that all have been blackened by the same sin. Some find fault with others for having been swindlers under the old regime and do not remember that all were guilty of the same vice, only to different degrees."[28] Der Nerses felt still greater indignation when some of the Armenians who had converted to Islam during the exile tried to take leading positions in the reconstructed Armenian people's newly reorganized institutions. He clearly spoke his mind in Hama upon learning that the Catholicos and the Armenian national bodies had sent Father Vahan Gyuldalian to Ayntab with the mission of restoring the diocese and Armenian national institutions. For Der Nerses, Der Vahan was an apostate, someone who had abjured his faith. It is not unlikely that the diarist from Ayntab considered himself the person most deserving of such a post:

> Oh times, oh mores! Der Vahan, an apostate who abjured his faith, although he had no reason to fear violent treatment, is now outstripping all the others in his eagerness to take control of Ayntab's church. Still more surprisingly, the Catholicos, who is aware of all this, has entrusted this post to him before all others, while the Ayntab Union has extended him the first invitation. But there is no reason to be surprised, because our Teacher said, two thousand years ago, "The world loveth its own."[29]

In time the process of national reconstruction succeeded in expunging the phase of the deported Armenians' collective conversion to Islam from the Armenians' collective memory, much like the whole "parenthesis" represented by their life in Bilad al-Sham. For decades thereafter, Armenian memoirists and historians rarely reflected on this phenomenon or subjected it to serious examination, as though description or narration of the genocide could not acknowledge the existence of such a collective "stain." In fact, in Armenian historiography or Armenian culture in general, the Armenian Genocide takes the form of an episode in which an entire people was martyred. With the sanctification of this image of the martyr nation, victims underwent a metamorphosis that made them objects of admiration and even veneration. In other words, this process of sanitization transformed the victims of the crime—both those who were killed and those who survived—into paragons of innocence and purity.

In a monolithic presentation of this sort, one important facet of the catastrophe is naturally overlooked: the struggle against mass violence by all available means, and the natural human tendency to try to survive at any cost. When the episode of collective Islamization suddenly appeared in this picture studded with powerful symbols, many were doubtless inclined to see it as a kind of desecration: in their eyes it might have tarnished the image of the hallowed martyr and sowed confusion in official discourse. The upshot of this situation was that people began collectively to forget the event that occurred "under the empire of Evil"—the conversion that had led Der Nerses to pronounce religious and national anathema on his compatriots. For him, apostasy and moral degradation were red lines beyond which lay "the greatest of the disasters" that could befall a human being. The priest from Ayntab had witnessed this tragedy and the crossing of the red line. Yet the deported Armenians had been liberated, the conditions of their lives were transformed, and tens of thousands of survivors had collectively returned to the national community and national church. The doors were open to them and Der Nerses, too, despite his abiding bitterness, probably found himself with no choice but to accept them and live and work with them.

Yet, the genocide and liberation had given rise to a new dividing line: solidarity and coexistence with Turks was now evidently deemed unacceptable. With his speech, Artin Efendi had crossed the new red line and therefore immediately become the target of verbal attacks from Armenian intellectuals that were tantamount to national anathema. The post-genocide, restructured Armenian historiography founded on the new principles treated Artin Efendi just as mercilessly. As editor of the periodical *Armenian Anteb* (subsequently renamed *New Ayntab*), Krikor Bogharian later memorialized the activity of a multitude of Armenian notables from Ayntab in its pages. He also wrote a book entitled *Ayntabagank* [Ayntabiana], in which he presented the biographies of 160 Armenians from that city. Finally, he contributed to a two-volume general history almost two thousand pages long called *Badmutyun Antebi hayots* [History of the Armenians of Ayntab], edited by Kevork Sarafian. Not once does Artin Efendi appear in any of these texts. He no longer had a place in the Armenian collective memory.

The present book has attempted to ignore the red lines and examine and analyze an episode of universal human history that opens up horizons that are perhaps as instructive as they were fraught with calamity: the struggle for survival waged from 1915 to 1918 by the Armenians deported to Bilad al-Sham, with its multiple facets. It is a history of ordinary people's catastrophe and survival that I have tried to make accessible to the public and to scholarship through the lenses of Krikor Bogharian's and Father Der Nerses Tavukjian's twin experiences.

In the field of Armenian Genocide studies, this book also marks a first known attempt at putting work in the genre of self-narration—in this case, two diaries—at the core of an academic study. The past few years have seen the publication of critical editions of memoirs in the genre of self-narration, investing genocide studies based on victim testimony with new meaning and new value. Nevertheless, I believe that appreciation of works in this genre has only just begun. They are, as a rule, written in Armenian, so a linguistic barrier blocks the general public's access to them. And whereas many have now been published in Armenian, hundreds of others are tucked away in people's drawers, institutional archives, or libraries, waiting to see the light of day. Among the unpublished works are memoirs, diaries, and correspondence of exceptional value. True evaluation of this material begins when certain of these micro-historical texts—such as the present book, based on just two diaries—become the principle object of academic monographs. Once the memoirist/diarist/letter writer has the floor, his or her testimony can be critically examined and analyzed, so that rather than being treated as a mere secondary source, it becomes the main voice and principal illustration of the events of the day.

In any event, it is certain that the study of the Armenian Genocide has entered a new phase. As Alexandra Garbarini and Boris Adjémian have written, the testimony of survivors "has considerably bolstered the historiography of that genocide."[30] Countless micro-historical texts with which the public was long unfamiliar have been given new life thanks to translations and critical editions. Krikor Beledian writes of such texts

Figure 6.1. Ruins of Baalbek (Beqaa Valley, Lebanon), 24 August 1928. During that summer, Father Nerses and his wife, Anitsa, as well as Father Karekin and his wife, Santukhd, traveled to Jersualem, where their sons, Nerses-Diran and Norayr, were attending the local Armenian Zharankavorats School. On the return trip to Aleppo, the travelers visited Baalbek. The identity of the two individuals on the left is unknown, though clearly they are an Armenian priest and his wife. The third person from the left is Father Nerses Tavukjian, and beside him is his wife, Anitsa Tavukijan (née Syulahian). To her left are Father Karekin Bogharian and his wife Santukhd Bogharian (née Tahtajian). The boy standing in the forefront is Father Nerses's and Anitsa's youngest son, Hagop, who was born after the Armenian Genocide. (Source: Krikoris Bogharian family collection)

that they waited a long time "to emerge from their 'period of latency,' or, rather, for us to face up to them, so 'unassimilable' was the event that gave rise to them."[31]

I hope that the present book has succeeded in breathing new life into Father Der Nerses Tavukjian's and Krikor Bogharian's diaries. Their personal and family micro-histories afford us the opportunity to research mass violence from the perspective of the victim. Their daily jottings are windows that allow glimpses of the details of their daily lives and observation of their own evolution as well as other deportees' gradual enfeeblement and irreversible decline, destined to plunge them, in Der Nerses's own words, into the "endless abysses" that are, ultimately, the crime of genocide itself.

Notes

1. The English translation is taken from Taner Akçam, *A Shameful Act*, p. 255.
2. Ibid. In the Armenian transcription of Boshgezenian's speech ("Haygagan godoradze khorhrtaranin mech" [The Armenian massacres in parliament], *Zhamanag*, 12, no. 3364 (11/24 November 1918), the phrase corresponding to "hooligan regime" is "çete government."
3. Cited in "The Armenian massacres in parliament," 11/24 November 1918, 12/3364.
4. Akçam, *A Shameful Act*, p. 255.
5. Der Nerses uses the Turkish word for bellwether, *kösemen*.
6. "Haygagan godoradze khorhrtaranin mech, Harutyun Ef(fendi) Gezeniani jare" [The Armenian massacres in parliament: Harutyun Efendi Gezenian's speech], *Zhamanag*, 12, no. 3365 (12/25 November 1918).
7. Ibid.
8. "Haygagan godoradznere khorhrtaranin mech, Harutyun Ef(fendi) Gezeniani jare" [The Armenian massacres in parliament: Harutyun Efendi Gezenian's speech] *Zhamanag*, 12, no. 3366 (13/26 November 1918).
9. "Haygagan godoradznere khorhrtaranin mech, Harutyun Ef(fendi) Gezeniani jare" [The Armenian massacres in parliament: Harutyun Efendi Gezenian's speech] *Zhamanag*, 12, no. 3368 (15/28 November 1918).
10. On the sessions of the Ottoman parliament held in the first few weeks after the war, see Taner Akçam, *A Shameful Act*, pp. 248–272.
11. A. Gebenlian, "Pari Turkere?" [The good Turks?], *Hay Tsayn* 1, no. 42 (2 January 1919).
12. A. Jyunbyushian, "Anonk mezme chen" [They are not of our number], *Verchin lur* 5, no. 1422 (19 November 1918).
13. Kevork-Mesrob, "Lretsek, mi khosik mezi hamar" "[Be quiet, do not speak on our behalf], *Nor gyank* 1, no. 33 (20 November 1918).
14. Mshetsi, "Kich me gshrelov khosetsek, hay mebusner" [Weigh your words a little before you take the floor, Armenian members of parliament], *Zhamanag* 12, no. 3368 (15/28 November 1918).
15. "Desagtsutyun me Halebi hay mebusin hed Wilsoni sgzpunkneru masin" [Interview with the Armenian member of parliament from Aleppo about Wilson's principles], *Verchin lur* 5 no. 1427 (25 November 1918).
16. Ibid.

17. Tavukjian, *Diary*, p. 144.
18. Ibid., pp. 176–177.
19. Ibid., pp. 170–171.
20. "Ashkhadagitsner/Krikor Bogharian" [Contributors: Krikor Bogharian], in Kevork A. Sarafian, ed., *Badmutyun Antebi Hayots* [*History of the Armenians of Ayntab*], vol. 2 (Los Angeles: Amerigapnag Antebtsineru miutyun [Association of Ayntab Natives Living in the United States], 1953), p. 636.
21. Tavukjian, *Diary*, p. 194.
22. "Nerses Kahana Tavukjian (Inknagensakragan noter)" [Father Nerses Tavukjian (Autobiographical notes)], *Shirag: Kraganutyan u arvesdi amsakir* [*Shirag: Monthly for literature and the arts*] 51, no. 8 (August 1987): 58–59; Krikor Bogharian, "Father Nerses Tavukjian," in *History of the Armenians of Ayntab*, pp. 470–471.
23. "Hay mamulin" [To the Armenian press], *Nor Gyank* 1, no. 32 (19 November 1918).
24. Kevork-Mesrob, "Gam Turk chek, gam sdakhos ek" ["Either you're not Turks, or you're liars"], *Nor Gyank* 1, no. 42 (29 November 1918): 1.
25. Ibid.
26. Onnig, "Pats namag Halebi yerespokhan Artin Ef. Gezeniani" ["Open letter to the member of parliament from Aleppo Artin Ef[fendi] Gezenian," *Nor Gyank* 1, no. 41 (28 November 1918).
27. Tavukjian, *Diary*, p. 171.
28. Ibid., p. 175.
29. Ibid., p. 178.
30. Alexandra Garbarini and Boris Adjémian, "Mass Violence from Experience to Knowledge," *Études Arméniennes Contemporaines*, no. 5 (June 2015): 18.
31. Missakian, *Face à l'innomable*, p. 122.

Selected Bibliography

Published Material

Akçam, Taner. *A Shameful Act: The Armenian Genocide and the Question of Turkish Responsibilty*. New York, 2007.

Alexandra Garbarini and Boris Adjémian, "Mass Violence from Experience to Knowledge," *Études Arméniennes Contemporaines*, no. 5 (June 2015): 18.

A. Jyunbyushian, "Անոնք մեզմէ չեն" [Anonk mezme chen] [They are not of our number], *Verchin lur* 5, no. 1422 (19 November 1918).

A. Gebenlian, "Բարի թուրքերը?" [Pari Turkere?] [The good Turks?], *Hay Tsayn* 1, no. 42 (2 January 1919).

Kevork-Mesrob, "Լռեցէք, մի խօսիք մեզի համար" [Lretsek, mi khosik mezi hamar] [Be quiet, do not speak on our behalf], *Nor gyank* 1, no. 33 (20 November 1918). "Կամ թուրք չէք, կամ ստախօս էք" [Gam Turk chek, gam sdakhos ek] [Either you're not Turks, or you're liars], *Nor Gyank* 1, no. 42 (29 November 1918).

Missakian, Chavarche, *Face à l'innomable Avril 1915*, trans. Arpik Missakian. Marseilles, 2015.

Mshetsi, "Քիչ մը կշռելով խօսեցէք, հայ մեպուսներ" [Kich me gshrelov khosetsek, hay mebusner] [Weigh your words a little before you take the floor, Armenian members of parliament], *Zhamanag* 12, no. 3368 (15/28 November 1918).

Onnig, "Բաց նամակ Հալէպի երեսփոխան Արթին Էֆ. Կէզէնեանի" [Pats namag Halebi yerespokhan Artin Ef. Gezeniani] [Open letter to the member of parliament from Aleppo Artin Ef[fendi] Gezenian]," *Nor Gyank* 1, no. 41 (28 November 1918).

Tavukjian, Father Nerses, "Օրագրութեան Մեքենագրուած Բնագիր" [Orakrutyan mekenakrvadz pnakir] [Typescript of the diary (Ms. Diary)].

———. Տառապանքի օրագրութիւն [Darabanki orakrutyun] [Diary of days of suffering]. Beirut, 1991. "Ներսէս Քհնյ. Թաւուգճեան (Ինքնակենսագրական նօթեր)" [Nerses Kahana Tavukjian (Inknagensakragan noter)] ["Father Nerses Tavukjian (Autobiographical Notes)"], *Shirag* 51, no. 8 (August 1987): 53–59.

"Աշխատակիցներ/Գրիգոր Պօղարեան" [Ashkhadagitsner/Krikor Bogharian] [Contributors: Krikor Bogharian], in Kevork A. Sarafian, ed., *Badmutyun Antebi Hayots* [*History of the Armenians of Ayntab*], vol. 2 (Los Angeles: Amerigapnag Antebtsineru miutyun [Association of Ayntab Natives Living in the United States], 1953), p. 636.

"Հայկական կոտորածը խորհրդարանին մէջ" ("Haygagan godoradze khorhrtaranin mech" [The Armenian massacres in parliament], *Zhamanag* 12, no. 3364 (11/24 November 1918).

"Հայկական կոտորածը խորհրդարանին մէջ, Յարութիւն Էֆ. Կէզէնեանի ճառը" [Haygagan godoradze khorhrtaranin mech, Harutyun Ef(fendi) Gezeniani jare] [The Armenian massacres in parliament: Harutyun Efendi Gezenian's speech], *Zhamanag* 12, no. 3365 (12/25 November 1918), 12, no. 3366 (13/26 November 1918).

"Տեսակցութիւն մը Հալէպի հայ մէպուսին հետ Ուիլսընի սկզբունքներուն մասին" [Desagtsutyun me Halebi hay mebusin hed Wilsoni sgzpunknerun masin] [Interview with the Armenian member of parliament from Aleppo about Wilson's principles], *Verchin lur* 5 no. 1427 (25 November 1918).

Glossary

al-salamu alaykum	a greeting in Arabic, "peace be upon you"
araba	cart
arazi mülkiye	the Sultan's properties
bâdiya	steppe, the land of the Bedouins
bastaci	a small vendor who spreads his wares out on the ground or on a table at market
basturma	salted and dried meat
*belediyeyi tambur*s	small carts belonging to the municipality
çavuş	sergeant
cherez	a mixture of raisins, walnuts, and pistachios
chorba	soup
değirmen	a type of milling machine
değlip	mills used to crush the boiled, dried wheat
direzin or *drezin*	the laid warp
düyunu unumiye	the Public Debt Administration
firman	imperial edict
han	an inn for travelers
harbiye kumandanı	military command
havale	money transfer
Heimat	native country, hometown, homeland
hummaai rajia	remittent fever
imalat hane	workshop
kadı	judge
kanon	a musical instrument
kavas	here, a bodyguard
kavurmahane	meat and dried-meat factory
kaymakam	county/kaza executive
kaza	sub-district or county

lahana	cabbage
talimâtnâme	ordinance
lider or *ratl*	units of weight for food
ma' âmura	area under cultivation
mal müdir	municipal treasurer
manusa	type of cloth
marhaba	hello, greetings
meclis-i idare	(local) governing council
mejid	a monetary unit
merkez kumandanı	garrison commander
mevsim	season
millet kahvesi	a club with a cafe
müdir	administrator
müdir muavin	assistant director
müfettiş	inspector
muhacir	emigrant, refugee
muhacir komisyonu	settlers' committee
muhtar/mukhtar	headman of a neighborhood or village
mutasarrıf	administrative governor of a sanjak, or district
mutemed katibi	clerk in charge of running accounts
nahiye	township
nazır	assistant
nikah	Muslim marriage
nivig	a dish
nufus teskeresi	identity papers
okha	1.28 kg
olchag	92.1 kg
prasa	leek
sadaret	the grand vizir's office
šahāda	the Islamic credo
sanjak	district
saray	the seat of the municipal government
sevkıyat	(in this context) a military term meaning dispatch or shipment
shireh	grape molasses
silejeks	big bath towels
sinameki	cassia
sucuk	a dry, spicy sausage
tahrirat katibi	(the *kaymakam*'s) general secretary
tayın	daily ration (plural *tayinât*)
tayın-kötek	*tayın*-beatings
tezgah	loom
tonir and *saj*	ovens
top	skeins
vali	governor-general of a province
vesika	document, in this context a pass
vilayet	province

INDEX

A
Abbasid rule, 62
Abdülhamid II, Sultan, 64, 114, 155
Abdülmejid I, Sultan, 63
Adana, 54, 70, 107, 139, 156, 158, 184
Africa, 62
Agha Khan, 64
Aghaton, Yervant, 103
Aghja Koyu (Akçaköy), 22
Agn (Eğin, Kemaliye), 67
Agricultural Bank (*Ziraat Bankası*), 100, 169
Ajlun, 38, 100
Al-Maghut, Muhammed, 58
Alawi, 63–64
Aleppo
  Allied forces in, 60
  Armenian deportees in, 7, 25, 28, 39, 43, 65, 71, 93, 95, 97, 100, 105, 110, 113, 116
  Armenian Prelacy (diocese), 94–95, 104–9, 139
  Armenian Prelacy Archives, ix, 9, 104
  Armenian Prelate, ix
  Armenian press, 184, 186
  Ayntab Armenians in, 64–65
  Committee for Settlers, 95, 97, 104
  Der Nerses in, 7, 66, 190
  distribution of aid by the Armenian Prelacy of, 104–9, 120
  food prices in, 90
  Krikor Bogharian in, 189
  orphanage in, 53
  Ottoman parliament representative from, 116, 184–85
  Prelacy's *kavas*, 117–18
  railway, 25
  U.S. consulate of, 102–3
  vali of, 95
Ali Kemal Bey, 158, 161
Allied forces, 33, 57, 60, 96, 113, 177–78, 188–90
Amasya, 29
American Committee for Armenian and Syrian Relief, 102
American missionaries
  in Ayntab, 22
  and dispatching financial aid to Armenian deportees, 102–6
Amja, Hasan, 55–56
Amman, 7, 25, 97, 156
Anatolia, 1, 6, 27, 30, 34, 52, 55, 60, 130
Anatolian
  anti-arab clichés, 61
  provinces, 16, 51, 61, 67, 137
  Rums, 102
Aneze, 28
Antioch, 16, 26, 101, 149
Aposhian, 157
Aprahamian, Der Bedros, 161

Arab regions, 24–23, 34, 53, 56, 60–61, 64, 88, 168, 176
Arabic (language), 19, 58, 163, 178
Arabs, 28, 53, 60–61, 64, 69–70, 113, 139, 156, 163, 177, 188. *See also* Bedouins
Aramian, Hayg, 9
Aramian, Sahag, 148–49
Armash (Akmeşe), 22, 54
Armenian Anteb (periodical), 7–8, 194
Armenian High Plateau, 1, 24, 37
Armenian National Delegation, 103
Armenian National Union, 189–90
Armenian Patriarch of Constantinople (Istanbul), 61, 103, 139
Armenian Patriarchate of Constantinople (Istanbul), 105
Armenian Prelacy of Aleppo, ix, 9, 94–95, 104–9, 117, 118, 139
Assyrian
  church, 26
  language, 19
  school, 19, 26
Atay, Falih Rıfkı, 52
Ayntab (Gaziantep), 5–8, 11, 16–25, 27, 29–34, 36, 38–42, 59, 62, 64–69, 72–73, 81, 83–88, 92, 94–96, 99–101, 110–16, 130, 133, 135–38, 140, 142–43, 145–50, 157–58, 160, 165–69, 171–74, 178–79, 185, 188–90, 192–94
Ayntabi Grtasirats school (Aleppo), 189
Ayntura, 55

B
Baalbek, 114, 195
Bab, 106–7
Baboyan, Kevork, 19, 40
Baghdad, 63, 168
Banque Ottomane, 100–1, 105
Barsumian, Hagop, 104
Basra, 177
Bedouin, 61, 63, 69, 83–84, 139
Beirut, 7–9, 55, 102, 189
Bekir Sami (Kunduh, *vali* of Aleppo), 97
Bern, 103
Beylan (Belen), 66
Bible House, 102, 105
Bilad al-Sham, 1–2, 4, 6–7, 9, 11, 25, 34–35, 40, 43, 51–56, 58–59, 61, 63, 65, 67–71, 73, 83, 88, 98, 105, 113, 117–18, 124, 129–30, 146, 155–57, 159–62, 164–65, 167, 170, 172, 176–79, 189–90, 192–94

Birejig (Birecik), 39, 106
Bogharian-Tahtajian, Santukhd, 12, 18, 38, 44, 166–68, 171–72, 195
Bogharian, Atam-Norayr, 38, 44
Bogharian, Father Karekin
  against the Islamization, 161, 174
  in Aleppo, 176
  in Baalbek, 195
  back to Salamiyya after his exile to Tafile, 170
  book-seller in Ayntab, 18
  correspondence with Der Nerses, 148, 170
  correspondence with Krikor Bogharian, 100
  diary of, 23
  exile in Buseyra (Tafile), 40, 82, 99, 158–59, 167, 171–72
  friendship with Der Nerses, 22–23
  in Hama, 101, 170
  and his family, 21, 38, 44
  priestly duties in Hama and Salamiyya, 26, 81
  opening a grocery store in Salamiyya, 170
  ordination in Sis, 22
  receiving *Byuzantion* newspaper in Hama, 21
  receiving money from abroad, 101
Bogharian, Hripsime, 38, 44
Bogharian, Khachig, 38, 40, 44, 82, 131, 170
Bogharian, Nubar, 38, 44
Boghigian, Der Khachadur, 107
Boshgezenian, Artin, 116, 184–86
Boshgezenian, Rupen, 39
British
  Empire, 64
  forces, 178, 190
Buseyra, 117, 159
Byuzantion (newspaper), 18, 21, 27

C
Catholicos
  of the Great House of Cilicia, 9
  Papken I Gyuleserian, 8
  Sahag II Khabayan, 61, 95, 107–8, 120, 139, 157, 173, 176, 178–79, 189, 192. *See also* Papken I Gyuleserian; Sahag II Khabayan
Caucasus, 102
Central Powers, 102

Cesaerea (Kayseri), 29
cholera, 130
Chorum (Corum), 100
Christian
  Armenians, 29, 174, 188
  Maronites, 56
  refugees in Iran and the Caucasus, 102
  religion/faith, 56, 141–42, 145, 147, 161, 163–66. *See also* conversion
Church
  Armenian, 23, 53, 189, 193
  Assyrian/Syriac Orthodox, 26, 174
  of the Forty Martyrs (Aleppo), 106, 108
  of the Holy Mother (Aleppo), 108
  services/custom, 21, 157–58, 165, 192
Cilicia, High School (Ayntab), 18, 22, 160
Circassians, 34, 53, 63
colonialism
  French, 55
  nationalist-colonialist policy of Jemal Pasha, 11, 56–57, 60
Commission of Abandoned Property (Emvâl-i metrûke), 98
Committee of Union and Progress (CUP, Ittihad, Ittihad Party, *Ittihat ve terakki*)
  Armenian genocide and, 2, 29, 55, 110, 177
  Artin Efendi Boshgezenian and, 116, 184, 186, 191
  internal political divisions, 51–55
  Islamization and, 158, 161–62
  pre-war activities in Ayntab, 114–115
Communist, 35–36
Compatriotic Union of Natives of Ayntab, 190
conscription, 42, 64, 67, 83, 109, 112, 128–30
conversion to Islam, 4, 54–55, 149–50, 155–66, 168, 192–93. *See also* Islamization

D
Dadrian, Vahram, 9, 61, 69, 88, 97, 100, 119, 129, 134, 156
Damascus, 6–7, 25, 31, 53–55, 60, 67, 70, 100, 106, 116, 129–30, 156, 158–61, 164, 173, 178–79
decline (disintegration of the social system in extreme conditions), 2–3, 5, 11–12, 30, 33, 37–38, 41, 80–81, 83, 93, 120, 128–29, 135, 137–150, 157, 160, 171, 192–93, 196

Der Zor, 16, 24–25, 28, 37, 39, 60, 93–94, 105–7, 117, 120, 129, 156–57, 176, 186
Dera'a, 25
Dutch Foreign Ministry, 102

E
economic crisis, 5, 7, 71, 73, 87–92, 96, 99, 117–19, 128, 130–31, 134, 150, 166, 170, 174–76
Edib, Halidé (Adıvar), 55–56
education, 9, 18, 21–22, 32, 36–37, 53–56, 160, 191
Egypt
  aid dispatched from, 178
  Allied armies' headquarters in, 177
  Egyptian front, 57
  money transfers from, 100
Ejzajian, Rupen, 104, 108
Ekmekjian, Father Kalusd, 7–8
Epidemics, 2, 5, 7–8, 12, 17, 25–26, 94, 128–136. *See also* cholera; fever; malaria; typhus
Erbid, 159
Erzurum (Garin), 37, 100, 112
Etmekjian, Der Hovhannes, 107
Euphrates
  river, 24, 31, 117
  valley, 51, 62, 116
European
  capitals, 101
  Great Powers, 24
  missionaries, 102–3
Everek, 114

F
famine, 17, 25, 56, 84, 102, 131, 137
Fatimid Caliphate, 62
Fendejak (Dönüklü), 26
Feruzan, Khairi (*mutasarrıf* of Hama), 156, 158
fever, 92, 131–33, 174–75, 199
food
  basic foodstuffs of the deportees, 83–87
  securing, 9, 80–82, 97, 107, 114, 116, 133, 135, 144, 148, 178
  shortage of, 41, 85, 93, 135, 142, 149, 160
  soaring prices of, 5, 7, 82, 87–92, 96, 119, 128
French
  colonialism, 55–56

language, 18
military authorities in Bilad al-Sham, 190
missionaries in Lebanon, 55
occupation of Syria, Lebanon and Cilicie, 57, 190

G
Garbarini, Alexandra, 17, 138, 194
gender, 167–72
Geneva, 99, 102–3
German
  army in Hama, 27
  missionary, 102
  Nazi, 57
  newspapers, 27
  officers in Der Zor, 117
Germany, 101, 103, 186
God (in Der Nerses diary entries), 16, 21, 23–24, 30, 33, 73, 96, 119–20, 131, 133, 136, 147, 149–50, 158, 164, 166, 174, 192
Gökalp, Ziya, 60
Great Britain, 64
Greece, 191
Gürün, 29
Gyuleserian, Bishop Papken (the future coadjutor Catholicos), 8, 100, 108

H
Hafez Bey, 185
Haigazian University, ix, 8, 20, 86
Hajin (Saimbeyli), 29
Hama
  Armenian deportees, 4–6, 8–9, 11, 26, 53, 71, 114–15
  Bogharian's friends, 19, 39
  books read by Bogharian, 19
  collective actions undertaken by Ayntab Armenian deportees, 27, 36, 42, 53, 111–13, 189
  conscription, 129
  deportees' degradation and decline, 12, 27, 29–31, 33, 117, 135, 137, 142, 146
  Der Nerses's personal and family life, 22, 29–33, 39–40, 71, 73, 119, 134–35, 141, 148–49, 174–75, 192
  distribution of aid through Armenian or missionary networks, 101, 103–4, 106, 108
  foodstuffs and prices, 83–90, 119

Islamization of Armenians, 12, 156–62
Krikor Bogharian's personal and family life, 18, 25–26, 38, 40, 167–72
money transfer, 100, 120
Ottoman army's retreat from, 177
post office in, 99
priestly duties in, 30
newspapers arriving in, 27
revival of the local market, weaving *manusa*, 67–69, 72
state-aid distribution, 94, 96, 98
transit station for many deportees, 30–31
Yervant Odian in, 16, 27, 69, 156, 158, 161–62
Hauran, 7, 25, 31, 38, 88, 159
Hay Tsayn (newspaper), 186
Hijaz railroad, 25
Hobbesian
  behavior, 160
  figure, 150, 173
  hero, 139–40, 147–48
  man, 139–40, 145, 147
  social contract, 144–47, 155
Holocaust (Jewish), 10, 57–58, 138, 140. *See also* Jewish
Homer, Frederic, 139, 144
Homs
  Armenian deportees in, 7, 39, 71–72
  Armenian prostitutes in, 146
  conscription in, 129
  Der Nerses in, 32, 101, 179
  Islamization in, 158
  market of, 73
  railway running through, 25
  sending money, 106
  starvation in, 84
  trade with, 68
Human Rights, 40, 190

I
Idlib, 106–7
imalat hane, 71, 113, 199
India, 64
Iran, 102
Irbid, 38–39
Islamization, 5, 12, 155–66, 171, 173–74, 150, 156, 159, 162–65, 193
Ismaili, 58, 62–64, 69, 168
Israel, 1
Istanbul, 16, 18, 27, 60–61, 64, 100–3, 105, 117, 139, 162, 185–88

Index

Izmir, 184

J
Jarash, 7, 67, 69, 88, 97, 100, 119, 129–30, 134, 156–57, 159, 163
Jebejian, Robert, 64–65
Jelal Bey (*vali* of Aleppo), 95, 97
Jemal Pasha, Ahmed, 11, 27, 42, 51–58, 70, 75n17, 75n18, 76n23, 97, 156–57
Jemil Efendi (director of the *ziraat bankasi* in Salamiyya), 169
Jerusalem, 32, 54, 107, 139, 158
Jevad Efendi (local official in Hama), 95
Jewish
  diarists, 17, 138
  Holocaust, 10, 57–58, 138
  forced laborers, 57
  Palestinian, 102
  population, 57
Jidejian, Tavit, 104
Jihan (Ceyhan), 66
Jisr Shoghur, 106
Jordan, 1, 159
Jounieh, 189

K
Kadmus, 63
Kaiser, Hilmar, 54–55
Kapigian, Garabed, 36–37, 93–94, 98, 100
Karaduran, 161
Karkemish, 22
Karlek, 106, 110
Kars Bazar (Kadirli), 161
Katma, 106
Kavafian, Vahan, 104
Kemal Bey (*kaymakam* of Salamiyya), 115
Kemal Pasha, Mustafa (later Atatürk), 190
Kemalist movement, 188–189
Kerek, 159
Kesab, 26, 29
Ketmenian, Garabed, 107
Kevork-Mesrob, 19, 186, 191
Kévorkian, Raymond H., ix, 25, 75n18
Kghi (Kiği), 29–30, 137
Khabur
  banks of, 51
  river, 24, 117
Khawabi River, 63
Kilis, 26, 29, 106, 112–13

Konya, 60
Kudulian, Krikor, 97, 159, 161
Kurds, 34, 53, 55, 60, 188
Kushagian, Torkom (Prelate of Egypt), 36

L
languages
  Armenian, 18, 53, 56, 189
  English, 18
  French, 18
  German, 117
  Ottoman Turkish, 18, 53, 56, 191
Lebanon, 1, 55–57, 84–86, 102, 177, 189–91, 195
Lejeune, Philippe, 3, 9
Levi, Primo, 19, 36, 51, 93, 140, 144, 147
Levonian, Hovhannes, 69, 94
liberation
  Allied forces occupation of the Hama region, 33, 113, 184, 193
  Der Nerses's daily life on the eve of, 174
  first months after the Ottoman army's retreat from the region of Hama, 177–79, 188, 193
Lodz (Litzmannstadt), 57

M
Ma'an, 25, 32, 159
Maara, 106–7
malaria, 40, 130–31
Manugian, Der Vahan, 107
manusa, 68, 72–73, 135, 141, 146, 200
Marash (Kahraman Maraş), 16, 26, 29, 30, 66, 106, 146, 170
Marat, 25
Margada, 25
Maronites, 56
Mazlumian, Armen, 104
Mazlumian, Onnig, 107–8, 124n106
Mejidabad, 63
Menber (newspaper), 188
Meskene, 106
Mesopotamia (Armenian deportees in the steppes of), 24–25, 52, 60–61
Meydan-Ekbez, 106
Mirza, Emir (notable in Salamiyya), 62
Missakian, Chavarche, 16
missionary activities, 22, 55, 102–6
Misyaf, 63
Mkhitarian, Bishop Kyud, 101, 157
Momjian, Der Sahag, 107

money
    bride, 37
    distribution by Armenian networks, 103–9
    distribution by missionary networks, 102–3, 105–6
    distribution to the victims of 1909 massacres, 16
    struggle for survival and, 25, 40, 81–82, 134–35, 149, 168, 174–75
    tayın (state-aid) distribution by the Ottoman authorities, 92–99, 115, 119
    transfers (*havale*), 99–101, 120
Mosul, 25, 93, 177
Msrian, 101, 103, 106
Mumbuj, 106
Murshid Efendi (Hama's mufti), 112
Musa Dagh (Mt. Moses), 26–27, 29
Muslim, 62, 139, 158, 162–64, 188, 192, 200
mutual assistance
    among family members, 4, 31, 37–38, 40–41, 43–44, 80–81, 116, 132, 148
    decline of, 120, 145–46, 167, 171, 178
    intra-community, 31, 35–38, 41–44, 73, 80, 111, 114, 116, 135, 149, 170, 173

N
Nalbandian, Harutyun, 113
Nalbandian, Kevork, 108, 112–13, 148–49
Nalbandian, Nazaret (Der Garabed), 113
Nazi
    concentration camps, 19, 35, 40, 51, 93, 139, 144
    crimes, 186
    officials, 57–58
Near East Relief, 102
Nejmeddin Bey (*kaymakam* of Salamiyya), 66, 111, 114–16
Nersesian school (Ayntab), 22
Nersesian, Artin, 156
Nersoyan, Kevork. *See* Tavukjian (Nersoyan), Kevork
Nichanian, Marc, 3
Nor Gyank (newspaper), 191
Nubar Pasha, Boghos, 103

O
Odian, Yervant, 16, 27–28, 60–61, 69, 100–1, 103, 113, 117, 156, 158, 161–64, 186

Orientalism, 60, 139
Orontes (al-Asi) River, 63, 142
Osman Bey (military commander of Hama), 42–43, 111–14, 142, 173
Ottoman Fourth Army, 11, 42–43, 51–53, 56, 70, 97, 116, 156–57
Ottoman
    army, 11, 29, 51, 60, 70, 83, 94, 97, 109, 116–17, 170, 172, 177–79
    authorities and the missionaries, 55, 102–3
    gendarmes/police, 16, 71, 107, 110, 115, 159
    gold lira. *See* food; money
    language (Ottoman Turkish), 18, 22, 55, 69, 83, 114, 168–69
    newspapers, 27, 97
    parliament representative, 116, 184–88, 190–91
    policy and the Arab provinces, 56, 60
    policy and the nomadic Bedouins, 83–84
    post office, 40, 99–100, 106, 108–9
    rule and the Ismailis in Salamiyya, 62–64
    state aid (*tayın*), 92, 98
    stock market, 82

P
Palestinian territories, 1
Peet, William, 102
Protestant (Armenian), 40, 99, 101, 159, 161
Public Debt Administration (*düyunu unumiye*), 100, 199

R
Rakka, 36–37, 67, 98, 100, 106, 112
Ras el-Ain, 25, 106, 108
Rayak, 7
Riha, 106–7
Rodosto, 70
Rohner, Beatrice, 105
Rums (Orthodox Greeks), 102

S
Sabka, 106
Sahag II, Khabayan (Catholicos), 61, 73, 95, 107–8, 120, 139, 157, 173, 176, 178–79
Sahagian, Sahag, 73

Salamiyya
Armenians in the surrounding villages of, 66–67
Ayntab Armenians in, 5–6, 11, 27, 39, 59, 66–67, 94, 113
conscription, 129
Der Nerses's personal and family life, 32, 39, 41, 72–73, 148
description of the town by Bogharian and Der Nerses, 58–62, 65–66, 68–69
diseases, 130–34
distribution of aid through Armenian or missionary networks, 99, 101, 103–4, 106
economic crisis, 71, 84, 117–19
foodstuffs and prices, 83–92, 119
intra-community mutual assistance, 36, 42, 116, 146
intra-familial mutual assistance, 37–38, 82, 116, 167–70, 172
Islamization of Armenians, 12, 156, 158–60, 162–63, 165
Ismailis and, 62–65
Krikor Bogharian's personal and family life, 19, 21, 26, 39–40, 82, 84, 167–72
life in the extreme conditions, 157–58
Nejmeddin Bey (*kaymakam*), 66, 68, 111, 114–15
prostitution, 145–46
state-aid distribution, 95–96, 98, 112
transformation of the local market, 66–69, 72–73
Salt, 7, 106, 129, 156, 159, 161
Samson (Samsun), 29, 33, 100–1, 161
Sarafian, Kevork, 194
Sarafian, Krikor, 19, 40, 92, 160
Sarkis (Kavas), 107, 118
Sarkisian, Khacher, 113–14
schools
in Aleppo, 189
in Ayntab, 9, 18, 20, 22, 32, 160, 169
Cilicia, High School (Ayntab), 18, 22, 160
in Damascus, 54
in Hama, 19, 26
in Jerusalem, 54, 195
missionary, 55
Nersesyan school (Ayntab), 22
in Salamiyya, 68, 115
in Sivas, 36

Turkey's Central College (Ayntab), 22
Vartanian school (Ayntab), 18, 20, 22
Zharankavorats School (Jerusalem), 54, 195. *See also* education
Settlers' committee (*muhacir komisyonu*), 95–98, 200
Settlers' Relief Committee (established by Aleppo's Armenian Prelacy), 97, 104–6
Sevag, Manase, 70
Severeg (Siverek), 66
sevkıyat, 26, 106, 200
Shalamov, Varlam, 36, 160
Sham (sanjak and vilayet), 25, 43
Sharifian Army (Arab), 177
Shedadiye, 25
Sheikh Khelil Efendi (director of the Banque Ottomane in Hama), 100
Sinai Peninsula, 25
Sis (Kozan), 22
Sivas (Sepasdia), 27, 29, 36, 67, 69, 94, 100
Soviet camps (Gulag), 36, 140, 160
Sublime Porte, 63
Suedia (Samandağı), 27
Suleiman, Emir (notable in Salamiyya), 62
Sultaniye (Karapinar), 60
Suriyye (vilayet), 25
Suruj (Suruç), 94, 100
Swiss, 102, 105
Switzerland, 103
Syria, 1, 4, 16, 30, 34, 43, 55, 57, 83, 129, 177, 190–91
Syriac Orthodox church, 174
Syrian steppes, 24, 34, 84, 95, 158
Syulahian, Hrant, 116
Syulahian, Mariam (Zantur), 39, 133, 175

T
Tafile, 17, 32, 40–41, 90, 100, 159, 167
Talaat Pasha, 52, 156
Tamir, Emir (notable in Salamiyya), 62
Taurus mountains, 24, 34, 60–61, 66–67
Tavukjian (Nersoyan), Kevork, 7, 40, 131–33
Tavukjian-Syulahian, Anitsa, 22, 39–40, 174–75, 195
Tavukjian, Diruhi, 128, 134–36, 174
Tavukjian, Hagop, 39, 73, 128, 134–36, 138, 148, 173–75
Tavukjian, Mariam, 40, 132–33

Tavukjian, Nerses (Der Nerses's son), 40, 132–33
Tavukjian, Shoghagat, 40, 134, 175
Tavukjian, Tshkuyn (Dudu), 40, 128, 132–33
Teotig, 19, 23
Tevfik Bey (Beybaba), 114
Tigris River, 24
Todorov, Tzvetan, 16, 19, 145, 147
Tokat, 29
Trabizon (Trabzon), 185
Turkey's Central College (Ayntab), 22
Turkification, 43
Turkish
  Armenian orphans or women living in Turkish families, 188
  elites, 60, 190
  language, 18, 22, 53–56, 69, 83, 92, 114, 133, 168–69, 191
  military troops, 190
  newspapers, 187–88
  notables in Hama, 113
Turks
  and Armenians, 34
  in Adana, 54
  in Ayntab, 22, 72
  coexistence with the, 187–88, 191, 193
  collective responsibility of the, 186
  hatred for the, 191
  opposed to the Armenian massacres, 185–86
  in Sultaniye, 60
typhus, 92, 130–31, 134

U
U.S. diplomatic presence in the Ottoman Empire, 102–3, 105
Ubayd Allah, 62
Ughurlian, Hmayag, 178
United States, 100, 102–3, 160
Urfa, 37

V
Vartanian school (Ayntab), 18, 20, 22
Verchin Lur (newspaper), 186

W
weaving trade
  Der Nerses as a weaver, 22, 72–73, 135, 146, 148, 173
  in Hama, 6, 72, 113
  in Salamiyya, 68. *See manusa*
Wilson, Woodrow, 187–88
World War I, 1, 12, 60, 85, 110, 156
World War II, 17, 57, 138

Y
Yesayan, Der Harutyun, 104

Z
Zahle, 160
Zaven (Patriarch). *See* Armenian Patriarch of Constantinople
Zeytun (Süleymanlı), 10
Zharankavorats School (Jerusalem), 54, 195

War and Genocide

General Editors:
Omer Bartov, Brown University; A. Dirk Moses, University of Sydney

In recent years there has been a growing interest in the study of war and genocide, not from a traditional military history perspective, but within the framework of social and cultural history. This series offers a forum for scholarly works that reflect these new approaches.

"The Berghahn series Studies on War and Genocide has immeasurably enriched the English-language scholarship available to scholars and students of genocide and, in particular, the Holocaust." —**Totalitarian Movements and Political Religions**

Volume 1
The Massacre in History
Edited by Mark Levene and Penny Roberts

Volume 2
National Socialist Extermination Policies: Contemporary German Perspectives and Controversies
Edited by Ulrich Herbert

Volume 3
War of Extermination: The German Military in World War II 1941–1944
Edited by Hannes Heer and Klaus Naumann

Volume 4
In God's Name: Genocide and Religion in the Twentieth Century
Edited by Omer Bartov and Phyllis Mack

Volume 5
Hitler's War in the East, 1941–1945: A Critical Assessment
Rolf-Dieter Müller and Gerd R. Ueberschär

Volume 6
Genocide and Settler Society: Frontier Violence and Stolen Indigenous Children in Australian History
Edited by A. Dirk Moses

Volume 7
Networks of Nazi Persecution: Bureaucracy, Business and the Organization of the Holocaust
Edited by Gerald D. Feldman and Wolfgang Seibel

Volume 8
Gray Zones: Ambiguity and Compromise in the Holocaust and its Aftermath
Edited by Jonathan Petropoulos and John Roth

Volume 9
Robbery and Restitution: The Conflict over Jewish Property in Europe
Edited by Martin Dean, Constantin Goschler and Philipp Ther

Volume 10
Exploitation, Resettlement, Mass Murder: Political and Economic Planning for German Occupation Policy in the Soviet Union, 1940–1941
Alex J. Kay

Volume 11
Theatres of Violence: Massacre, Mass Killing and Atrocity throughout History
Edited by Philip G. Dwyer and Lyndall Ryan

Volume 12
Empire, Colony, Genocide: Conquest, Occupation, and Subaltern Resistance in World History
Edited by A. Dirk Moses

Volume 13
The Train Journey: Transit, Captivity, and Witnessing in the Holocaust
Simone Gigliotti

Volume 14
The "Final Solution" in Riga: Exploitation and Annihilation, 1941–1944
Andrej Angrick and Peter Klein

Volume 15
The Kings and the Pawns: Collaboration in Byelorussia during World War II
Leonid Rein

Volume 16
Reassessing the Nuremberg Military Tribunals: Transitional Justice, Trial Narratives, and Historiography
Edited by Kim C. Priemel and Alexa Stiller

Volume 17
The Nazi Genocide of the Roma:
Reassessment and Commemoration
Edited by Anton Weiss-Wendt

Volume 18
Judging "Privileged" Jews:
Holocaust Ethics, Representation,
and the "Grey Zone"
Adam Brown

Volume 19
The Dark Side of Nation-States:
Ethnic Cleansing in Modern Europe
Philip Ther

Volume 20
The Greater German Reich and the Jews:
Nazi Persecution Policies in the Annexed
Territories 1935–1945
Edited by Wolf Gruner and Jörg Osterloh

Volume 21
The Spirit of the Laws: The Plunder of
Wealth in the Armenian Genocide
Taner Akçam and Ümit Kurt

Volume 22
Genocide on Settler Frontiers:
When Hunter-Gatherers and
Commercial Stock Farmers Clash
Edited by Mohamed Adhikari

Volume 23
The Making of the Greek Genocide:
Contested Memories of the Ottoman Greek
Catastrophe
Erik Sjöberg

Volume 24
Microhistories of the Holocaust
Edited by Claire Zalc and Tal Bruttmann

Volume 25
Daily Life in the Abyss:
Genocide Diaries, 1915–1918
Vahé Tachjian

Volume 26
Let Them Not Return: Sayfo—The Genocide
Against the Assyrian, Syriac, and Chaldean
Christians in the Ottoman Empire
Edited by David Gaunt, Naures Atto,
and Soner O. Barthoma

www.ingramcontent.com/pod-product-compliance
Lightning Source LLC
Chambersburg PA
CBHW072153100526
44589CB00015B/2208